The Sandy Knoll Murder

Legacy of the Sheepshooters

by

Melany Tupper

Central Oregon Books, LLC, Christmas Valley, Oregon

Central
Oregon
BOOKS LLC

PRINTED IN THE UNITED STATES OF AMERICA

Visit our website at: http://www.christmasvalley.net

Second edition published 2011

ISBN: 978-0-9831691-1-6

To Mom

My first editor

CONTENTS:

"The truth is only arrived at by the painstaking process of eliminating the untrue."

-Sherlock Holmes

Author's Introduction

John Creed Conn was murdered in 1904 in the midst of central Oregon's bloody range war period, and that circumstance has always been believed to have precipitated his death. Sensational and intriguing, the details of the murder held the reading public in rapt attention with articles appearing on the front page of the *Oregonian* for nine months after Conn's mysterious disappearance. It is not very often that a prominent man, a celebrity, vanishes from the main street of an Oregon town in broad daylight. And even less often does a missing man's body reappear on a small, sandy knoll outside of that same town seven weeks later.

This work is the result of six years of painstaking research that encompassed eighty other homicides and suspicious deaths of the period, Conn's life and relationships, the circumstances of his death, and all that was ever written by and about the sheepshooters.

Conn's lifestyle presented some challenges that the killer had to overcome if he wanted to pull off the crime. He had to eliminate the possibility of being seen; to leave no tracks or trace in the area around town; he would need to use his own gun and take it away with him so that it would not be found; he would kill fast to avoid detection; and do what he could to buy time to keep the investigators off of his trail. All of the planning that the killer put into making Conn vanish showed a high level of control and organization on his part. But, he did unwittingly leave some clues to his identity, and they could be traced like fingerprints through the ink of the newspapers of the day. Other clues were left like footprints in the soil surrounding the Sandy Knoll and in the behaviors that he exhibited there.

Considering all of the planning that went into the crime, the killer had to be aware of who Creed Conn was, and what the consequences of killing him would mean. Conn was the brother of a district attorney and a member of a politically prominent and well-connected family. He was a celebrity and a respected figure, and there could be no doubt that a massive man hunt and investigation would quickly ensue. It seemed certain that Conn was singled out and specifically targeted, and that meant that he had a relationship of some kind with the killer, that they were closer than mere acquaintances.

The writer has made every effort to adhere to the actual facts of the case, long-held as the legacy of the sheepshooters. The Creed Conn murder was then, and remains today, one of the most sensational in the history of the state of Oregon.

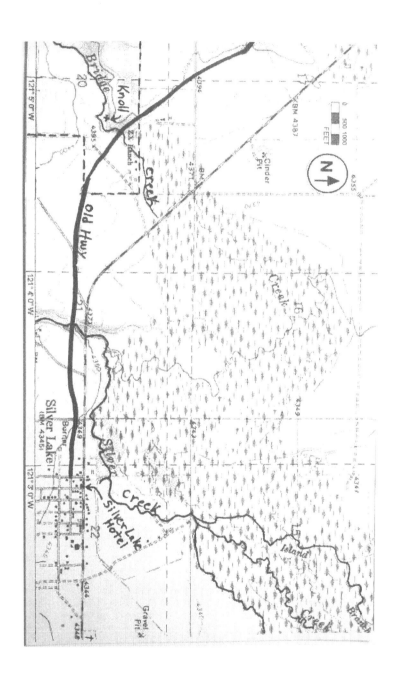

Chapter One

The Sandy Knoll

"The body lay on a small sandy knoll within a fenced field," reported the *Oregonian* on its front page. "It could have been seen from any point for some distance. The place is easily identified. Why was it that the searchers did not discover the body sooner?"

John Creed Conn, a prominent citizen and merchant of Silver Lake, Oregon, vanished from that town on March 4, 1904. Then, just as strangely as he had disappeared, the body of Conn materialized 48 days later at a point one and a quarter miles from town.

During the interviews with citizens who had spoken with Conn on the morning of his disappearance, it was revealed that his departure had been very sudden. So sudden, that he left no word of his leaving, and no instructions with the clerk in his store. Conn had gone off on foot without an overcoat or overshoes when the temperature outside was around 25 degrees. He had left with no suggestion of suicide; no instructions for the disposition of his property, no will, and no suicide note.

The county papers, however, leapt to the conclusion that Conn was dead, even though death is usually not a foregone conclusion in a disappearance. "It is thought that some imaginary trouble has preyed upon his mind and he thought to end it all in the grave," said the *Lake County Examiner* on March 10. The writers refer to Conn in the past tense only a few days after he was last seen alive, and ended like obituaries, recounting his life and listing next of kin.

The remains were found by a young vaquero, Fred Austin, and the knoll was located near the west bank of Bridge Creek about 150 yards from the main highway. No one believed that the searching parties that had scoured the countryside for several weeks after the disappearance could have missed the body in such an obvious spot. Even stranger though, was the condition the body was in, and the way it was positioned. There had been snow at Silver Lake the night before. It was the first significant snowfall to occur in the month of April, and Lakeview received six inches of accumulation, but the body had not been covered with enough snow to dampen it.

"All through March the weather was very severe and stormed almost every day. The precipitation was unprecedented in that part of the country for that month.... If the body of J.C. Conn had lain on that knoll all that time, would it not, too, have become rain-soaked? He wore a white starched shirt and cuffs. Never a drop of moisture had touched these articles of apparel where he lay. They were as smooth as the day he put them on. Rain would have wrinkled them," reported the *Oregonian*. "Where was the body of J.C. Conn during all those storms of March? It surely never lay in that pasture.... The body, after being exposed to the elements for seven weeks was still well preserved. The skin underneath the clothing was still clear white. Only the hands and face were blackened. It goes to show that the body had not been exposed to the elements, but had been concealed in a manner to preserve it."

Although the cause of death would later be named as two gunshot wounds to the chest, Conn had not fallen forward in a heap like most gunshot victims do. "The body was lying on its back, the arms thrown up over the head, the legs straight and feet close together, and the clothing neatly arranged as if by someone after depositing the body." Conn's hat was pushed back and pulled down tight, while his arms were up over his head, like he was sleeping, "as if in repose," said one writer.

An antiquated, 38-caliber six-shooter with two empty shells was found near Conn's left side. During the coroner's inquest that followed the discovery, examining doctors Thomas V. Hall and Albert A. Witham found that the first bullet passed through the upper part of the heart and lodged in the spinal column, and that shot was believed to have been the fatal one. The course of that bullet showed that it was fired from the front and to the left. The second shot entered the chest about three inches above the first, passed completely through the body without striking any vital organ, and was found later in the ground, about six inches underneath the body. The doctors believed that Conn had been standing or in an upright position when the first shot was fired, and were certain that the body had not moved at all after the second shot.

Conn's remains were guarded for four days by six men who worked in shifts until the jury, doctors, and witnesses were assembled. The body guards were Charles D. Buick, James F. Wyman, Robert H. Mosby, Josiah L. Smith, Samuel L. Porter, and Thomas C. Hamilton.

On April 24, Warren Duncan hauled the body to the school house in town where it was held overnight. On the day of the inquest the body was first examined by doctors Hall and Witham who stated their opinions as to the cause of death. Twelve witnesses were questioned by John D. Venator, who was appointed by Lafe Conn to act for the state. The coroner's jury, comprised of cattlemen, returned a verdict of suicide by gunshot, a verdict that did not jibe with the injuries, even to the untrained mind. "A verdict of suicide was returned, which was entirely unsatisfactory to Mr. Conn's friends, who do not hesitate to assert that politics influenced the verdict," said the

Oregonian of May 10. Their finding of suicide was widely viewed as an outrage and a scandal.

> *"We, the jury impaneled by the coroner, F.E. Harris, to enquire into and investigate the death of the body before us, report as follows: After uncovering the remains and hearing the testimony, we find as follows:*
>
> *The body is that of J.C. Conn, a resident of Silver Lake, Lake County, Oregon, aged 44 years. That he came to his death by two wounds inflicted with a 38-caliber revolver. That the wounds were self-inflicted, on or about 8 o'clock a.m., on the 4th day of March, at Silver Lake, Lake County, Oregon.*
>
> *Dated at Silver Lake, Lake County, Oregon, April 24, 1904.*

Conn himself was right-handed, and it was unlikely that he would shoot himself with his left hand, as the direction of the first shot indicated. The gun itself did belong to Conn. It was one that he kept in the drawer of his desk at the mercantile store. But it did not fit with the two gun shot wounds. The bullet holes themselves seemed to have been made by a .38 caliber weapon like Conn's, but his gun was a very old design, and had to be hand cocked between shots. "Was a man already mortally wounded with a bullet through his heart likely to stop to cock this weapon to fire another shot?" Asked the *Oregonian*. "Even had he fired this himself when he fell, the gun would have dropped from his nerveless grasp and he could not have picked it up again to fire the second shot. Nor would he have arranged his legs so neatly on the ground, but would have tumbled in a heap." A final argument was that Conn never carried a gun with him, and no one had seen him take the gun from the store on the morning of his disappearance.

There were other injuries, to the head. Conn's face was described as "maimed" and "mangled." His features were "obliterated" to such an extent that his gold pocket watch had to be used to identify the body. There was an odd hole in his right temple, that was not made by a bullet, but by some heavy instrument. Surely Conn did not inflict these additional injuries on himself. The doctors, probably confused by the extent of the injuries, would not name the manner of death, unwilling to state whether it had been a suicide, murder, or accident. Yet the coroner's jury was unswayed by their professional opinions.

One person, Mrs. R.H. Mosby, reported seeing Conn walking west out of town on the Morning of March 4. He disappeared from her sight as he neared Silver Creek, and shortly after, two men standing at different points, Royal E. Ward and George S. Parker, reported having heard the sound of a single pistol shot emanating from the vicinity of the Silver Creek Bridge. Silver Creek flows past the west edge of the town, only about one quarter mile from where Conn's store was located. As the result of that testimony, Silver Creek had been thoroughly searched, dragged, and even dynamited in attempts to find the body. But, where was Conn found? One mile further west, at Bridge Creek. Two 'ear witnesses' stated that they heard a single pistol shot near Silver Creek, and yet, here was a bullet in the ground underneath the body one whole mile away from that place.

Items found on the body included: a promissory note for $450 that Conn had paid at Lakeview a few days before his death; the keys to Conn's store; an intact, unopened bottle of an opiate solution known as laudanum in his vest pocket; his gold watch; about $30 in cash; and some other papers. Missing was a journal that he always carried with him, and used as a bookkeeping tool for recording transactions made outside of the store. "It is believed that in this book he had made notes bearing upon the recent sheep-killing, and that it bore damaging evidence against the perpetrators," reported the *Oregonian*. "The book may have been appropriated to destroy such entries."

Criticism rained down on the members of the jury for months to come. Two of the men owned cattle, and the other four were all employees of cattlemen. One, George Lovegrove, was secretary of the Chewaucan Land and Cattle Company, better known as the ZX Ranch, the largest cattle company in the county. The other jurors were William D. West, Jason E. Sullivan, Ervin K. Henderson, Clarence Z. Harris, and Clifford Smith. Their occupations were pointed out by writers who wanted to insinuate that there was a connection between Conn's murder and an attack that had been made on a band of sheep on February 2, allegedly by cattlemen. "It was the men that did that slaughtering that murdered Conn," asserted the *Oregonian* of June 9.

The first paper to implicate the sheepshooters was the far away *Deschutes Echo* of March 19, published at a place just north of present day Bend, Oregon. "J.C. Conn, a merchant of Silver Lake, is missing, and the circumstances of his disappearance are very strange. It is said that Conn regarded the recent sheep killing raid in Lake county as an outrage and freely expressed such opinion."

"Mr. West, another Democrat, candidate for Assessor, who did not denounce the sheep-killing and who was one of the men who rendered the verdict of suicide, received the unanimous 98 votes of his precinct," reported the *Oregonian*. The thoroughness of the proceedings was also questioned. "It is to be regretted that at the Coroner's inquest a complete autopsy was not made and the first bullet fired into Conn's body through the heart, located," complained the *Oregonian*. "The jury thought such an examination was not necessary. The inquest seems to have been only perfunctory."

"The *Plaindealer* under such circumstances admires the spirit of a governor of Colorado who, when the law was being trampled on and peaceful citizens murdered, said: 'The laws of Colorado shall be enforced and citizens be protected if blood flows up to the bridle bits.'"

In an editorial to the *Central Oregonian* at Silver Lake, juryman Ervin K. Henderson responded to some of those attacks by pointing a finger at Creed Conn's district attorney brother. "Lafe Conn was present at the inquest and assisted in the examination of the witnesses, as was also his brothers, Virgil and George, and if they knew of any evidence that would have caused a different verdict, they should have introduced it."

The weeks before the inquest had seen other curious behavior on the part of District Attorney Conn. On April 4, one month after Creed Conn disappeared, 18 days before the body was found, and without any eye witnesses or any jurisdiction whatsoever, Lafe Conn declared Creed Conn dead and filed a petition with Lake County Judge, Bernard Daly, for permission to liquidate the estate.

In the Mater of the Estate of J.C. Conn, Deceased.

Petition for letters of administration.

To the Honorable B. Daly, County Judge of Lake County, Oregon: The Petition of L.F. Conn, of Lake County, Oregon, respectfully shows:

That Petitioner is a brother of said J.C. Conn, and resides in Lake County, Oregon;

That the said J.C. Conn was a resident of and residing in said Lake County, Oregon, at the town of Silver Lake, on the 4th day of March, 1904;

That on said date the said J.C. Conn was at his usual place of business between the hours of 7 o'clock A.M. and 8 o'clock A.M., the said place of business being a general merchandise store in

*said town; that he disappeared from his place of
business between the said hours of 7 and 8 o'clock
without giving any notice of his purpose or
intention of absenting himself, and was seen
shortly thereafter walking along the County road
leading westerly from said town of Silver Lake to
where the same crosses Silver Creek; that shortly
after he was seen traveling along said road,
affiant is informed, and therefore alleges it to be
a fact, that a pistol or gun shot was heard in the
direction toward which said J.C. Conn was
traveling, by divers persons living in that
vicinity; that Petitioner and other members of the
family of said J.C. Conn have made, and caused
to be made diligent and thorough search in and
about the vicinity of the said town of Silver Lake,
and for miles distant thereabouts, and have
caused an exhaustive search to be made in the
surrounding mountains, streams and valleys, for
some trace of the body of said J.C. Conn, and that
not the slightest clue or trace has been
ascertained or found, and by reason of his
mysterious disappearance, and long and
continued absence from his home and wonted
place of business, and from the further reason
that there was not and is not the slightest
probability of his having departed from the
community where he was residing on said March
4th, 1904 your Petitioner believes, and therefore
alleges, that the said J.C. Conn is dead, having
expired on said last named date;*

*That said Deceased left an Estate in the County of
Lake, State of Oregon, consisting of real and
personal property of the probable value of Fifteen
Thousand Dollars, and also real property in the
County of Douglas, State of Oregon, of the
probable value of Two Thousand Dollars.*

The petition goes on to name Conn's surviving eight
siblings, and requests that brother Virgil Conn be appointed as
administrator of the estate. Was the young district attorney
leaping to a conclusion in a missing person case, or did he have
inside information? What made him so certain of his brother's
death that he was willing to risk his entire career and
reputation?

SOURCES:

"Was Not Suicide," *Oregonian,* June 9, 1904.

"Body of J.C. Conn Found," *Prineville Review,* April 28, 1904. Story was picked up from the *Central Oregonian* at Silver Lake.

"Murder or Suicide," *Oregonian,* June 12, 1904. This letter to the editor was written by Ervin K. Henderson, a member of the coroner's jury (see Appendix B).

"Body is Found," *Lake County Examiner,* April 28, 1904.

"Reign of Terror," *Oregonian,* May 10, 1904.

"J.C. Conn Murdered," *Plaindealer,* May 12, 1904.

"First in Heart," *Oregonian,* July 14, 1904.

"Creed Conn is Missing," *Lake County Examiner,* March 10, 1904.

"Mysteriously Disappeared," *Plaindealer,* March 17, 1904. Article was originally published in the *Central Oregonian* at Silver Lake less than one week after the disappearance.

"J.C. Conn's Body Found," *Crook County Journal,* April 28, 1904.

Editorial, *Crook County Journal, June 23, 1904.* Picked up from the Central Oregonian at Silver Lake.

"Weather Report for March," and "Weather Report for April," *Lake County Examiner,* July 21, 1904.

Bill for services rendered to the County of Lake in holding an inquest over the remains of J.C. Conn, dated at Lakeview May 2, 1904, by coroner Farnham E. Harris. Schmink Museum basement storage, Lakeview, Oregon.

"Anarchy in Lake County," *Plaindealer,* May 16, 1904.

Petition for letters of administration, In the Mater of the Estate of J.C. Conn, Deceased, Probate file of John Creed Conn, Probate Case Files, 1875-1927, Clerk's Basement South Storage Room, Lake County Courthouse, Lakeview, Oregon.

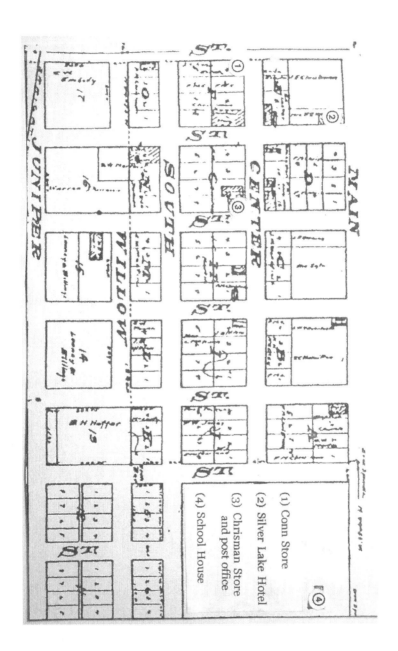

(1) Conn Store
(2) Silver Lake Hotel
(3) Chrisman Store and post office
(4) School House

Chapter Two

Thin Air

The most detailed accounting of the events of the morning of Creed Conn's disappearance was printed at Silver Lake in the *Central Oregonian*. And, although no copies of that issue of the long-extinct newspaper survive, the article was picked up by The *Plaindealer* at Roseburg, printed near the place where the Conn brothers had grown up. That article suggested both suicide and foul play as possibilities. It asserted that the missing man was dead, referred to Conn in the past tense, and ended by reviewing the man's life and naming his next of kin, just like an obituary, although Conn had only been missing for a few days.

> *"No one had noticed anything strange in Mr. Conn's manner as he seemed to be in his right mind up to the time he disappeared. Mr. Conn, in company with Prof. R. B. Jackson and one or two others, ate breakfast at the Silver Lake Hotel about 7 o'clock. Mr. Conn and the Prof. left the hotel together. Mr. Jackson went to the school house while Mr. Conn made his way direct to his place of business. Frank Payne, who is clerking for Mr. Conn, was sweeping when Conn walked in and asked the clerk if he had been to breakfast. Frank informed him that he had, he then asked if the Prineville mail had arrived being told that it had, he turned and walked out.*
>
> *T.J. Roberts who is clerking for F.M. Chrisman, was in the post office at this time and says he is confident that Mr. Conn called for his mail. He was seen a short time after he left the post office by Mrs. R.H. Mosby and her two small boys as he was walking up the Prineville road about one half mile west of town. Mrs. Mosby says after he passed the house a short distance he stopped and looked back toward town, then went on up the road, this was the last time he was ever seen. A very short time after he had vanished from Mrs. Mosby's sight, R.E. Ward who resides about three-quarters of a mile west of town heard a pistol shot somewhere near the Silver Lake bridge, thinking it was some of the boys*

that were hunting, he thought nothing strange and gave it no further attention until Saturday noon when Mr. Payne began to grow uneasy as to the whereabouts of his employer as he had left early Friday morning without leaving any word with him and had gone without his overcoat or overshoes. After investigating it was found that he had not occupied his room or had not been seen by anyone since Friday, Mr. Payne suspecting something was wrong went to the drawer where Mr. Conn kept two revolvers. He discovered that one was gone and the one missing had not been in use for a year or more. Payne immediately informed the citizens of the full details of the strange affair, and a searching party was organized at once composing of at least 50 men. Mrs. Mosby and R.E. Ward were interviewed, in which it was found that the lady had seen Mr. Conn pass up the road about 8:15 o'clock. A short time after Mr. Ward, hearing the report of a shot near the Silver Creek bridge and upon inquiry in the matter it was found that no one in the valley had fired a shot of any kind in that vicinity at any time during that day. This is strong evidence of either suicide or foul play, which leads the citizens of the valley to believe that the body of the missing man lies in the bottom of Silver Creek, and the distance will not exceed one mile from this place.

No searching for Conn was done until Saturday afternoon, more than 28 hours after he was seen at the post office. "Mr. Conn had been gone a day before any alarm was felt for his safety," said the *Deschutes Echo*. "Conn was last seen Friday morning. Nothing was thought of his absence until the next day, and search was not instituted till Sunday. Thus two nights had intervened without any investigation," was a complaint made by the *Oregonian*.

On Saturday Frank Payne phoned Lakeview with news of the disappearance, checked Conn's hotel room, and sent some men out on horseback to inquire at neighboring ranches. On Sunday the real search began. "Searching parties composed of every able bodied man in the valley were organized, horsemen scoured the entire country to the snow line and a thorough search was made in which Silver Creek was dredged for over a mile, but in vain," reported the Silver Lake paper. The interest in the stream seems to be based upon the accounts of Mosby, Ward, and Parker, which were seen as "strong evidence of either suicide or foul play, which leads the citizens of the valley to believe that the body of the missing man lies in the bottom of Silver Creek, and the distance will not exceed one mile from this place."

On the 15th of March Morgan L. Troth built a boat to use in dragging Silver Creek for the body of Conn, and worked in that stream with Thomas C. "Cull" Hamilton for the remainder of that week and part of the next. Silver Creek was dragged for a distance of over two miles. They believed that Conn's body had sunk to the bottom of the stream and been covered in sand during the high water that occurred at the time of the disappearance. During the first week of April, clerk Frank W. Payne and William D. Robinett worked further from town, searching the banks of Buck Creek, about two miles northwest of Silver Lake.

George Conn was probably the first of the brothers to arrive on the scene, arriving at Silver Lake on Monday or Tuesday to assist with the investigation. He did this even though the Chewaucan River at Paisley was at flood stage. It had taken out 40 feet of bridge, and threatened to flush his flour mill down stream.

On Sunday and Monday Silver Creek was dynamited in an attempt to dislodge the body. "The general opinion is that he has taken his life and that some day his body will be found in the creek that flows near this place," said the *Central Oregonian* at Silver Lake. "Mr. Conn's two brothers, Hon. Virgil Conn of Paisley and District Attorney L.F. Conn of Lakeview were here on the ground several days this week in the interest of their brother's business. They went over all his private letters and business correspondence together with the books and say that his business affairs were in good standing and there was nothing among his private letters that gave any evidence of why he so strangely left and say the whole affair is a strange mystery to them." Had the family and friends of Conn relied too heavily on the statements that suggested Conn had disappeared from the vicinity of Silver Creek?

The closest thing to an eye witness was Mrs. Mosby, who was supposed to be the last person to have seen Conn alive. Creed Conn had been living at the Silver Lake Hotel up until March 4, and it was there that he had eaten breakfast with the school teacher, and would have left about 7:30. It would have taken Conn about five minutes to walk the two blocks from the hotel to his store, where he spoke to clerk Payne for a few minutes, then walked to the post office which was located about a block away inside of the Chrisman store. Conn probably would have left the post office before 7:45. The distance from the post office to the bridge on Silver Creek was about one half mile. A man in his prime, as Conn was, walking on a brisk morning could have easily reached the approach to the bridge by 7:50 or 8 o'clock. Why then does Mosby say that she did not see Conn approaching the bridge until 8:15? Is it possible that she saw someone else?

When the U.S. census was taken in 1900, Mrs. Mosby and her husband Robert were working for and living with Mr. and Mrs. William O. Hough. The Houghs sold that property in 1907 to Minnie L. Ward. It was located in the southwest corner of the northwest quarter of section 22, or about one quarter mile south of the Silver Creek Bridge. Further evidence of Mrs. Mosby's position was found in the inquest records, which showed that she was compensated for traveling two miles round trip back and forth from the inquest, which was held at the school house. The distance from the school to where she was living matched the location of the Hough's house.

The man that Mrs. Mosby saw was traveling away from the sun, which had risen about one hour before. If the man was wearing a hat, as Conn was that morning, his face would have been in deep shadow, and from one quarter of a mile away, it is doubtful that Mrs. Mosby could have identified his facial features. Her claim was not corroborated by anyone.

Also somewhat doubtful are the accounts of Royal E. Ward and George S. Parker, who did not see anything, but say that they heard a single pistol shot from the vicinity of the Silver Creek Bridge. Even Ward himself dismissed this as irrelevant, "thinking it was some of the boys that were hunting, he thought nothing strange and gave it no further attention until Saturday noon." Because Conn had not one but two bullet wounds in his chest, these 'ear witness' accounts have to be taken with a grain of salt.

The claims that Conn disappeared from the stream were later refuted by some. "Right after him went the stage, and if Conn had taken the road where his body was found seven weeks later, the driver would have observed him," argued the *Oregonian*. "Another team at that same time passed over the road, and the ill-fated man was not seen."

Just how did the coroner's jury arrive at a verdict of suicide? The verdict seems to have been the product of poor information. There were no real witnesses to the moment that Conn disappeared. None of the witnesses questioned were able to say that they saw what happened. When no one was able to state that they had seen a murder committed, the jury eliminated that possibility and selected a verdict of suicide, a verdict based on hearsay testimony more than physical evidence.

"The charitable view that the public took of the Coroner's jury that rendered the verdict of suicide in the death of J.C. Conn in Lake County was that the men on the jury had not fully weighed the evidence, that they were honestly deceived by the efforts to make it appear a case of self-destruction," was the opinion of one *Oregonian* writer.

Juryman Henderson admitted that, "Mr. Venator the Assistant District Attorney, made a searching examination of all the witnesses and he was unable to find a single fact or circumstance that would point to murder."

By the middle of April, the 'death plunge' suicide theory no longer held water with the people of Silver Lake, and there was considerable talk of murder. "When questioned in Portland about the Conn mysterious disappearance, a citizen of Lake County said:

> 'The body of Conn had not been found and that many citizens did not believe that the man had committed suicide the same as the first reports indicated. He also stated that many citizens of Lake County believed that murder had been committed and the body made away with; and there were men who at first thought that Conn had shot himself and then plunged into the creek to finish up the job, but as days and weeks have elapsed, and an almost constant search and watch kept up to find the corpse without any result being obtained, that many are wondering if a mistake was not made in supposing that Conn had committed suicide and that he might have been murdered instead. 'True or false,' the Lake County man said, 'there is one man who will be suspicioned as the cause of Conn's taking off if the body is not found.'"

If the shaky, uncorroborated testimony of Mrs. Mosby is thrown out, as it should have been, then the last place that Conn was seen, with any certainty, was at his own store. Clerk Payne had stated that Conn had asked if the mail stage from Prineville had arrived, but T.J. Roberts, who the paper said was confident that he saw Conn at the post office, was not questioned as a witness at the inquest. For whatever reason, Roberts was not viewed as a reliable witness, and his information was thrown out.

When only the testimony of the school teacher and Payne is relied upon, Conn vanished into thin air before 8 o'clock A.M. somewhere near his own store. It was perhaps unfortunate that so much of the investigation and searching focused on the area of the bridge and the country surrounding the town.

On March 8, four days after the disappearance, a report out of Paisley offered information about a suspect:

"*A horse was stolen from the Chas. Innes ranch in Summer Lake, and from all appearances the party came from the north, and after taking the horse--which was a fine saddle animal--proceeded on south until near Paisley, when he took an easterly course and was tracked toward Alkali. It has been suggested here that the party who took the horse is in some way connected with the disappearance of Mr. Conn, but at this time sufficient evidence to connect the two incidents is unattainable.*"

The suspicion against the horse thief was strong enough at the time that Charlie Campbell of Paisley decided to attempt to track the man. He did not succeed however, because he accidentally shot himself in the leg when he was strapping on his holster. The horse was apparently turned loose or got away from the thief when he attempted to cross the Chewaucan River where the bridge had recently washed out, because the animal wandered back home riderless and was found in an adjoining field. Fred Collins was arrested for the crime at Summer Lake, where he had been working for William Sherlock under the alias of "Rhodes." The young man was jailed at Lakeview until his trial on May 16 and was found guilty of larceny of a horse, and nothing else. His attorney requested leniency on account of his youth, but District Attorney Conn objected and Collins was sentenced to three years in the penitentiary.

In May of 1904 reward offers began to spring up all over central Oregon for the arrest and conviction of the murderers and the sheepshooters. Governor George Chamberlain was appealed to, both editorially and through private letters, to take executive action and stop the violence. The governor's first reaction was cool. "The trouble seems to be due entirely to local conditions and local differences, and I think local people must find a remedy," said Chamberlain on May 12.

"The terror-stricken citizens have appealed to the governor for protection. They prayed for bread and our governor has given them a stone," said the *Plaindealer*, reminded Chamberlain that he had taken an oath to support the laws and constitution of the state of Oregon. "Is he not pandering to crime when he fails to send the state troops there to protect lives and property of citizens of Oregon? There is no time to play politics."

The first to act were the citizens of Lake County, who circulated and signed a petition requesting that the county court offer a reward for the men who killed sheep at Reid Rock on February 2, and at Benjamin Lake on April 28. On May 19, Lake County offered a reward of $1,000 for the arrest and conviction of the sheepshooters.

Finally, acting on "the suggestion of prominent citizens of Lake County," Governor Chamberlain stepped in on May 19th.

> *"Whereas, it has been charged that there is reasonable ground to believe that J.C. Conn, late of Silver Lake, in Lake County, Oregon, was assassinated on March 4th, 1904, and*
>
> *Whereas in has been charged that on April 28, 1904, a band of about 2,500 sheep were shot and killed by masked men in said county, the herders thereof blindfolded and compelled to stand by while the property of their employers was destroyed:*
>
> *Now, therefore, I, George E. Chamberlain, as governor of the state of Oregon, hereby offer rewards as follows:*
>
> *$2,500 for the arrest and conviction, or for information which will lead to the arrest and conviction of the murderer or murderers of said J.C. Conn;*
>
> *$300 for the arrest and conviction, or for information that will lead to the arrest and conviction of each and every one of the men who destroyed or participated in destroying said sheep on or about April 28, 1904.*
>
> *The payment of these rewards is conditioned upon an appropriation to be made by the legislature, which I promise to do all in my power to bring about in case said rewards, or any part thereof is earned.*
>
> *Given under my hand and the great seal of the state of Oregon at the capitol in Salem, this 19th day of May, A.D. 1904.*
>
> *George E. Chamberlain, Governor*
>
> *F.I. Dunbar, Secretary of State*

Through his authority as governor, Chamberlain had overruled and reversed the suicide verdict of the county and finally opened the way for a serious investigation into the murder two and half months after Conn's disappearance.

Copies of the governor's proclamation and rewards were printed and sent out to be posted around central Oregon, and he sent letters to Sheriff Dunlap and District Attorney Conn "urging them to do all in their power to apprehend the outlaws." The reward from the state was promised to be paid, "to any person having the information, even though he be an accomplice who confesses."

"The state seems to be impressed with the murder theory or the governor would not have offered a reward for the murderer of J.C. Conn," responded the *Examiner*. "Whether or not the relatives of Mr. Conn are satisfied with the verdict of suicide we are not informed, but if they are not, the governor's reward will probably be increased."

Shortly after Chamberlain's action, the stockmen of Lake County formed an organization so that they too could offer a reward, this time for $2,000 "for the arrest and conviction of the party or parties guilty of unlawfully killing sheep in the northern part of this county." The stockmen pooled their reward money together at once, and voted to apply it to all sheep kills, past or future.

In June, the Oregon State Wool Growers Association offered $1000 reward for "information as shall lead to the arrest and conviction of any person or persons guilty of shooting, killing, or maiming any member of the above association, or any employee of such member while engaged in their duties in attendance of the herds of a member, or guilty of killing, maiming, or otherwise unlawfully and with malicious intent destroying the sheep of a member."

All told, $9,200 would be the prize for the man that could bring to justice the nine sheepshooters of north Lake County, and the assassins of John Creed Conn, and yet, no arrests were ever made. "Nothing has ever come of the Governor's offer of $2,500 reward last Spring for the arrest of the men who murdered Creed Conn at Silver Lake, or the reward of $300 each for arrest of the men who killed sheep in Lake County," complained the *Examiner* in December. "Neither the Sheriff nor District Attorney, so far as known, paid any attention to the offer of reward, for neither even acknowledge receipt of the Governor's letter."

"A coroner's jury said it was suicide," continued the *Examiner*, "but the circumstances pointed so strongly to murder that there was a loud cry for a more thorough inquisition into the facts and for punishment of the supposed assassins. The Conn tragedy became a living issue in southeastern Oregon politics, and led to the defeat at the polls of public officers who appeared to have taken the side of the criminals, or to have hesitated to procure their arrest and conviction."

Throughout the spring of 1904, the ZX Ranch, owned by the Chewaucan Land and Cattle Company, took a protective stance in relation to the murder, largely because the *Lake County Examiner* printed a news item that was in the hands of every subscriber on the day that Creed Conn disappeared.

> *J.C. Conn, the Silver Lake merchant was transacting business at the county seat last week. A few days previous to his arrival here, Mr. Conn had the misfortune to lose three fine freight wagons by fire, valued at $600. They were standing under an old stock shed belonging to the ZX company. The cause of the fire is not known, but is thought to be the act of some boys who threw down a lighted cigarette.*

That fire was dismissed as an accident by most of the citizens of Silver Lake. Until seven weeks later, when Conn's body was found by a ZX employee at the Sandy Knoll. Because everyone in town knew that the Sandy Knoll was located on ZX property.

SOURCES:

"Mysteriously Disappeared," *Plaindealer,* March 17, 1904. Article was originally published in the *Central Oregonian* at Silver Lake during the week following the disappearance.

"Was Not Suicide," *Oregonian,* June 9, 1904.

Town Plat for Silver Lake, T28S R14E Sec. 22, Schmink Museum basement storage room, Lakeview, Oregon. Map shows names and locations of many of the original buildings.

Annie C. Hough and W.O. Hough to Minnie L. Ward, November 5, 1907. Deed and title records, vol unknown p 434-435, Lake County Courthouse, County Clerk's Office, Lakeview, Oregon. This is where the Houghs and Mosbys lived in early 1904.

List of Taxable Property of J.C. Conn and F.M. Chrisman, Silver Lake pct., in the County of Lake, State of Oregon, for the year 1901, J.B. Blair Assessor. Schmink Museum basement storage room, Lakeview, Oregon. These records provide a detailed description of the property of both men.

U.S. Census Bureau, Twelfth Census of the United States, 1900, Silver Lake, Lake County, Oregon.

Bill for services rendered to the County of Lake in holding an inquest over the remains of J.C. Conn, dated at Lakeview May 2, 1904, by coroner Farnham E. Harris. Schmink Museum basement storage, Lakeview, Oregon.

"The Conn Case," *Prineville Review*, April 7, 1904. Picked up from the *Central Oregonian* at Silver Lake.

"News Notes From Paisley," *Lake County Examiner*, March 10, 1904.

"Has J.C. Conn Killed Himself," *Plaindealer*, March 14, 1904.

"A Mysterious Disappearance," *Deschutes Echo*, March 19, 1904.

"Whereabouts of J.C. Conn Yet Unknown," *Prineville Review*, March 24, 1904. Article was originally published in the *Central Oregonian* in mid-March.

"Reign of Terror," *Oregonian*, May 10, 1904.

"First in Heart," *Oregonian*, July 14, 1904.

"Murder or Suicide," *Oregonian* June 12, 1904.

News Notes from Paisley, *Lake County Examiner*, April 9, 1903. George P. Lovegrove is named as bookkeeper for the Chewaucan Land and Cattle Co.

"The J.C. Conn Mystery," *Plaindealer*, April 18, 1904.

"Range Men Must Settle," *Oregonian* May 13, 1904.

"Anarchy in Lake County," *Plaindealer*, May 16, 1904.

"County Court," *Lake County Examiner*, May 19, 1904.

Editorial, *Ashwood Prospector*, May 24, 1904.

"News Notes from Paisley," *Lake County Examiner*, March 10, 1904.

"Collins is Arrested," *Lake County Examiner*, March 17, 1904.

Inmate record for Fred Collins, #4900, May 30, 1904, Oregon State Archives, Salem, Oregon.

"Rewards Offered," *Lake County Examiner*, May 26, 1904.

"State Offers Big Reward," *Burns Times-Herald*, May 28, 1904.

"Murder or Suicide," *Lake County Examiner*, June 16, 1904.

"$1,000 Reward," *Crook County Journal*, June 30, 1904.

"Sheep Killing Again Unearthed," *Lake County Examiner*, December 22, 1904.

In the Mater of the Estate of J.C. Conn, Deceased, Probate file of John Creed Conn, Order Appointing Appraisers, April 9, 1904. Probate Case Files, 1875-1927, Clerk's Basement South Storage Room, Lake County Courthouse, Lakeview, Oregon. Frank Payne and Gilbert Wardwell assisted Lovegrove in the appraisal.

"Local News," *Lake County Examiner*, March 3, 1904.

C.P. Marshal to G.P. Tarpey and Johanna Tarpey February 11, 1903. G.P. Tarpey and Johanna Tarpey to Chewaucan Land and Cattle Company, March 25, 1903. Deed and Title Records, vol 13, p 318 , Lake County Courthouse, County Clerk's Office, Lakeview, Oregon.

"Silver Lake The Way It Was," by Robert L. Fitch, 1991, Western Printers, Eugene, Oregon, p 1, 38. Fitch, who arrived in Silver Lake in 1923, described the route of the old highway that went west through Silver Lake, then curved toward the northwest as it passed the Sandy Knoll. The old highway is still visible on some maps, and on the ground in places. See map on page 8.

Reid Rock, viewed from the West, has a spongey, volcanic appearance. There are natural enclosures inside of it, and it is generally shaped like a crater. It is located on BLM land in township 26 South, Range 17 East, section 6.

Philip P. Barry, was the herder in charge at the time of the sheep kill at Reid Rock. Descendants believe that this is a photo of Barry's father, Philip K. Barry.

Chapter Three

Reid Rock

The murder of John Creed Conn has long been attributed to the sheepshooters of central Oregon, but more specifically to a group of five men who attacked the sheep of Benham and McKune in north Lake County, about one month prior to his disappearance, on February 2, 1904. The very first suggestion of the sheepshooters' connection to Conn was printed in the *Deschutes Echo,* published by George Schlect with Patrick Rowan as editor, on March 19 and during the time when Conn was still missing:

> *"It is said that Conn regarded the recent sheep killing raid in Lake County as an outrage and freely expressed such opinion. Reports have it that he afterwards received threatening letters commanding silence on the subject."*

The slaughter of sheep was viewed as an outrage by many people, primarily because of the importance of the sheep industry to the local economy. So, why was Conn, the brother of a District Attorney, singled out for murder from amongst all of those people angered? Did that one suggestion, not attributed to any source, give birth to a legend that has far outlived the man? In 1906, a writer for *Pacific Monthly* wrote, "You will find a lot of men down in Crook County who do not consider it a very healthy conversation to talk about Conn at all." The assassination of the brother of a district attorney was a high stakes proposition, not to be entered into lightly. The sheep destroyed prior to his murder had a probable value of about $4500, which made the crime a felony.

During the first two weeks of March, and until the time the *Echo* article was printed, other writers attributed the disappearance of Conn to either suicide or foul play. "It is now believed that Mr. Conn committed suicide on the banks of Silver Creek and that his body was washed down stream during the high water," reported the *Crook County Journal.* "It is supposed that in a fit of despondency he went to the top of the bridge and there shot himself and the body falling into the swollen stream has been carried into Silver Lake about ten miles away," said the *Plaindealer* at Roseburg.

The *Lake County Examiner* speculated broadly about the fate of Conn. "It is feared that during a moment of aberration of his mind he has wandered away, and either perished in the mountains or taken his own life.... it is thought that some imaginary trouble has preyed upon his mind, and he thought to end it all in the grave. Some however, are reluctant to believe he would do so rash an act, and think there has been foul play."

But, after the *Echo* suggested that the sheepshooters were involved, the idea caught fire and spread through papers across the state, even though the Silver Lake paper still held to the theory of suicide. "The general opinion is that he has taken his life and that some day his body will be found in the creek that flows near this place."

The next to seize upon the sheepshooters idea was another Crook County paper, the *Prineville Review*, of April 21. "It is the general supposition among the inhabitants of the region that he was murdered and buried by the parties to the deed instead of having suicided by drowning himself. Mr. Conn, it is said, knew more about the wholesale killing of sheep that occurred sometime before than was good for his health, and after his business had been injured in an attempt to induce him to leave the country, without effect, he was quietly made away with."

The McKune family suffered more harassment after the attack on their sheep. In mid-June Charles McKune, brother of sheepman Guy McKune, was the victim of arson. He found his sheep corrals in Thompson Valley in flames.

Probably the most sensational story tying Conn's death to the sheepshooters appeared on the front page of the *Oregonian,* after the body was found, on May 10, 1904. The article described a "reign of terror" taking place in Lake County, and sandwiched a mention of the Conn murder in between two sheep kill accounts. "The circumstantial evidence leading up to the belief that the death of Creed Conn was a murder and that it was committed to conceal the identity of the outlaws is shown in the following narrative," said the article, that went on to suggest that Conn was killed because of his close association with his brother, the District Attorney, and that Creed Conn "lived among the outlaws and knew each one of them personally." It also tried to suggest vaguely that Conn had sold ammunition to the sheepshooters with, "He had sold the ammunition and the guns that killed the sheep." The article made the assertion that Conn was considered an enemy by the sheepshooters simply because he had spoken to his brother at Lakeview twice during the spring.

The "information" in the reign of terror article regarding Conn's connection to the sheepshooters was all questionable. The occurrence of his disappearance between two sheep shooting events could have been coincidental. He may have met with the District Attorney twice simply because they were brothers, or had some personal business to discuss. The idea that Conn would knowingly aid and abet men whose objective was to damage an industry upon which most of

Conn's livelihood depended was ridiculous in the extreme. Finally, the assertion that he "lived among the outlaws" was not an opinion shared by the men investigating the slaughters.

On May 18 the Lake County Court reviewed a petition from citizens, and decided to offer a reward of $1,000 for the arrest and conviction of parties who had wantonly and unlawfully killed a band of sheep at Benjamin Lake on April 28. "It appears from such evidence as has been obtained by the officers of said county that the parties who killed said sheep are non-residents of Lake County."

The court order pointed to the men who committed the sheep kill at Benjamin Lake almost two months after Conn's disappearance, saying that they were not residents of Lake County. But what about the men who committed the sheep kill near Reid Rock one month prior to Conn's murder? The inflammatory "Reign of Terror" article made no distinction between those groups of men, lumping them together in one single band of outlaws.

In an editorial picked up by the *Plaindealer* on June 16, one writer referred to the Benjamin Lake sheepshooters as being responsible for Creed Conn's death, with the phrase, "those who killed 2300 head of sheep that led to Mr. Conn's murder." The number of sheep killed matched the Benjamin Lake slaughter.

There were many similarities between the two sheep shooting events. They occurred close together, both in space and in time, and the methods used for disarming the herders and killing the sheep were very similar. For that reason, and because those most knowledgeable about the Conn homicide pointed to both sheep shooting events, the perpetrators of both events warrant careful study.

By June 9 the *Oregonian* had changed its tune, and in another sensationalistic front page story pointed to the sheepshooters who attacked at Reid Rock on February 2 as the murderers: "It was the men who did that slaughtering that murdered Conn." The first report about Reid Rock came out of Silver Lake:

> "The sheepherder for the McKune sheep came in from the sheep camp near Christmas Lake Wednesday bringing the startling news that the camp had been visited by five masked men the night before and the larger part of the band of sheep were slaughtered.
>
> The five masked men were all heavily armed and proceeded to do their work in a deliberate way. The herder was first taken care of and while one man guarded him the

other four proceeded with their part of the work.

The sheep had been corralled for the night and were easy to get at. They took the night for their work, using knives, clubs, and guns in the wholesale slaughter. With the approach of day they took their departure with the parting injunction that other sheep using that range would be treated in a similar manner unless they were moved soon.

They had done their work well, and only a small remnant of a band of over 3,000 sheep were left. Upon receipt of the news, Guy McKune came to this place and telephoned Sheriff Dunlap who will make a thorough investigation of the affair.

While only a meager account of the killing can be had at this time, enough has been learned that the killing was done by five masked men and certain parties are suspected and startling disclosures are expected to take place in the near future.

The cause for the killing is attributed to the fact that the sheep were on range used by cattlemen.

While the amount of sheep reported killed may be over estimated, it is a hard loss to Mr. McKune and he will leave nothing undone to hunt down the parties who did the killing."

The exact location of this slaughter was not given, and other details like the name of the herder, the number of sheep killed, and the exact methods of the sheepshooters were lacking, but could be found elsewhere. Important clues pointing to the identities of the the sheepshooters were left in the printed publications of the day.

At the end of February a team of men was hired by the owners of the sheep to go to the site and salvage some of the wool, which at the time was selling for about twenty cents a pound. One of those men, Jason S. Elder, wrote an account of what he found at the scene of the slaughter, in which he gave its location as being "ten miles northwest of Christmas Lake."

Another reliable source of information as to the location of the sheep kill was a petition signed by over 40 taxpayers requesting that the Lake County Court offer a reward for the sheepshooters. "It is currently known throughout said County, that on the night of February 2nd, 1904, unknown parties wearing masks, at a place in said County some 25 miles or so North-easterly from the town of Silver Lake, set upon and killed from 1000 to 1400 head of sheep in the possession of William Benham and Guy McKune."

When two arcs are drawn on a map, one arc 25 miles northeast of Silver Lake, and another 10 miles northwest of Christmas Lake, the two arcs cross at a point about three miles north of a feature named "Reed Rock." The feature is a familiar one to explorers of north Lake County, and was mentioned in the book, "Pioneer Homesteaders of the Fort Rock Valley," by Raymond R. Hatton. In his book, Hatton interviewed Louise Godon who pointed to Reed Rock, a few miles from the Godon Ranch, as the site of one of the sheep kills. Although Godon, who did not live in the valley during the range war period, was mistaken on several facts about the slaughter, she offered one detail from firsthand information that was probably correct. She told Hatton that for years after the sheep kill, bones of sheep could be found at the site. Reed Rock is about six miles from the Godon Ranch, and the name Reed, correctly spelled "Reid," is an important one.

John M. Reid was related to both of the men described as owners of the sheep killed on February 2, 1904. He was a brother-in-law of William Benham, having married Eliza Benham, and he was a father-in-law of Guy McKune, who had married his daughter, Lola Reid.

When all of the above clues are combined: the account of a man who visited the site; the petition of the men who knew of the sheep kill and wanted a reward offered; and the account of a woman who lived near the site for many years; it becomes abundantly clear that the first sheep kill in Lake County occurred in the vicinity of Reid Rock. Even more detail about the scene appeared in "An Illustrated History of Central Oregon," published one year after the slaughter.

> *"The Particular locality of Christmas Lake is a rough sagebrush plain, cut up by rim-rocks and ridges covered with scrubby juniper timber. Standing upon one of the high points of these ridges or rim-rocks, one can see for miles around; drop down into a valley or ravine, and you are sheltered from storms. At many places on the desert almost complete enclosures can be found, where sheepmen with a little work can make corrals by piling rock and brush across gaps in the rim-rock and pitching camp in an outlet. In some*

instances these enclosures cover several acres of ground."

It was in one of these enclosures that a band of sheep, most of which belonged to Benham Brothers, was corralled on the evening of February 3, 1904.

Although the writer was off by one day, "Benham Brothers," was probably the business name used by the men who owned the sheep, identified as William Benham and Guy McKune in a warrant issued by Lafe Conn for the arrest of the sheepshooters. The makeshift corral, created by fencing gaps in the rimrock, explained the clubs that were used to kill some of the sheep, described as, "juniper limbs about four feet long and the size of a man's wrist." Twelve of those branches were found at the scene of the slaughter. The description of the area was corroborated by Elder, who wrote that it occurred, "up against a small rimrock, over which there was no escape."

The author spent considerable time in the vicinity of Reid Rock in the summer of 2009 searching for a natural enclosure like the one described in "Illustrated History." The most likely site was found inside of Reid Rock itself, at 43 degrees 20'25.5" north and 120 degrees 44'19.8" west. The large outlet where the herders pitched their camp is on the east end, and there are two smaller gaps in the rimrock to the northwest. The place is well sheltered from the winds that prevail out of the southwest, and is at a low elevation at the edge of the valley floor, so it would have been accessible to sheep in the winter. Juniper trees seem to have persisted in the area for a very long time, and there are some at or near the enclosure that appear to be over 100 years old.

The area surrounding Reid Rock was on the winter range used by stockmen of all kinds in 1904. The land belonged to the Department of the Interior, but was outside of the forest reserves. Some ranchers who owned sufficient pasture would keep their stock at home during the winter months, but owners of either little land or many head of cattle or sheep would turn them out onto the open range until spring.

So, who were those masked men? The newspapers do not name them, and neither did Lafe Conn when he issued a warrant for their arrest on May 20. To that warrant the district attorney attached the name of one witness, Julius Escallier. Escallier is a Basque name, and it is likely that he was a camp tender for the slaughtered band, working with Philip P. Barry, who was the herder.

There were, in 1904, three members of the Barry family with the first name of Philip, all living in Lake County.

A first cousin of Philip P., Philip S. Barry, at the age of 19 had already shot a man to death, and at the time of the sheep kill was out on $3,500 bail awaiting trial. Defense attorneys for the shooting death of Timothy Ahern were Eldon M. Brattain and James A. Boggs.

Aside from herding sheep, the Barrys had another pastime, which was driving and shooting jackrabbits. In late January of 1903, Philip and William K. Barry, and a few friends, drove 2,000 rabbits into a corral against a rimrock and killed them. Afterward William K. Barry, under the pen name, "McCarty Come Down," wrote an amusing account of the event for the *Examiner*.

The method used by the Barrys for herding and killing jackrabbits with clubs and guns bore an uncanny similarity to the method used by the sheepshooters at Reid Rock and Benjamin Lake. "The sheep were killed like rabbits in a drive," was the opinion of the *Ashwood Prospector* after Benjamin Lake.

What else can be learned about the sheepshooters by a study of their methods? When they convened on the band at Reid Rock, they were far from efficient, which could indicate inexperience. The warrant issued for their arrest stated that out of 3,000 sheep, only 900 were killed. When the cleanup crew arrived to recover the pelts, they reported having found only about a thousand dead. The account in "An Illustrated History" said that the sheep stampeded at one point, and a large number escaped.

The clubbing of the sheep must have been done after the shooting, because if men were in the corral among the milling animals, they would have been shot, too. After the shooting, some or all of the men pulled juniper branches from the makeshift fence across the outlet and clubbed to death the sheep that were still alive. But why? Was that the behavior of a ruthless mob? Why not just attack and go? The wounded sheep were as good as dead anyway.

The sheepshooters were believed to have lain in wait for the band to enter their rimrock corral to bed down for the night, so the crime was premeditated, not an impulsive act committed by men who just happened along. Cattle on the desert were customarily left unattended until about May when they were rounded up for branding. "No sooner had the herder corralled his sheep, than five masked men rode up to him, emerging from a hiding place nearby, where they had evidently awaited this opportunity."

The herder and camp tender were held at gun point while the outlaws put sacks over their heads, tied their hands, and relieved them of their guns and ammunition. At Benjamin Lake the grain bags used were described as barley sacks by the *Oregonian* of May 10. Barley was the grain most used by sheepmen to ensure that the animals made it through the winter and produced strong lambs in spring. And, sheepmen would have been the obvious source for numerous barley sacks. At Benjamin Lake, around a dozen of those sacks were used to disguise the sheepshooters and to blindfold the sheepmen.

At both of the sheep kills that occurred in north Lake County in the spring of 1904, the sheepshooters left the herders with stern warnings that may have pointed to their motives and identities. "They returned to the herder and told him what they had done, and warned him that other sheep found grazing on certain range would be treated the same way. They also stated that they had drawn dead lines, and that it was death to all sheep crossing them. The men rode away, leaving the herder to contemplate the situation. Not, however, until they had cautioned him about 'talking too much.'" Another version of the warning at Reid Rock from the Silver Lake paper was, "With the approach of day took their departure with the parting injunction that other sheep using that range would be treated in a similar manner unless they were moved soon."

At Benjamin Lake, "The gang of masked men who did the slaughtering informed the herder that the next band which crossed the Wagon Tire and Silver Lake road would be dealt with similarly and the herder thrown in. It is believed that this is the same gang which killed another band of the same number a few weeks ago." And, "Destroying almost the entire band, they then informed the employees of the band of sheep that they would give them time to gather up what sheep remained and get them across the dead line as soon as possible. Before they took their departure they warned the men not to come north of the Wagontire road with another band of sheep in the future. The sheep-killers told the camp tender to inform every sheepman he saw that the next band of sheep found in around Benjamin would meet with the same result and they would not spare the herders hereafter. These fellows informed Mr. Wilcox to have this report published in the Lake County papers so all sheepmen could take warning in the future."

After Creed Conn's disappearance, the *Lake County Examiner* was edited and published by Oscar Metzker, who was a personal friend of the Conn family. Metzker had previously operated the *Paisley Post*, the office of which was located inside of Virgil Conn's store building. That close association made Metzker's insights into both the murder and the sheep kills worthy of special attention. In December of 1904, he described "a gang of outlaw cattlemen," who used the sheep kills to wreak vengeance on their enemies and "the feud between them led to the shocking and mysterious death of leading citizen, J.C. Conn."

On May 26, Metzker described the strange and unexpected nature of the sheep kills. "There never has been any range trouble in Lake County until the past few months as has occurred in grazing counties farther north.... nothing of the kind has ever before occurred and the feeling between sheepmen and cattlemen has ever been of the warmest nature."

"It is the belief that the best of feeling exists between sheepmen and cattlemen of this section. No range wars exist here as do in the northern portion of the state. The whole affair is a mystery," was the reaction of the *Paisley Post*. And, the Portland *Telegram* charged that the slaughter was done "wantonly and without excuse whatsoever."

"Enough has been learned that the killing was done by five masked men and certain parties are suspected and startling disclosures are expected to take place in the near future," stated the Silver Lake paper after the sheep kill at Reid Rock.

One clue as to the identities of the sheepshooters came from the ammunition that they used. The "Reign of Terror" story attempted to blame Conn for having provided ammunition to the outlaws, "a broad assertion, to say the least," said Ervin K. Henderson, a member of the coroner's jury. "Mr. Conn's clerk informs me that at no time within the past year has there been one half the amount of cartridges in the store that were found where the sheep were killed."

The ammunition left behind at one of the Lake County sheep kills was later referred to, when the *Oregonian* admitted, "cartridge boxes were found with a Prineville firm's cost mark on them." A Prineville family's genealogical record, written many years later, referred to the store again as having, "sold cartridges to the members of the Crook County Sheep-Shooters Association, his store having received the unofficial commission as arsenal for that body." The establishment referred to was owned in partnership by Otto and Bruce Gray, Columbus J. Johnson, Rennie Booth, and Naomi Salomon.

Immediately after the first sheep kill at Reid Rock, the *Examiner* offered, "It appears that the cattle men of that vicinity, which is understood to lie partly in Crook and Lake counties, drew a dead line and warned sheepmen not to cross it with their sheep under penalty of having their bands destroyed without mercy." That deadline was later described as the road that ran from Wagontire to Silver Lake. The combination of those two clues indicates that the sheepshooters came from the north.

A final hint about the identities came from Oregon Governor George Chamberlain in his annual address to the

Twenty-third legislative assembly of 1905. "Since the last session of the Legislature, range difficulties in Lake and Crook counties have reached an acute stage, resulting in the willful killing of many hundred sheep, and it is charged, in the loss of one human life in the former county," he said in reference to the Conn homicide. "I fully appreciate the difficulties of the local authorities in attempting to suppress the prevailing acts of lawlessness. A few men bent upon the ruthless destruction of personal property might travel by night a distance of sixty miles from one county into another, apply the torch, perform their nefarious mission of slaughter, and return to the point of departure before the setting of another sun." It is interesting to note that both Reid Rock and Benjamin Lake are approximately 60 miles from Prineville.

The belief that John Creed Conn was killed by the sheepshooters became a legend. In the pages of Jackman and Long's "The Oregon Desert." Long, apparently a graduate of the old west school of creative writing, claimed to remember having seen Conn at his home leaving the scene of the Benjamin Lake sheep kill. Long was six years old at the time. "The first big jerk-line team that I remember that stopped at our place had a full load of pulled wool, taken from dead sheep killed in a sheepman-cattleman range dispute near Benjamin Lake. I was a small boy, but this was such an unusual load that I remember it. This was a mule team owned by Creed Conn and driven by Ed Henderson."

By the time the Benjamin Lake sheep kill occurred, Creed Conn was dead and buried. Conn's freight wagons had been destroyed in a fire about two and a half months prior, and Ed Henderson drove for Chrisman, not Conn, and was not in the recovery crew.

"This is the West, sir. When the legend becomes fact, print the legend."

Quote attributed to Editor Dutton Peabody, played by Edmond O'Brien, in John Ford's "The Man Who Shot Liberty Valance"

All through 1904 the newspapers attempted, circumstantially, to tie the Conn homicide to the sheep kills with things like derogatory statements made by Conn against the sheepshooters, or his alleged sale of ammunition to someone involved, which was later disproven. The only physical evidence of the alleged connection was the enigmatic lost journal that Conn had always carried with him, and that had not been found on the body. "A private memorandum book in which he was supposed to have noted the evidence against the outlaws," raised serious questions about the contents of that volume.

SOURCES

"A Mysterious Disappearance," *Deschutes Echo*, March 19, 1904.

"The War for Range," by Arno Dosch, *Pacific Monthly*, vol 15, February 1906.

"Forest Growth and Sheep Grazing in the Cascade Mountains of Oregon," 1898, by Frederick V. Coville, p. 13-15, USDA, Division of Forestry, Government Printing Office, Washington, D.C.

"Mysteriously Disappeared," *Plaindealer*, March 17, 1904. Article was originally published in the *Central Oregonian* at Silver Lake during the week after the disappearance.

"J.C. Conn Disappears," *Crook County Journal*, March 17, 1904.

"Has J.C. Conn Killed Himself," *Plaindealer*, March 14, 1904.

"Creed Conn is Missing," *Lake County Examiner*, March 10, 1904.

"Reign of Terror," *Oregonian*, May 10, 1904.

Editorial, *Prineville Review*, June 23, 1904. Picked up from the *Central Oregonian* at Silver Lake.

"County Court," *Lake County Examiner*, July 14, 1904.

Untitled editorial, *Plaindealer,* June 16, 1904. Reprinted from the Salem Statesman.

"Ban on Range Feuds," Oregonian, January 4, 1905. Steiner was a member of the lower house of the Oregon Legislature and a doctor at Lakeview.

"Marriage Records, vol. 2, 1895-1909, County of Lake, Lakeview, Oregon," 1995, Oregon Youth Conservation Corps, Lakeview, Oregon. Steiner was the best man at Lafe Conn's wedding on May 21, 1902.

"Was not suicide," *Oregonian*, June 9, 1904.

"2000 Sheep Killed," *Prineville Review*, February 11, 1904. Story was picked up from the *Central Oregonian* at Silver Lake.

"Local News," *Lake County Examiner*, March 3, 1904.

"Days of Bitter Sheep War in Oregon Described by One who Say Results," *Oregonian*, August 25, 1920.

"Masked Men Kill Sheep," *Lake County Examiner*, February 11, 1904.

"A History of the Fremont National Forest," by Melva Bach, 1990, Forest Service, USDA, Pacific Northwest Region, Fremont National Forest. Bach names the herder as Phil P. Barry on page 11.

"Petition, to the Honorable County Court of Lake County, Oregon." Schmink Museum basement storage, Lakeview, Oregon. Document is undated, but describes the sheep kills at Reid Rock and Benjamin Lake.

"Metsker's Map of Lake County, Oregon," undated, Metsker Map Company, Tacoma, WA.

"Settlers in Summer Lake Valley," by Teresa Foster, 1989, Maverick, Bend, Oregon, p 148.

"Local News," *Lake County Examiner*, March 3, 1904.

"An Illustrated History of Central Oregon," Western Historical Publishing, 1905, Spokane, WA, p.827.

"Information for Maliciously Killing Animals, the Property of Another," May 20, 1904, Record of the Circuit Court, 1886-1982, Circuit Court Basement West Storage Room, Lake County Courthouse, Lakeview, Oregon.

Bureau of Land Management, Oregon State Office, Land Status and Cadastral Survey Records, Willamette Meridian, Oregon and Washington, Historical Index, Township 26 south, Range 16 east, http://www.blm. gov/or/landrecords/ or/ 260s16oehwd.pdf

"Preliminary Examination," *Lake County Examiner*, December 3, 1903.

"Phil Barry Out on Bail," *Lake County Examiner*, December 10, 1903.

U.S. Census Bureau, Thirteenth Census of the United States, 1910, South Warner, Lake County, Oregon.

"2000 Rabbits Run Down," *Lake County Examiner*, January 29, 1903. It is not known which of the three Phil Barrys was involved in this rabbit drive.

""Survived Tragic Christmas Eve Fire, pioneer reminisces about early-day Silver Lake life," *Bend Bulletin*, August 10, 1970. Small, who lived in north Lake County in the early 1900's recalled that rabbits in drives were killed with juniper clubs, and guns and dogs were not allowed.

Editorial, *Ashwood Prospector*, May 3, 1904.

"Valedictory," *Lake County Examiner*, March 10, 1904.

Editorial, *Lake County Examiner*, March 10, 1904. Metzker entered into negotiations to purchased the Examiner the day after Conn disappeared. He took over as editor with the March 10 issue.

Editorial, *Lake County Examiner*, March 3, 1904. Describes the return of the recovery crew, and says the number of sheep killed had been overestimated.

"Rewards Offered," *Lake County Examiner*, May 26, 1904.

"Murder or Suicide," *Oregonian*, June 12, 1904.

"Lake County Sheep Killing," *Ashwood Prospector*, May 10, 1904.

"Sheep Killing Again Unearthed," *Lake County Examiner*, December 22, 1904.

"Masked Men Kill 1,500 Sheep," *Burns Times-Herald*, February 20, 1904. Story was picked up from the *Paisley Post*.

Editorial, *Crook County Journal*, March 17, 1904. Comments on an article in the *Portland Telegram*.

"2000 Sheep Killed," Prineville Review, February 11, 1904. Article was originally printed in the *Central Oregonian* at Silver Lake.

"Drive Out Sheep," *Oregonian*, December 12, 1904.

"The Married Life of Otto and Jessie Gray, 1901-1951, p.1, Gray-Ketchum genealogy file, Bowman Museum, Prineville, Oregon.

"Masked Men Kill Sheep," *Lake County Examiner*, February 11, 1904.

Message of George E. Chamberlain Governor of Oregon, to the Twenty-third Legislative Assembly of 1905. Oregon Messages and Documents, 1905, Governor's Regular Session Message, Salem, Oregon, J.R. Whitney, State Printer, 1905. Available on the web site of the Oregon State Archives at: http://arcweb.sos.state.or.us/governors/chamberlain/message1905.html

"The Oregon Desert," E.R. Jackman and R.A. Long, 1969, Caxton, Caldwell, Idaho, p 277.

'Killed 2,300 Sheep in Two Hours," *Crook County Journal*, May 5, 1904.

The author searched through many photos of freight teams, and this was the only one found that matched the description of Conn's team as given by his nephew, Ted Conn, and the probate records from the estate of J.C. Conn.

Chapter Four

Mr. Silver Lake

Creed Conn was strongly identified with the excellent freight team that made him what he was, a celebrity, and a prosperous one at that. Around the year 1900, the coming of a big freight team pulling three wagons was an exciting event that marked the arrival of oodles of new merchandise. And what a show! The mules were enormous, tall and wide, and the loud thudding of their feet could be heard far in the distance. They strutted into town amidst cries of excitement, a huge cloud of dust, snorting as they came in a cacophony of chiming bells. Bells were suspended above the collars of the mules, between the hames, and each set of bells represented the conquering of another freight team by passing it on a steep grade. The greater the number of bells, the greater the team, and Creed Conn's team had many, many bells.

John Creed Conn, who went by "Creed," arrived at Paisley in 1886 and began clerking at the mercantile store established several years earlier by his older brothers, George and Virgil. In 1892, Creed Conn moved to Silver Lake and established a mercantile store there, although he remained in partnership with Virgil under the firm name of "Conn Brothers." The store was about one block west of the store owned by Francis Chrisman. Creed and Virgil Conn were named together in their business in the tax roll of 1895 for Silver Lake as "V. and J.C. Conn."

Chrisman had suffered near financial ruin when the famous Christmas eve fire of 1894 destroyed the contents of his store. As soon as Chrisman's creditors received news of the fire, they garnished all of his insurance money. Just prior to the fire, Chrisman had bought out his brother's share in the mercantile business, and was leasing the building, still owned by J.H. Clayton. The Christmas eve fire is still considered one of the most appalling tragedies in Oregon history and claimed the lives of 43 people.

Most of the settlers that arrived in the Lake County communities of Silver Lake, Paisley, and Summer Lake in the 1870's were stockmen from the Eugene area of Lane County. The Oregon Trail had brought a crush of homesteaders to the Willamette Valley, creating a shortage of grazing land and an escalating real estate market. The Oregon Central Military Road was a project that gained strong support from Eugene stockmen that needed range land and were looking for an easier route to take their cattle to hungry soldiers at the cavalry forts that dotted eastern Oregon.

Congress provided a land grant for the road project in 1864 that allowed promoter B.J. Pengra to sell land on either side of the road as a means of paying for construction. The first usable section of the road was completed and allowed settlers to breach the mountains in 1865. Union Army supply trains began using the road almost immediately, and many men who enlisted in Eugene found themselves mushing food and other goods to forts around the region, an experience that exposed them to the country and led many to eventually settle in Lake County. One of those soldiers was George Conn, older brother of Creed. George became receiver of the US Land Office at Lakeview from 1877 to 1882, and had handled homestead filings at Linkville prior to that time.

A man by the name of Stephen Rigdon kept a fairly complete record of those who passed through his "Pine Openings" toll station, located on the Oregon Central Military Road, from 1873 to 1896. The road was the only one between the Lake County settlements and the Willamette Valley for several years, and Rigdon's books were a sort of guest registry that provided details as to the names of persons in parties, their direction of travel, type and number of livestock, wagons, and the purpose o f their ventures.

Peter Chrisman, who often spelled his name as "Christman," was a Cottage Grove cattleman who liked to introduce himself as "Major." Chrisman was named in Rigdon's records as coming and going from the Silver Lake area seven times before 1882, but probably crossed more frequently than that because there are gaps in the record. The Major was shown bringing his wife and three children over the pass heading east in September of 1874, and he and his brother Gabriel and son Francis were shown to be associates of other cattle-raising families like the Martins, Smalls, and Brattains. In June of 1881, Peter Chrisman and eight men took 600 head of cattle over the pass bound for Silver Lake, the cattle probably originating from the 500 acre ranch of the Major's brother Scott, a stock dealer in Cottage Grove.

The family had immigrated to Oregon in 1851, and Peter Chrisman was a teenager driving a team of oxen when his family reached Lane County in 1853 to settle in Cottage Grove. Chrisman had five siblings, and his father Campbell was an Oregon state senator from 1862 to 1866. The Peter Chrisman family was one of the first to settle in Silver Lake, and the Major was thought of as the founder of the town, and so was also referred to as, "Mr. Silver Lake." The original town site was located on the west side of Silver Lake, and that was where the Major built a log cabin school house and hired a teacher so that his children could begin their education in 1880.

The town of Silver Lake did not really start to develop until about 1885. Chrisman sold all of his interest in the cattle business in 1882, and his Silver Lake ranching headquarters to Fred Cox and John Jackson. After relocating to Lakeview, Peter Chrisman established the first bank in the county, The Lakeview Bank, and served as its president for 11 years. The first mercantile store was established at Silver Lake in 1885 by J.P. Roberts, and the following year, a second store owned by J.H. Clayton opened there. In 1890 Francis Chrisman, Mr. Silver Lake's heir, became a business partner in the Clayton mercantile store.

Most of what has been written about Creed Conn has focused on the peculiar circumstances surrounding his disappearance and death in 1904, and little is known about him and the life that he lived. He was born in January of 1858 in Roseburg, Oregon, the ninth child of Henry Conn, an affluent farmer who had extensive land holdings along the south Umpqua River.

Creed Conn was a Republican and very politically active, as were most members of the Conn family. The father, Henry, was a prominent free soil Democrat and took an active interest in organizing the Union Party that later evolved into the Republican Party.

The Conn family had ties to the politically powerful family of General Joseph Lane. According to a transcribed interview with Katherine Diller Conn, the Lanes befriended the Conns upon their arrival at the Roseburg area. "Their first stop was at the ranch of General Joseph Lane, to whom Henry Conn Senior carried a letter from an eastern friend. The Lane's ranch of 640 acres was located a short distance northwest of Roseburg. Here Mr. Henry Conn and his family visited a few days until he could look around for a location. The Conn family went to what was then known as French Settlement, where Henry Conn Senior bought a donation land claim of 640 acres, to which he later added considerable acreage in that vicinity, becoming an owner of a great deal of land."

As a young man, Creed's brother Virgil went to work for the mercantile store of Floed and Company at Roseburg. Floed had been a business partner of General Lane's son, Simon, and Virgil Conn worked for the store for 11 years until he opened his own store at Paisley in 1882. The crypt of General Lane is located near the Conn family plot in the old Masonic section the Roseburg Memorial Gardens, on land that once belonged to Henry Conn.

Creed's brother, George, had significant pull with senator John Mitchell, demonstrated in 1904 when his letter to Mitchell resulted in the appearance of a team of US engineers that came to study the water supply of the Chewaucan River. Creed's brother James became an Oregon state representative in 1898, and brother Virgil was in the legislature twice, in the sessions of 1859 and 1897.

In February of 1903, it was announced that Creed's younger brother, Lafayette, who went by "Lafe," had been appointed as the new district attorney for Klamath and Lake counties. The appointment was the result of the creation of a new prosecuting attorney district that had been split off from Jackson and Josephine counties by senator Emmitt's bill.

Creed Conn was a member of the Baptist church and a friend of fellow church member Al Dunning, with whom he boarded around the year 1900. Conn never married, although he was a strikingly handsome man with dark hair and light blue eyes. He was described as business-minded, with his business being his main focus and 'raison d'etre.' Around the time of his death, the newspapers described him as "prosperous," with a business that was in a most flourishing condition. "Mr. Conn was recognized as one of the leading merchants of Lake County and was always found upright and honest in all his dealings. He was a man that was very conservative, although he had many warm friends. He took very little interest in anything outside his own business."

At the time of his death, Creed Conn had accumulated about $17,000 in personal wealth, and there can be little doubt that he benefited from the devastation of the Chrisman store in the fire of 1894. By 1900, Chrisman must have realized that the competing Conn Brothers' store was a force to be reckoned with, because their Paisley store was the largest and most successful mercantile business in Lake County.

The secret of Creed Conn's success seemed to stem from having carefully integrated his mobile freighting business with the commercially viable store location in Silver Lake where he stocked a large variety of goods. Unlike other store owners, Conn had determined early on that he could haul wool from the sheep camps of the county to the railhead at Shaniko, and bring back groceries and store inventory on the return. The money that he charged the sheepmen for hauling their wool offset the expense of bringing inventory to the store.

Supplying food, whisky, grain, and other essential items to the sheep camps on the desert was an integral part of Conn's success, and he hired a skilled teamster to handle the freighting end of the business. It is not known who was freighting for Conn at the time he was killed, but during his early days at Silver Lake, Thomas J. "Tommy" LaBrie, an old friend from Roseburg, brought freight in for Conn all the way from The Dalles. By 1900, LaBrie was no longer driving for Conn, and had settled down into the life of a farmer. Conn's teamster has been incorrectly identified by some writers as Ed Henderson, who was actually working for the competing Chrisman store after December of 1903. Up until his death,

Conn was still bringing his freight in from the railhead at Shaniko.

Conn's freight team was unique, one of the best in Oregon, and also the envy of many other operators. While some team owners opted for fashion over function, choosing animals that looked good together, Conn obviously selected his animals for performance. He owned 12 mules that were shades of dapple gray, and a pair of super smart white horses that worked as the leaders, but generally ran with a team of ten. "This is one of the best known freighting outfits in eastern Oregon, and many snap-shot photos have been taken of it," claimed the *Ashwood Prospector* in 1904

The clever lead horses were white to make them easily visible to oncoming traffic through dust, or in any light conditions. Nimble and knowledgeable, the leaders were not controlled by reins, but by voice commands and a single "jerk line" that was used to communicate directions to the left end of the bit in the mouth of the left, or "nigh" leader. A steady pull on the line would turn the team left, and a series of short jerks would turn them right.

Next after the leaders was the massive swing team. Taller, wider, and darker than all the others, they were mules with a draft horse in their family tree. Behind them were the pointers, trained to jump the chain, and with a difficult sideways gate, would pull at an angle about 45 degrees away from the direction that the leaders were pointing. This enabled the team to pull a string of wagons around a sharp corner without going off the road. After the pointers were two more teams, and the rear mule on the left provided the driver's seat for the teamster, who controlled the team and the wagon brake. The last team was known as the "wheelers," and it was their job to hold back the wagons on down grades. Creed Conn owned and operated with three deep and heavy freight wagons.

At the time that Creed Conn opened the Silver Lake Store in 1892, he appeared to have been a silent partner of brother Virgil, and was paid in wages and in shares in the company. By 1904, Creed Conn was operating as a sole proprietor of the Silver Lake store that had originally been a profitable adjunct to the main store at Paisley, and Virgil Conn was loosing business to his younger brother. Virgil and George Conn seem to have been often at odds over petty issues in the partnership, unable to act as true partners in any sense of the word. "George Conn's younger brother, Virgil, moved to Paisley and also set up a store and built a house. He and his brother George had difficulty in getting along.... What the difficulty was concerning them I never knew, but they were not friendly," said nephew, Ted Conn, in a 1982 interview.

In 1892 George sued Virgil in a rather embarrassing court case in which everything from soup to nuts was the object of bickering. Virgil Conn had bought out George's interest in the business in 1889, and in the court's sorting out of "sundry items" from their past partnership, Virgil appeared to be the more petty and niggardly of the two brothers. The store had earned some money from the receipts of the post office inside of it, of which Virgil was postmaster, and Virgil wanted all of those earnings returned to him; George refused to lease out the company's flour mill at Paisley, so Virgil claimed that he lost money while the mill was not leased; Virgil felt the mill lost business because it needed some repairs, and George would not pay for the repairs; George paid Creed some money owed him in salary, and Virgil resented that and wanted the money returned; Creed had also earned interest on his shares of stock in the company, and Virgil asked to have that money returned. In the end, George Conn came out on top, and Virgil was ordered by the court to pay over to him $820.

Creed Conn, was a member of the AF&AM, the Ancient Free and Accepted Masons. The Conns immigrated to Oregon in 1854 from Indiana, and there is some genealogical evidence that the first Conn's in Oregon were of German-Irish extraction. Creed, Lafe, George, and Virgil Conn all graduated from Willamette University, at the time one of the finest private colleges in the nation.

Creed, like his brothers, played an important role in local politics. When the Lake County Republicans met on March 23, 1902, he was one of the delegates to the county convention from Silver Lake and a proxy for the other delegates from his town. He was one of three men that comprised the committee on credentials, the role of which was to approve or disapprove delegates entitled to seats and votes in the county convention.

The *Lake County Examiner*, like other newspapers of the day, carried small tidbits of personal news about county citizens. Those "local mention" columns seemed to focus more on prominent families and business people, and when combined with innuendo found in other articles, provided important clues about the life and disappearance of John Creed Conn. On February 11, 1904, just days before his disappearance and less than a month from the planning meeting of the Lake County Republican Central Committee at Lakeview, the *Examiner* quipped, "J.C. Conn, the Silver Lake merchant, was transacting business in Lakeview Monday. Isn't it about time candidates for the coming June election were announcing themselves?"

Was Creed Conn planning to run for county office? With his family's strong political ties and history of political involvement, brother Lafe's position as district attorney, and his own strong role in north county politics, it has to be considered a possibility. In May of 1904, an article submitted to the Roseburg *Plaindealer* from Lakeview by an unknown writer seemed determined to blame Conn's death on cattlemen. "After hearing the evidence, a verdict of suicide was returned, which was entirely unsatisfactory to Mr. Conn's friends, who do no hesitate to assert that politics influenced the verdict."

Creed Conn never made it to the March 2 planning meeting of the Republicans at Lakeview. He had been at the county seat on February 26, just five days earlier, and at that time had borrowed $200 from his district attorney brother, Lafe. He was said to have paid a note for $450 at Lakeview just a few days prior to his disappearance, which may have been what the loan was used for.

Lafe Conn went to Silver Lake about that same time, and asked a proxy to represent him at the county Republican Central Committee meeting. Lafe probably left Silver Lake on March 3, the day before the disappearance. The reason for the district attorney's visit was not stated. However, it is likely that he was there to investigate the poisoning of Creed's team that caused the death of one of his leaders on March 1.

"It is said that Conn regarded the recent sheep killing raid in Lake county as an outrage, and freely expressed such opinion," said the *Deschutes Echo* two weeks after the disappearance. "Reports have it that he afterwards received threatening letters commanding silence on the subject."

The threat letters were again referred to in "An Illustrated History of Central Oregon," published in 1905. "One morning when one of the merchants of Silver Lake went to open his store he found a small piece of rope tied to the door knob and a note advising him to 'keep quiet.' All these warnings came from mysterious sources; some of the letters were mailed at distant post offices, and no clue could safely be traced."

Conn was threatened again, on February 29, when his team was poisoned. "One of his fine horses took sick and suddenly and died," stated the same writer, "Creed Conn had one of the best freight teams in Oregon. It was said the horse was poisoned, and Conn was afraid the others might suffer the same fate."

On April 21, the *Prineville Review* reported, "Mr. Conn, it is said, knew more about the wholesale killing of sheep that occurred sometime before than was good for his health, and after his business had been injured in an attempt to induce him to leave the country, without effect, he was quietly made away with." Conn's body would be found later that same day.

District Attorney Lafe Conn may himself have had a rival in William J. "Joe" Moore, who had aspired to be named as district attorney. Moore, a Lakeview lawyer and Democrat, probably considered himself first in line to become D.A. because he had served as the deputy D.A. under A.E. Reames for three years between 1900 and 1903. Prior to that, the prosecuting attorney district had been comprised of Klamath, Lake, Jackson, and Josephine Counties. Emmitt's bill split it in half, creating a new district out of Klamath and Lake counties early in 1903. Lafe Conn was appointed as D.A. of the new district, and his choice for Deputy District attorney was John D. Venator. A.E. Reames continued in Jackson and Josephine Counties, and W.J. Moore was left out in the cold.

The action to divide the territory may have been due to abuses of the public money by Reames and Moore. Emmitt, a Republican, succeeded in passing the measure by citing heavy travel expense incurred by the two men in covering the four county area. District attorney Reames was indignant over the choice of Lafe Conn. "I understand that certain parties claiming to be Democrats, are circulating in Lake County the report that I am responsible for the putting in office in that county a Republican," wrote Reames. "This is absolutely false, and has no truth in it whatever. The bill was submitted to me at the time of its introduction. At that time no one was mentioned in the bill for Eastern Oregon, nor was the salary mentioned. When the bill came back from the Committee, it had Mr. Conn's name in it, though I was not present at the legislature at that time."

While Lafe Conn was accepting his appointment as the new district attorney, the *Examiner* reported that Creed Conn's town of Silver Lake was, "on the eve of a big boom." The article came from George Duncan, who frequently served as a correspondent from his Lone Pine Ranch on the west side of Silver Lake. In the same article, Duncan described a meeting in which Creed Conn had introduced him to a man by the name of Baldwin, and another man who were planning to build an office and start a newspaper.

Duncan's article also described the arrival of 26 persons hoping to locate on timber land in the vicinity. "There is considerable excitement among the present population," wrote Duncan, who took the attitude of a somewhat indignant expert on local properties who resented Conn and the outsiders.

"They tell us that here will be four hundred emigrants looking for homes and locations on the desert, and that Silver Lake will be the centralized point of Lake County," wrote Duncan. "A man was hired to haul out a load of hay to the McCarthy ranch about 12 miles from town, and he was given twenty dollars per ton. There is undoubtedly a 'nigger in the woodpile,' and these parties are on a hot track." Duncan pointed out that the man hauling hay was grossly overpaid, possibly as a part of a plan to convince potential buyers that the land was able to produce grass.

The county was definitely turning its attention to the north end by 1904, and if Creed Conn had chosen to run for the office of county clerk or assessor, he would have been a tough man to beat. Politically connected, well-educated, good looking and charismatic, Creed Conn was well on his way to becoming the new "Mr. Silver Lake."

SOURCES:

"The Growth of Lake County, Oregon," by G.E.B. Stephenson, 1994, Book Partners, Inc, Wilsonville, OR. Photo of a freight team on page 34 of this book is the only photo that the author has found of a team that matches the description of Conn's team, which was comprised of 10 mules, with white leaders that were sometimes mistaken for horses because they lack the tan faces common in brown mules.

"Mysteriously Disappeared," *Roseburg Plaindealer,* March 17, 1904. Article was picked up from the *Central Oregonian* at Silver Lake.

Petition for letters of administration, In the Mater of the Estate of J.C. Conn, Deceased, Probate file of John Creed Conn, Probate Case Files, 1875-1927, Clerk's Basement South Storage Room, Lake County Courthouse, Lakeview, Oregon.

Town Plat for Silver Lake, T28S R14E Sec. 22, Schmink Museum basement storage room, Lakeview, Oregon. Map shows names and locations of many of the original buildings.

List of Taxable Property of J.C. Conn and F.M. Chrisman, Silver Lake pct., in the County of Lake, State of Oregon, for the year 1901, J.B. Blair Assessor. Schmink Museum basement storage room, Lakeview, Oregon. These records provide a detailed description of the property of both men.

Tax Roll for Silver Lake, Lake County, Oregon for the year 1895, Oregon State Archives, Salem, Oregon.

"An Illustrated History of Central Oregon," Western Historical Publishing, 1905, Spokane, WA, p914-915.

"Illustrated History of Lane County," by A.G. Walling, 1884, Portland, Oregon, p351.

"The Oregon Desert," by E.R. Jackman and R.A. Long, 1969, Caxton Printers, Caldwell, Idaho, p 34.

Diary of George Conn, Lake County Museum, Lakeview, Oregon.

Central Oregon Emigrant Military Wagon Road, Cascade Mountains East and West, Stephen Rigdon papers, Oregon Historical Society Manuscripts Department, Lake County, Pine Openings, 1873-1896.

"Brief Description of Life History of P.G. Chrisman," *Lake County Examiner,* May 1, 1911.

"F.M. Chrisman, Pioneer of Silver Lake, Dies at 82," *Oregonian,* August 23, 1948.

U.S. Census Bureau, Eighth Census of the United States, 1860, Roseburg, Douglas County, Oregon.

U.S. Census Bureau, Twelfth Census of the United States, 1900, Silver Lake, Lake County, Oregon.

"The Centennial History of Oregon," vol 4, S.J. Clarke Publishing Co., 1912, Chicago, Illinois, p 1064-1065.

"The Conn Family," oral history, by Katherine Diller Conn (wife of H.P.), undated, Douglas County Museum of Natural and Cultural History, genealogical collection.

"Reminiscences of Southern Oregon Pioneers," interview with Henry R. Conn, April 3, 1939, Douglas County Museum of Natural and Cultural History, genealogical collection.

"Historic Douglas County, Oregon," Douglas County Historical Society, 1982, Roseburg, Oregon, p. 108-109.

Research conducted by author at the archives of Willamette University.

"An Illustrated History of Central Oregon," Western Historical Publishing, 1905, Spokane, WA, p. 909.

"Virgil Conn Succumbs," *Oregonian,* March 1, 1931.

"Measuring the Chewaucan River," *Lake County Examiner,* June 23, 1904.

"L.F. Conn, District Attorney," *Lake County Examiner,* February 26, 1903.

"Reames' Insult to Lake Co. Democrats," *Lake County Examiner,* May 28, 1903.

"Not the Right Man," *Lake County Examiner,* May 12, 1904.

Probate file of John Creed Conn, Lake County Courthouse, Clerk's Basement South Storage Room: Probate [Case Files], 1875-1927, Lakeview, Oregon. The first semiannual accounting of his estate November 28, 1904 shows that his team of 13 horses and mules were sold to Wurzweiler and Thomson for $1,200.

"Reflections, Short Stories of Old Lake County," Lake County E.S.D., 1982, Lakeview, Oregon. During his interview for this book, Ted Conn said that Conn's team included two horses.

"A History of the Deschutes Country in Oregon," Deschutes County Historical Society, 1985, Redmond, Oregon, p 317.

"Local News," *Bend Bulletin,* December 11, 1903. Identifies Chrisman's new driver as Ed Henderson, who started that job around December 1.

"Hitch for Jerk Line Freight Team," Illustration by Ivan Collins, 1903-1971, Oregon Historical Society negative #68441, Portland, Oregon.

"The Wagonmasters," by Henry P. Walker, 1966, University of Oklahoma Press, Norman, Oklahoma.

"A Mysterious Disappearance," *The Deschutes Echo,* March 19, 1904.

"Reports of Cases Decided in the Supreme Court of the State of Oregon During the October Term 1891, March Term 1892, and May Term 1892, vol. 22, by George H. Burnett, 1892, Oregon State Printer's Office, Salem, Oregon, p. 452-456.

"Republicans Hold Their Primaries," *Lake County Examiner,* March 13, 1902.

"Republicans Hold Their County Convention," *Lake County Examiner,* March 27, 1902.

"Reign of Terror," *Oregonian,* May 10, 1904.

"Was Not Suicide," *Oregonian,* June 9, 1904.

"Local News," *Lake County Examiner,* March 3, 1904.

"Silver Lake on the Eve of a Big Boom," *Lake County Examiner,* February 26, 1903.

"An Illustrated History of Central Oregon," Western Historical Publishing, 1905, Spokane, WA, p 827.

This tree on Wolf Creek, about four miles northeast of Paulina, was one of two trees in Crook County believed to have been meeting places of the sheepshooters. The second tree was on Committee Creek on the East edge of the Horseheaven area.

Chapter Five

The Notorious Sheepshooters

In February 1927, a district ranger by the name of Charles S. Congleton wrote a report at the request of Forest Supervisor Vern Harpham about events in the history of the Ochoco National Forest. "While out on my rounds of the district this winter I have made it a point to get what information I could from the old timers relative to the range wars in the early days between cattlemen and sheepmen," wrote Congleton, who had recently interviewed a mysterious figure he referred to only as "Mr. B.," and described as a man who "was in the ranching game and cattle business in Camp Creek country for a good many years in the early days and during the range wars in the Camp Creek, Bear Creek and desert countries." The Camp Creek area described is found south of the Maury Mountains in south central Crook County, just north of Hampton Buttes.

Although the mysterious Mr. B was wrong about the year of the Benjamin Lake sheep kill, he convinced Congleton that he himself had been there. "Mr. B goes into so much detail about this slaughter that naturally one would think that he was there himself, and I really think he was, and I do not doubt a single statement he has made," wrote Congleton. One insight in particular offered by that elusive character did ring true. He related how sheep shooting in Oregon had originated in Grant County.

In July of 1896, a powerful newspaper, the *New York Times*, carried the powerful headline "The Sheep War in Oregon," above a small story that described two sheep kills that were miniscule by later standards. In early July a band of sheep belonging to Scharff Brothers was shot into, with eight sheep killed. Also in early July, a band of sheep belonging to John Nealon was shot into with 15 dead, and about 60 wounded. The Nealon's herder caught some lead in the shoulder, and his dog was killed. Both incidents occurred in Fox Valley, located about 17 miles northwest of John Day.

What was significant about the article was its description of a very early, organized effort to keep sheep out of a particular area, that agreed with Mr. B's account of the origins of sheep shooting in Oregon. "Early this Spring the people of Fox Valley decided that sheep could no longer be promiscuously herded in their valley, and notified all to that effect. As a result of their determination, bands were fired upon and many sheep killed and wounded."

A 1906 article in the magazine *Pacific Monthly* agreed that range violence in Oregon got its start in Grant County around 1896. "At that time the sheep men from the north drove their flocks into the south fork of the John Day River, and insisted upon staying there until the settlers were forced to make a 'dead line' and form a local organization. That was the first range war in Oregon."

In 1896 and 1897 there was a decided uptick in violent encounters between stockmen all over the west that was largely attributed to the creation of various forest reserves and other actions by the federal government. In January of 1893 a proclamation had been submitted to President Harrison establishing the boundaries of the Cascade Range Forest Reserve in Oregon. On April 14, 1894 the Department of the Interior issued regulations to protect the reserves that prohibited the "driving, feeding, grazing, pasturing or herding of cattle, sheep, or other live-stock within the reservation." The creation of the reserves dramatically changed the landscape for stockmen, and forced sheep out of the mountains and into the low valleys that had traditionally been the spring and summer range of cattlemen. In 1897 the Organic Act was passed, allowing for the appointment of men to supervise and patrol the reserves.

"More than 400,000 head of sheep have each recurring summer been driven from the hot and dried-up plains to the cool shades of the mountain slopes, which they are now prohibited from using for grazing purposes by reason of the creation of the reserve," reported the *Oregonian* in May of 1897. By the summer of that year, the Department of the Interior realized the error of their ways, and decided to allow sheep back on the reserves of Oregon and Washington, with a few stipulations: The sheep could not injure forest growth; could not interfere with the grazing rights of others; and sheep owners were required to apply to the commissioner of the general land office for permission to graze their flocks on the reserve.

Despite that reversal, the stage had already been set for increased range violence in Oregon. The status quo had been upset, and certain stockmen had learned to take the law into their own hands in a system with few rangers and forest officers to provide enforcement. Bands of sheep were shot into or poisoned, corrals were burned, sheep camps were robbed and destroyed. Events were scattered, random, and fairly minor at first, but became increasingly more organized and more damaging as time wore on.

1896 was the year that several men were arrested and brought to trial for grazing sheep on the reserves. In 1897 the General Land Office issued a set of regulations to govern grazing. Stockmen of all types had serious doubts about the new system that promised each man exclusive grazing rights in a certain area. They feared that the range would not be divided fairly, that their stock might not have access to water, but mostly they feared that the pathetically understaffed Interior Department could not possibly provide adequate enforcement. That fear set the stage for some to take the law into their own hands.

Another man interviewed by Congleton in 1927 was William D. Officer, who Congleton described as "an old timer of the Izee country" southwest of John Day in Grant County. According to Officer, "The Izee sheep shooters were organized in the Izee country in 1896. The cattlemen formed this organization for their protection from sheepmen encroaching on their cattle range. The cattlemen state that the sheepmen from far distant winter and spring ranges would bring their sheep during the summer to the Snow Mountain and Izee country, and would herd their sheep right down to the cattlemen's pasture fences, 'eat out their door yards,' as they put it. The cattlemen felt that the only thing to do was to form this organization and when the sheep came too near their ranches, a bunch of sheep shooters would get together and go out and hold up the herder and camp tender and then would kill a good portion of the band of sheep, inflicting unbearable losses on the sheepmen. Naturally the sheepmen moved out and had more respect for the cattlemen after that. This sheep-shooters organization of the Izee cattlemen was in excellent working order, and killed thousands of sheep in the Snow Mountain, Izee, and Bear Valley country from 1896 'til 1906, the later date being the year the National Forests were put under administration and the Forest Service made lines between sheep and cattle ranges for administrative purposes and incidentally put a stop to the range wars."

Officer seems to have arrived in the Izee area around 1890, and lived in Grant County continuously until the time he was interviewed by Congleton. He had 160 acres five miles southeast of Izee patented to him by the U.S. government in 1891, so his claim of knowledge of history of the area seems legitimate. Range violence did continue in the southwest corner of Grant County through the early 1900's, just as Officer said. Bear Valley lies in the south central portion of Grant County and South of John Day. Silvies River and Canyon Creek flow through the region. Izee is in the southwest corner of Grant County, south of Dayville on the south fork of the John Day River, and about 12 miles east of the Crook County border.

The Paulina Valley in east Crook County was supposed to be the next area where the practice of shooting sheep was taken up, and the outlaws there have been associated with a meeting place under a lone pine tree. The Sheepshooter Tree was for many years an important symbol of the sheepshooter culture in Oregon.

Congleton interviewed another mystery man, "Mr. A," parenthetically identified as Fred Powell, who described an organizing meeting of the sheepshooters that took place one night in July of 1898 under a lone pine tree at Wolf Creek about four miles northeast of the town of Paulina. Fred Powell had a large stock ranch near that tree, on Wolf Creek.

> "Mr. A went, arrived at the designed place about 11 P.M. and found a big bon fire burning and some twenty-five to forty men sitting in a circle around the fire. Mr. Henry Snodgrass, Izee cattleman, was speaker of the night. After Mr. Snodgrass had outlined the purpose of the meeting and the methods used in sheep killing in the Izee country, he stated that if there was anyone present who did not want to join the Paulina sheep-shooters, it was time for them to get up and leave the meeting, go home and go to bed. Then Snodgrass called each man by name in rotation around the circle and asked them if they agreed to join.
>
> Mr. Snodgrass had called the names almost around the circle and each man in turn had agreed to join, until he called Billie Congleton's name, then Billie asked Snodgrass, 'Now Mr. Snodgrass, I understand you to say that it is the agreement that if we go out to kill sheep and it becomes necessary for us to kill a herder or camptender we are to bury them there and say nothing about how it happened; and furthermore you state that if any of our crowd is ever arrested or brought to trial for any sheep killing we agree to go on the witness stand and swear to lies in order to obtain an acquittal of the accused in court?' Mr. Snodgrass said, 'Yes, that must be the agreement.' Then Billie said, 'Well, that lets me out, I can never agree to that kind of compact, so I will go home and go to bed.' Then Sam Courtney said, 'That also lets me out,' and Mr. A Said, 'That lets me out also.' And the three of them, Congleton, Courtney, and Mr. A got up and left the meeting and went home."

State Representative John N. Williamson of Prineville, a major sheep owner himself, had been instrumental in the successful effort to allow sheep back into the reserves. In the spring and summer of 1902, some Crook County stockmen were crowded out of their rightful, government ordained grazing allotments on the reserve by "outside sheep." The Crook County men were careful to avoid trouble in these cases, because they had been warned by officials of the Interior Department that if they could not settle their differences themselves, those in conflict would have their future range privileges revoked. It was believed at the time that there had been collusion between the forest rangers of the Department of the Interior and the outside sheepmen who received grazing allotments.

In June of 1901 a group of cattlemen in Crook County made what appeared to be a first gesture toward defending the range that they considered theirs by publishing a notice in the newspaper. Despite its small size, that notice bore a tone that would become familiar in years to come.

Notice
To whom it may concern: The Crook County Cattlemen's Protective Association have located for its exclusive use the territory bounded on the north by the summit of Mowry Mountain, on the south by the desert, and extending from the north fork of Bear Creek on the west to Camp Creek on the east.
By order of the Executive Committee

The territory described by the cattlemen covered an area about 25 miles wide. The north boundary of their claim, Maury Mountain, is about 23 miles southeast of Prineville. The south boundary, "the desert" was vague and could have extended all the way to the county line. Deschutes County would not be created until 1914, so in 1901 the south boundary of Crook County was the north boundary of Lake County. The Crook County Cattlemen's Protective Association may have been supplanted by the Crook County Cattlemen's Association, formed in September of 1902, because the two organizations were structured in the same way, with officers forming an "executive committee" and a written constitution and bylaws.

In the spring of 1902 diverse stockmen of Crook County decided to organize to protect their interest in the range, and formed the Crook County Stockgrowers Association. They wanted to protect the home range, and they organized themselves like a corporation, with a set of officers and a constitution and by-laws. Sixty men attended the meeting in response to an invitation published in the *Crook County Journal*. One of their stated purposes was to settle "range disputes and to hold Crook County range for Crook County stock as far as practicable." The first official act of the association was to draft a resolution reflecting their thoughts on the subject of grazing on the Cascade Forest Reserve. The committee on resolutions was comprised of Andrew Morrow, Roscoe Knox, and Judge W. C. Wills.

The main gripe of the stock growers seemed to be having been put at a disadvantage to stockmen of northern counties by the creation of the reserves. They believed that their grazing grounds had been usurped by the sheepmen of Wasco County. Anyone wishing to graze stock on the reserves had to apply to the Interior Department's office at The Dalles one hundred and twenty miles away. A factor that was "both inconvenient and expensive for our stock growers, resulting in an advantage to the non-residents and in a discrimination against the people of this county in choice of allotments, and a great injury to the local grower in the destruction of his grass and ranges by the passage of enormous herds of sheep from other counties through this county going to and from the Reserves."

In December of 1902, the Crook County stockmen met with Inspector Harold D. "Doug" Langille of the Department of the Interior's forestry branch, known as "Division R." Langille made a presentation at the stock growers' quarterly meeting at Prineville, and laid out the government's plan for managing and dividing the range inside of the Cascade reserves. "He also inquired into the conditions confronting the cattle men who must have the summer pasturage on the reserve and said that certain portions would be set apart for their especial use and that they would be subject to the same restrictions as were the sheepmen." Langille explained his vision of the future, saying that the government wanted to gradually decrease the number of stock grazing on the reserves, and that "by that time conditions would be such that there would be a definite series of lines established to the ranges and no trouble would be encountered."

After his appearance at the stock growers' meeting, Langille was 'roped' into a meeting with a committee from the Crook County Cattlemen's Association, that on the same day formed a permanent organization and elected officers. Marion R. Biggs was elected president; Amos Thompson, vice president; John Henry Gray, secretary; and C. Sam Smith, treasurer. Langille was questioned on the subject of the grazing of cattle on the Cascade reserve.

In his memoirs, Langille described the atmosphere in Crook County at the time. "At Prineville I addressed what I supposed to be a stockmens' meeting. After adjournment I was informed that only sheepmen were present; I was scheduled to talk to the cattlemen in the afternoon. So bitter was the feeling that cattlemen would not sit in the same room with sheepmen. Division and segregation of the range was promised."

At a meeting the summer before, the cattlemen had appointed some temporary officers, and signed a petition that they sent to the Secretary of the Interior on July 28, 1902. What the cattlemen requested was "that a strip of land six miles wide along the south and west boundary of the Blue Mountains Reserve in Crook County and all of the Maury Mountain Reserve be held for cattle and horses only." The document was signed by temporary president Biggs and temporary secretary Edgar T. Slayton.

"The sheepmen and cattlemen who are summering in the Blue mountains are on the verge of a conflict," warned the *Deschutes Echo* in July of 1903. "The cattlemen have given the sheepmen such part of the range as they considered just and are holding the sheep to that part. The sheep range is already exhausted and the sheepmen will have to break over the line or see their bands starve."

In the spring of 1904, Biggs traveled to Washington D.C. to again request that the range be segregated between cattle and sheep. Chief Forester Gifford Pinchot took his time with the request of the Crook County cattlemen, and did not respond in writing until March 28 of 1904. He denied the request to have two large portions of the reserves set aside for the exclusive use of cattlemen.

"Mr. Langille states that in his opinion the only way in which the matter can be satisfactorily settled is for the representative of the Government to make a detailed investigation of the ground itself, taking into consideration the character of the range in each particular locality and hearing at length the claims of both cattle and sheep men. I can assure you, however, that the recommendations of this Bureau will be based upon the following general principles:

1. Local questions will be settled on local grounds.

2. Sudden changes in industrial conditions will be avoided by gradual adjustment, after due notice.

3. Prior users , small users, and actual home makers and home owning residents will have a preference in the allotment of range.

4. Range questions will be decided as far as possible in cooperation with the grazing interests and especially in cooperation with live-stock associations.

I shall be exceeding glad to arrange for a field examination of the range problem on the proposed Blue Mountains Forest Reserve in the early summer."

So, the two new livestock groups formed in Crook County were not unique by any means, but were another manifestation of government control of a previously open, public range. Men like Langille encouraged stockmen to form into associations, empowering them to facilitate the division of the range and the drawing of lines between themselves. Local associations of sheepmen or "woolgrowers" were formed during the earliest days of the reserves, and were well established by 1904.

In early 1903, the range trouble pot began to boil in the vicinity of Fife and Buck Creek in southeastern Crook County. William W. Brown, a major sheep operator with headquarters there, had been cited by agents of the Interior Department for having illegally fenced a large amount of government land. As the result of the government order, and a report made by special agent Edward Dixon, Brown was forced to remove 100 to 200 miles of fence. Brown reacted by reporting on neighboring ranchers who also had illegal fences, approximately 35,000 acres of government land had been enclosed. Cattlemen had fenced the range to keep off sheep, and the papers predicted that they would take revenge on Brown.

"There is a strong probability that a large number of Brown's sheep will go the way of others that have come in the way of the cattle men of that section and, as Brown has large bands of sheep that will be ranged in close proximity to a great deal of the land that has been thrown open, and is looked upon by the cattle owners as the cause of the opening of the fences, he will naturally be the object of their vengeance."

Their predictions were correct. In late February 1903 a flock of sheep belonging to Brown was attacked in Riddle Canyon near Hampton Buttes, even though the illegal fences were allowed to remain up until that fall. Very little information about the attack made it into the news of 1903. Rifles were used in the slaughter, but the herder was allowed to flee the scene before the shooting began. Between four and five hundred of Brown's sheep were killed. Years later the herder was identified as Monroe Miller by his cousin, Fred Houston. Like the sheep kills to follow in 1904, the attack on Brown's sheep was done early in the year while the animals were on winter range.

The Interior Department flatly denied any responsibility for Brown's trouble. "While Federal officials have no intimation that the threats of trouble between sheep and cattle growers in Eastern Oregon may have had any connection with the Government's crusade, it is felt that trouble may possibly occur after the public lands are restored." Was it a mere coincidence that the attack on Brown's sheep occurred during the week that Harold D. Langille, Forest Inspector of the Department of the Interior, was meeting with stockmen at Burns?

In a 1979 interview, Sam Boyce, who knew Brown, said that after the sheep kill Brown had tracked the sheepshooters to the east side of Hampton Buttes and questioned people living in the area. Boyce speculated that cattlemen living there were involved, and sang a few lines of a folk song that described the event.

> *"Bill started out for Buck Creek with his pockets full of chuck, but he thought he'd go to Hampton for to try and change his luck. The weight of 30-30s came a whizzin' down the draw, Bill was mighty certain that the work was pretty raw."*

The witnesses against Brown in the government case were Nimrod Comegys and Joseph Street and the sheriffs of Crook, Lake, and Harney counties. According to the notes of A.R. Greene, a special agent of the Interior Department, Brown had unlawfully enclosed one entire township of land in Lake County. In 1900 Street was a close neighbor of Brown's, occupying the same census page, and a stock raiser in Hardin precinct, which lies in the extreme southeast corner of Crook County. Comegys was skipped in the 1900 census, but he and his wife had land patented to them by the U.S. government in 1906 and 1908 northeast of Wagontire Mountain.

When asked about the attack on Brown's sheep, Mr. B told Congleton, "Cattlemen in that part of the country picked up the methods of sheep-shooting from the Paulina men.... there was never any meeting or formal organization of the sheep-shooters in that part of the country, a bunch of them just got together and went out and 'touched up' Bill Brown's sheep for a few hundred head in the early spring of 1903."

In April of 1903 another brief "notice to stockmen" appeared in the *Crook County Journal* with more of the language common to the propaganda of the sheepshooters. "We the citizens of Ochoco respectfully request the sheepmen to respect the range enclosed by the following described boundary lines, viz:" began the warning, that went on to describe, by naming natural landmarks, an area of about two townships lying 15 miles east of Prineville. The warning closed with the words, "By order of committee." One of the natural boundaries described in the notice was Horse Heaven Creek, home to some of the men who claimed to be responsible for the later, sensationalistic, sheepshooter letters.

Edwin Z. Wakefield of the Newsom Creek and Post area lost 150 sheep in what was described as a "shooting scrape." The newspaper of the account offers no additional details about the incident, which probably happened in early April of 1903.

A neighbor of Wakefield's, Diedrich Koopman, had considerable trouble in the Newsom Creek area beginning in 1900. That year he lost five cabins and a house to arson. In 1902 unnamed parties killed 100 of his sheep. In 1903 arson took 30 tons of hay and another 200 sheep were killed. In April of 1904 vandals cut his fence on both sides of the posts for an entire mile.

In February of 1904 the sheepshooters struck at Reid Rock in north Lake County. Then on April 28 the largest sheep kill ever to occur in Oregon happened at Benjamin Lake. The first report of the attack came out of Silver Lake:

> *"The affair took place about three o'clock in the afternoon. The day was very warm and the sheep were camped. The blood-hunters first came to the camp tender. They put a flour sack over his head and mounted him on one of his pack horses and took him to where the sheep were about a mile away. They also blindfolded the herder and two men guarded them while the other seven proceeded to destroy one of the finest bands of sheep in Lake County. After two hours of slaughtering with knives, guns, and clubs, about 300 was all that were spared out of 2700 head. Destroying almost the entire band, they then informed the employees of the band of sheep that they would give them time to gather up what sheep remained and get them across the dead line as soon as possible. Before they took their departure they warned the men not to come north of the Wagontire road with another band of sheep in the future. The sheep-*

killers told the camp tender to inform every sheepman he saw that the next band of sheep found in around Benjamin would meet with the same result and they would not spare the herders hereafter. These fellows informed Mr. Wilcox to have this report published in the Lake County papers so all sheepmen could take warning in the future."

News of the slaughter spread quickly around the state. At Ashwood, the *Prospector* reported that the sheep of "Grube and Parker" had been attacked by 10 masked men at Benjamin Lake and the sheep "were killed like rabbits in a drive.... it is charged that cattle men are at the bottom of it. This is believed to be the beginning of a very bitter range war."

The *Crook County Journal* provided additional details by naming some of the owners of the sheep, which was a band of whethers, or castrated males about two or three years old, belonging to several men. Chester B. Parker of Paisley, and Howard Mulkey and Harrison Price of Lakeview were among the owners. "It is believed that this is the same gang which killed another band of the same number a few weeks ago," claimed the *Journal*, referring to the slaughter at Reid Rock. The sheep kill at Benjamin Lake lasted only two hours.

On May 20 District Attorney Lafe Conn filed warrants with the county for the arrest of nine unnamed men for maliciously killing animals, the property of another. Jonas Norin was named as another of the owners of Benjamin Lake sheep, and claimed to have lost 500 head there. Witnesses named by Conn were Scott H. Wilcox, the herder; A. T. Robinson; George Winkleman; and Jonas Norin. Separate warrants were issued for the arrest of the Reid Rock sheepshooters on the same day.

As in the sheep kill at Reid Rock, the Benjamin Lake band was on the low desert and winter range, just inside the Lake County line. Knives, clubs, and guns were used in both attacks. The herder was allowed to go free after both incidents. The sheepshooters wore sacks over their heads and used sacks to blindfold the herder and camptender at both sheep kills. The only differences in the two attacks seems to be that, at Benjamin Lake there were four more sheepshooters in the party, and the Benjamin Lake sheepshooters wanted and asked for publicity, as though they had a broader agenda. The sheepshooters, in the months that followed, showed a real penchant for propaganda, and were eager to draw attention to themselves. They sent several sensationalistic and inflammatory letters to the editors of newspapers in 1904, two of which have survived in print and are reproduced here because they contain important clues about the identities of those men.

The first surviving letter was addressed to one of the officers of the Antelope Woolgrowers Association, and was received at Antelope shortly after the return of three sheepmen from a meeting with cattlemen to negotiate range lines in the Blue Mountains Reserve. An agreement was not reached at that meeting. The letter was reproduced in the *Prospector* at Ashwood, a Crook County town about 15 miles south of Antelope. It was from the stockmen of "Horseheaven, Crooked River, and Beaver," a vast area that stretches from just southeast of Prineville, all the way east to Grant County. Although the letter was not officially claimed as the work of the sheepshooters, the similarities in the threatening tone and in the language used are almost unmistakable.

Prineville, Or., July 14, 1904

Mr. H.C. Rooper,
Antelope, Oregon

You will please notify the members of your association that the contracting parties in the agreement made at Howard last Tuesday represent only a small part of those who are entitled to range privileges which conflict in interest with that agreement, and that any attempt to follow out the agreement on the part of your members who own sheep will result in a contest for the range involved that will not be pleasant. If any of your members are unwise enough to presume upon the strength of the agreement mentioned they must take the consequences.

Horseheaven, Crooked River, and Beaver Stockmen

P.S. Perhaps you have never realized that the reward offered by your association makes it rather hard on your sheepherders and camp-tenders, as it is not our purpose to be testified against, no matter what reward and inducements are offered, and the offering of money rewards simply makes your employees existence in Crook county the more strenuous. You will understand exactly what we mean.

Another letter was dated December 29, 1904 and addressed to the editor of the *Oregonian* at Portland, but was never published in that paper, probably because it was such an obvious tool of terrorism. The editors of "An Illustrated History of Central Oregon" reproduced the letter in its entirety, and claimed that it had been published in the *Oregonian* on July 16, 1905. A thorough search of all issues of that paper for January and July has failed to produce the original.

Crook County, Oregon
December 29, 1904

Morning Oregonian
Portland, Oregon

Mr. Editor;

Seeing that you are giving quite a bit of publicity to the Sheep Shooters of Crook County, I thought I would lend you some assistance by giving you a short synopsis of the proceedings of the organization during the past year. Therefore, if space will permit, please publish the following report:

Sheep Shooters' Headquarters, Crook County, Oregon

December 29, 1904

Editor, Oregonian;
I am authorized by the association (The Inland Sheep Shooters) to notify the Oregonian to desist from publishing matter derogatory to the reputation of sheep-shooters in Eastern Oregon. We claim to have the banner county of Oregon on the progressive lines of sheep-shooting, and it is my pleasure to inform you that we have a little government of our own in Crook County, and we would thank the Oregonian and the Governor to attend strictly to their business and not meddle with the settlement of the range question in our province.

We are the direct and effective means of controlling the range in our jurisdiction. If we want more range we simply fence it in and live up to the maxim of the golden rule that possession represents nine points of the law. If fencing is too expensive for the protection of the range, dead lines are most effective substitutes and readily manufactured. When sheep-men fail to observe these peaceable obstructions we delegate a committee to notify offenders, sometimes by putting notices on tent or cabin and sometimes by publication in one of the leading newspapers of the county as follows:

'You are hereby notified to move this camp within twenty-four hours or take the consequences. Signed: Committee

These mild and peaceful means are usually effective, but in cases where they are not, our executive committee takes the matter in hand, and being men of high ideals as well as good shots by moonlight, they promptly enforce the edicts of the association.

We have recently extended our jurisdiction to cover a large territory on the desert heretofore occupied by sheepmen, and we expect to have to sacrifice a few flocks of sheep there this winter.

Our annual report shows that we have slaughtered between 8,000 and 10,000 head during the last shooting season and we expect to increase this respectable showing during the next season providing the sheep hold out and the Governor and Oregonian observe the customary laws of neutrality.

We have burned the usual number of camps and corrals this season, and also sent out a number of important warnings which we think will have a satisfactory effect.

We have just received a shipment of ammunition that we think will be sufficient to meet any shortage which might occur on account of increase of territory requiring general protection.

In some instances the woolgrowers of Eastern Oregon have been so unwise as to offer rewards for the arrest and conviction of sheep-shooters and for assaults of herders. We have heretofore warned them by publication of the danger of such action, as it might have to result in our organization having to proceed on the lines that 'Dead men tell no tales.' This is not to be considered a threat to commit murder, as we do not justify such a thing except where flock owners resort to unjustifiable means in protecting their property.

Mr. Editor, please excuse the lack of systematic order in preparing this, our first annual report. Our office is not yet supplied with the necessary printed forms so useful in facilitating reports. We have thought of furnishing the names of our officers, and also those of honorary members of the order, but as your space will probably not admit of a supplementary report at this time, we will not be able to furnish a roll of honor that will be complimentary to the cause.

Signed: Corresponding Secretary
Crook County sheep-Shooting
Association of Eastern Oregon

SUPPLEMENTARY REPORT

The New Year was duly observed by our brave boys by the slaughter of about 500 head of sheep belonging to a gentleman who had violated our rules or laws. The names of the active participants in this last brilliant action of the association have not yet been handed in. When they are we will take pleasure in recording them on the roll of honor above mentioned.

The Crook county papers have recently said some uncomplimentary things about our order which may invite attention later on. Our work is now of too much importance to justify a diversion from the regular order of business.

Cor. Sec. C.C.S.S. Association

The careful reader will note that that the "executive committee" that printed an earlier notice in 1901 claiming territory up to the edge of the desert, referred to themselves again in 1904 claiming to have extended their territory *into* the desert and having taken issue with winter ranging bands of sheep like those at Reid Rock and Benjamin Lake. And, that the writer of the sheepshooter letters seems to have been a past member of the "Crook County Cattlemen's Protective Association."

With the summer of 1904, sheep shooting returned to Crook County in a relatively minor raid on a band of sheep belonging to Alvis P. Jones on Monday, June 13. It was the first significant incident to happen in Crook County since the attack on Bill Brown's sheep in February of 1903.

Masked men killed about 65 sheep that day on Mill Creek, which flows out of the Blue Mountains northeast of Prineville. Three weeks prior to the attack, a group of men representing the Antelope Woolgrowers had visited the same site with some Crook County cattlemen in an attempt to negotiate lines for sheep and cattle, but were unsuccessful. The owner of the sheep, "Allie" Jones, was a resident of Crook County. The herder was guarded by one man while the shooting took place, and afterward was "told to turn the remainder back and keep them out of the territory in which they had been found." Knives and clubs were not mentioned in this attack, or the time of day, or a corral.

The next violent outburst occurred in far away Baker County, at a sheep camp on the slopes of Old Baldy Mountain, located about 15 miles south of Baker City. The methods used in that attack were different from those used around Crook and Lake Counties. Six men who wore no masks or disguises struck a band of sheep at 9 o'clock at night. The camptender had left the flock to go to town for supplies, and the sheepshooters did not bother to check the tent for the herder, so may have believed the flock was unattended. The herder, G. W. Brooks, snatched up his rifle when he heard the shooting start and dashed into the woods. The sheepshooters were thwarted in their attack by Brooks, who returned fire and wounded one man. "He seized his rifle and ran out of the tent, when he saw six men a short distance away firing into the band of 2300 sheep as they lay scattered about camp on the mountain side." No official complaint was filed by the owner, Miles Lee, and the amount of damage to the flock was not reported.

"The trouble results from the sheepmen being driven out of the mountain ranges by the United States forest rangers, as about all of their former grazing ground has been taken into the new forest reserves," claimed an *Oregonian* article datelined at Baker City. "The sheepmen, being forced out of the mountains have, it is claimed, encroached on the ranges that have been used for years by ranchers in the valley for their Summer cattle range. One peculiarity about these raids is the unwillingness of the sheep owners to invoke the law. Mr. Lee declined today to make complaint and have the Sheriff investigate this raid."

Another notice, seemingly very benign, appeared in the *Crook County Journal* in July of 1904. It was a "Notice to Sheepmen," warning them that outside sheep, meaning transient herds from other counties, "would not be permitted to graze in the territory south or east of Lookout Mountain," and was signed, "Crooked River and Beaver Creek Stock Association." The area it described contained Gray Prairie, Horse Heaven, and the shearing plant and corrals of John N. Williamson.

A third piece of propaganda from 1904 did not take the form of a letter, but was instead an attempt by the sheepshooters to draw attention to themselves through the media with a published interview with one of their members. That interview was datelined at Prineville on December 10, published on the front page of the *Oregonian* on December 12, 1904, and had this introduction: "The writer has been fortunate in getting the story of a sheep shooting affair from a participant, and the fact that it was unsolicited enables him to give it without any qualms of consoence.* His story follows:"

Tale of a Sheep-Shooter

"About 3 o'clock in the afternoon the scouts that had been posted during the entire day had ascertained that the herder was alone and unarmed, and that we ran no chances in getting possession of his band. This was done by our party, numbering some dozen men, after we had indulged in a few preliminaries such as firing off our guns and giving vent to a few oaths, just to make the poor cuss stand pat, for if he had attempted to run, we would have had to kill him. He was bound and gagged to prevent his getting away and giving the alarm, and was then placed by the side of a tree.

The band of sheep, numbering about 2000 was then driven to a corral on deeded land, which was done for a double purpose, as we could then shoot without their scattering, and we could also point to the carcasses and say: 'Well, they were on deeded land and whoever killed them did so merely as an act protecting

*their own property.' We then knelt with our
knees on the ground, that every shot from our
30-30's might take effect in more than one
sheep, and thus save ammunition. In this
manner more than 1500 shots were fired, and
as a result 1200 sheep were killed.*

*Those of the band that succeeded in getting
away were without a herder for two days, and
many succumbed to the attacks of the coyotes.*

*Yes, we had our faces blackened so that we
could not be recognized, and it was a veritable
picnic. Had everything our own way from
start to finish. You're d - - d right, that
sheepman will never get within miles of our
range again, that's a sinch."*

The sheepshooter interview more or less described the
attack made on the sheep of Morrow and Keenan, who had a
ranch at Willow Creek in Crook County. The number of
sheepshooters was reported elsewhere as 20, not 12, and the
herder was not alone at the time of the attack, a camptender
was also present. Because of those errors this alleged
sheepshooter interview seems to be a fraud, and a propaganda
tool written over three months later by someone who had not
been present, but who did have an agenda. It was signed with
the initials C.B.W., clearly identifying the piece as a submitted
editorial. Whoever the mysterious C.B.W. of Prineville was, he
or she must have been a person of some influence to have
arranged for the placement of a sensational editorial like that
on the front page of the *Oregonian*.

The sheep kill, which occurred at Little Summit
Prairie on August 26, 1904, was witnessed by one of the sons
of Mr. Keenan who had been working as camptender and was
in hiding nearby. After the incident he reported what he had
seen to the newspapers. The weapons used were described as
Winchester rifles. As before, the herder had a grain sack over
his head. The criminals had blackened their faces by rubbing
them with charcoal.

The methods used in the attack at Little Summit
Prairie differ from the two Lake County sheep kills in several
other ways: The sheepshooters did not wear grain sacks on
their heads; they neglected to 'scare up' and capture the
camptender as had been done in the past, and so allowed him
to witness the whole affair; and they did not use knives and
clubs as had been done at Reid Rock or Benjamin Lake.
Furthermore, the sheep were on summer range, not winter
range. The true number of sheep killed was only 600.

Sheepshooters struck again on October 15, 1904 near Wildcat Mountain on Mill Creek, about 26 miles northeast of Prineville. One hundred sheep were killed outright, and another 100 scattered and were lost when ten men, with faces blackened, held up the herder in the afternoon. The only weapons mentioned in that attack were guns, and the owner of the sheep was Ulysses S. Cowles. The methods used on Cowles' sheep made it most similar to the Morrow and Keenan sheep kill.

Various writers in modern times have pointed to a man by the name of Roscoe Knox as the author of the now infamous sheepshooter letters. The article linking Knox to the mysterious letters appeared in a 1939 history tabloid in Crook County. It described his involvement like this: "Knox took an active part in quelling the range war. Pretending to be a sheep shooter in order to expose the sheep shooters' depredations, he wrote arrogant letters to the *Oregonian*. He signed these letters 'The Sheep Shooters' Corresponding Secretary.'" What was unfortunate about the 1939 claim was that it was made long after Knox had died, and did not attribute the information to any source, such as a family member.

Roscoe Knox was a sheepman of Crook County who lived at Newsom Creek during the range war period, and died in 1908. His daughters were friends of Otto and Bruce Gray, who were neighbors. Their father, John Henry Gray, and Knox were both members of the Crook County Stock Growers' Association in the early 1900's, and Gray was also a member of the Cattlemen's Association. Knox and Gray both had close ties to John N. Williamson, who had a ranch in their neighborhood and was a U.S. Congressman from 1903 through 1907.

In late 1904, before the December 29 sheepshooter letter was written, an unidentified sheepman of Crook County did correspond with Governor Chamberlain, which was a whole different thing than being a publisher of sheepshooter propaganda. "The Governor has recently received several personal and confidential letters from a resident of Crook County, telling him of the reign of outlawry in that section of the state. The name of the informant is not made public for the reason that the outlaws would burn his property, kill his sheep, and perhaps assassinate him, if they knew who made the complaint."

"According to the letters received by the Governor, the cattlemen have recently established new "dead lines" to be observed this Winter, and have announced the intention to shoot all sheep found on the public domain in the territory which they have selected for their cattle. In some instances the territory they have selected includes land upon which sheepmen have grazed flocks for years unmolested."

"The informant says that cattlemen have fenced whole townships of the public domain and hold it for rent to men who need it for the grazing. This man implores the Governor to come to the aid of the law abiding sheepman, for the coming Winter promises to be worse than any previous time for outlawry of the kind mentioned."

1904 closed with the shooting of 500 mutton sheep belonging to Fred M. Smith of Paulina. Reports were conflicting as to the exact date of the attack, which occurred on either Friday the 30th or Saturday the 31st of December. The shooting was done by six masked men on Grindstone Creek, near the headwaters of Crooked River, and southeast of Paulina near the Grant County line. It occurred in the afternoon on a traditional winter range for sheep that had been used by Smith for many years. As far as Smith knew, the grazing right to the place had never been contested. Smith had leased the land from the government.

"The slaughter is looked upon by both sheepmen and cattlemen alike to be one utterly inexcusable in every detail. The sheep were on their own territory and were in no wise molesting the cattlemen's district." The herder of the band was blindfolded, and knives, clubs, and guns were used in the incident which lasted three or four hours. The method used differed from that used in the major sheep kills of 1904 at Reid Rock, Benjamin Lake, and Little Summit Prairie in that the sheep were not corralled and the sheepshooters fired from horseback.

"Unknown men approached the band, which were ranging some distance from the Smith ranch proper, and began shooting indiscriminately," reported the *Oregonian*. "The assailants were mounted. They rode pellmell into the band, using both Winchesters and revolvers, and riding many of the animals down. In their wake was left a string of animals dead and dying, some with broken limbs, some with bullets through parts not vital, and some killed outright."

All of the noteworthy sheep kills that happened around Crook County, from February 1903 through December of 1904, took place around the perimeter of the county, with the exception of the two attacks in the spring of 1904, which occurred just over the county line in Lake County. Reid Rock was the farthest out, being about 18 miles from the old county line that is now the south boundary of Deschutes County.

This widely reproduced photo was taken during the range war period, and has been associated with several different sheep kills, including Benjamin Lake. It first appeared in the *Oregonian* on December 13, 1904, with the caption, "Scene showing slaughtered sheep near Willow Creek, central Oregon." The ranch of Morrow and Keenan was at Willow Creek, but their sheep were killed at Little Summit Prairie.

SOURCES:

"History of the Ochoco," by Charles S. Congleton, dated at Paulina, Oregon, February 8, 1927. The Crook County Historical Society has reproduced Congleton's report in their history pamphlet #141, "Sheep and Cattle Wars," available at the Bowman Museum at Prineville.

"Forest Growth and Sheep Grazing in the Cascade Mountains of Oregon," 1898, by Frederick V. Coville, p. 11, 36, 51, USDA, Division of Forestry, Government Printing Office, Washington, D.C.

"The Sheep War in Oregon," *New York Times*, July 14, 1896. Article has a dateline of July 13 at Portland.

"The War for Range," by Arno Dosch, *Pacific Monthly*, vol 15, February 1906.

"Notice," *Crook County Journal*, June 8, 1901.

"What Hermann Said," *Oregonian*, May 23, 1897.

"Sheep on Reserves," *Oregonian*, July 15, 1897.

"The USDA Forest Service, the First Century," by Gerald W. Williams, Ph.D., July 2000, USDA Forest Service, Washington D.C., p 19.

"A Misconstruction," *Crook County Journal*, March 20, 1902.

"Our Stockmen Meet," Crook County Journal, December 4, 1902.

"Stockmen Meet," *Crook County Journal*, March 13, 1902.

"Cattlemen Organize," *Crook County Journal*, December 4, 1902.

Editorial, *Deschutes Echo*, July 25, 1903.

"Mostly Division 'R' Days," Harold D. Langille, December 1956, Oregon Historical Quarterly, p 301-313, Abbott, Kerns & Bell, Portland, Oregon.

"Cattlemen Hold Annual Meeting," *Crook County Journal*, October 20, 1904.

"The Ochoco National Forest, a History," by Allen H. Hodgson, Deputy Forest Supervisor, 1913. http://www.fs .fed.us/r6/ uma/history/ochocohistory.pdf

"No Funds at His Disposal," *Oregonian*, December 13, 1904.

"William 'Bill' W. Brown 1855-1941, Legend of Oregon's High Desert," by Edward Gray, 1993, Your Town Press, Salem, Oregon, p 36.

"Fences Must Go," *Crook County Journal*, February 5, 1903.

Editorial, *Lake County Examiner*, April 30, 1903.

Local News, *Ashwood Prospector*, January 12, 1904.

Local and General, "Harney Valley Items," February 7, 1903.

Song lyrics are by an unknown author, as recorded by Grant Barney and Sam Boyce in a 1979 interview for the Harney County Oral History Project, #260.

"Cattle Barons of Early Oregon," by David Braly, 1878, American Media Co., Prineville, Oregon, p 46

Cases pending March 1, 1905, land fraud cases under investigation by A.R. Greene, memoranda for use of Francis J. Heney, U.S. Attorney, p 2, Thomas Neuhausen papers, University of Oregon special collections.

U.S. Census Bureau, Twelfth Census of the United States, 1900, Hardin Precinct, Crook County, Oregon.

Bureau of Land Management, records of the General Land Office, land patent of Nimrod Comegys serial #ORBAA 075929 , land patent of Sarilda A. Comegys serial #ORBAA 075928 . Both pieces of land are in T25S R24E, section 20. http://www.glorecords.blm.gov/PatentSearch

Bureau of Land Management, records of the General Land Office, land patent of William D. Officer, serial #ORLGAA 080099. Land is in T18S R28E, sections 8 and 9. http://www.glorecords.blm.gov/PatentSearch

"Killed 2300 Sheep in Two Hours," *Crook County Journal*, May 5, 1904.

"Lake County Sheep Killing," *Ashwood Prospector*, May 10, 1904. Story was originally published in the *Central Oregonian* at Silver Lake.

Editorial, *Ashwood Prospector*, May 3, 1904.

"Information for Maliciously Killing Animals, the Property of Another," May 20, 1904, Record of the Circuit Court, 1886-1982, Circuit Court Basement West Storage Room, Lake County Courthouse, Lakeview, Oregon.

"Notice to Stockmen," *Crook County Journal*, April 23, 1903.

"Another Sheep Slaughter," *Plaindealer*, June 20, 1904. Article describes the meeting between the Antelope Woolgrowers Association and cattlemen of southeastern Crook County.

"Pioneer Memories," *Bend Bulletin*, May 17, 1935.

"Cattlemen Declare War," *Ashwood Prospector*, July 26, 1904.

"An Illustrated History of Central Oregon," Western Historical Publishing, 1905, Spokane, WA, p 718-721.

"Attempts to Repel Raiders," *Oregonian*, July 16, 1904.

"Range Trouble Again," *Ashwood Prospector*, June 21, 1904.

"Drive Out Sheep," *Oregonian*, December 12, 1904. * "Consoence" is not a word in the English language, so must contain typographical errors. The word "consonance," fits the context of the sentence.

"Heney Lets Fall Scathing Words," *Oregonian*, August 1, 1905. This article is the only one found to contain the true number of sheep that Morrow and Keenan lost.

"Notice to Sheepmen," *Crook County Journal*, July 21, 1904.

"Williamson Says He is Innocent," *Oregonian*, July 18, 1905.

"Has Reason to Complain," *Crook County Journal*, April 28, 1904.

"One Thousand Sheep Killed," *Ashwood Prospector*, August 30, 1904.

"Range War Still Continues," *Lake County Examiner*, September 1, 1904.

"Another Sheep Killing," *Prineville Review*, November 3, 1904.

"Roscoe Knox Early Pioneer," *The Crook County News*, Pioneer Edition, August 4, 1939.

"A Hundred and Sixty Acres in the Sage," 1984, by Beverly A. Wolverton, self published.

Biography of John Newton Williamson, Biographical Directory of the United States Congress, http://bioguide.congress.gov/scripts/biodisplay.pl? index=W000552

"No Funds at His Disposal," *Oregonian*, December 13, 1904.

"More Sheep Slaughtered," *Oregonian*, January 3, 1905.

"Masked Men Shoot Sheep," *Crook County Journal*, January 5, 1905.

"Much Interest Taken in Sheep Killing Law," *Crook County Journal*, January 19, 1905.

Benjamin Lake, located in township 24 South, range 20 East in Lake County, was the scene of the largest sheep kill in Oregon, with an estimated 2,300 dead. The attack took place on April 28, 1904.

Chapter Six

Conspiracy Against the Commonwealth

"Go out into Oregon, Mr. Langille, and have an interview with the people of that state from the fifth story of Hotel Portland, come back to D.C. and inform the powers that be that there is a steadily growing sentiment among Oregon people favoring forest reserves," said Mr. Hitchcock. Mr. Langille did.

-Klamath Falls Express

"If the Express is right about this, the Portland Hotel ought to be razed for sheltering a conspiracy against the commonwealth under its roof."

-Deschutes Echo

In 1903 there were still many people in the commonwealth of Oregon who were against the reserves, including constituents of Congressman Williamson. Some wanted the forest reserves abolished completely. A statement made by Williamson at the annual meeting of the Oregon Woolgrowers reflected that sentiment. "Who is doing this reserve business, and for what purpose? The people of Oregon should be consulted and their lands should not be taken away by the wholesale in sagebrush plains." Williamson believed that the reserves were impairing the growth of the state by discouraging settlement and the extension of the railroads.

"Representative Williamson's stand in opposition to the formation of a reserve in Crook, Klamath, and Lake Counties is worthy of commendation," said the *Deschutes Echo*. "There is no doubt that the sentiment of the people of this district is voiced in what he says." The same issue accused the authorities in Washington of holding sagebrush in high esteem and contained the following bit of verse:

> *Oh! Woodman, spare that tree,*
> *Touch not a noble bough,*
>
> *In youth it sheltered me*
> *And I'll protect it now."*

"The Republicans turned down Moody for Williamson in this district and in the meantime it will render its congressman every aid in his fight against the reserves," said the *Echo* in the fall of 1903. "His stand is popular in this vicinity and all over Oregon and he will succeed, we hope."

"The Republicans of this district elected Mr. Williamson and will see that he has a fair and open field to make his mark. That he is on the right side of the forest reserve question passes without argument," said the Echo in October of 1903. Apparently one of the major planks in Williamson's platform was to oppose the reserves.

"When one-fourth of the area of the State of Oregon, including some of its most valuable lands, has been withdrawn from all form of settlement and entry, with the intention of ultimately making these withdrawals permanent, it is time for the people of that great commonwealth to pause and consider the situation which confronts them," began a full page rant in the *Oregonian* of September 7, 1903.

"The reserve as it now stands completely bottles Lakeview up," said the *Lake County Examiner* in the summer of 1903, "and if made permanent will eventually drive every sheep man out of business."

Many additional, minor incidents of range violence, too numerous to describe, occurred throughout eastern Oregon from 1897 to 1905. The sheep were almost always the losers, although cattle were occasionally shot at or had their stacks of winter hay destroyed by arson. Sheep were shot in winter, spring, summer, and fall. The southeast corner of Grant County continued to be a hot spot, with many bands of sheep fired into. There seemed to be no discernible pattern to the violence. Sheep were shot at night and during the day, in corrals, out in the open, or while en route to and from grazing grounds. Sheep were sometimes killed when they ranged far from home, but more often were killed in the county where their owners lived. Contrary to popular belief, all of the animals killed in the four largest slaughters of the period were killed inside of the counties where their owners resided. Sheep were shot on government land, and also on land leased or owned by the sheepmen. Shot on winter range. Shot on summer range. Sometimes they were killed in large numbers, and sometimes individually picked off by sniper fire. Sheep were sometimes poisoned or clubbed to death.

How does one make any sense out of this seemingly random violence? The answer lies in a study of what life was like for the cattlemen, primarily the small operators, during the period. Few owned adequate real estate to grow enough hay to provide winter feed for their herds, or adequate pasture to feed them year round. They had always relied on the free, government owned, open range as a means to feed their cattle most of the year, and had brought them in to a home pasture to feed them only in the depths of winter snows or at branding time.

The open range became crowded by 1897 with settlers and transient stock, primarily sheep, and the cattlemen were not able to adapt quickly enough to survive. There was no grass left on the range for their cattle in the spring and fall, and when they bought hay to feed their cattle, they were lucky to break even when they sold their beef. "It will be remembered that last fall nothing but the best beef was taken from this section of the country, and that at a very low figure," reported the *Lake County Examiner* in the spring of 1904.

About 1903 the government began to crack down on cattlemen who had fenced public land or had claimed a section of grass by acquiring title to the land that surrounded it. The grazing areas that the cattlemen would have preferred to use, those best suited to cattle, were the stream and river valleys and in the 'juniper belt' of mountain foothills. All now stripped bare by an overpopulation of sheep, for which there was a high demand in both meat and wool. The sheep found ideal summer grazing in the forest reserves. Despite paying their fair share of taxes, the cattlemen did not feel they were provided with the same privileges as the sheepmen. Under the new range management system being proposed, spring through fall, the sheepmen would have areas in the reserves set aside for their individual use, complete with a water source, and government officers on hand to enforce their grazing rights. In the spring and fall the sheep would travel in and out of the reserves, stripping bare the meadows surrounding the cattle ranches and everything in between. What were the cattlemen left with?

"It has been my purpose at all times to eliminate timberless grazing lands, particularly in the vicinity of settlements," wrote Langille in his report on the proposed Blue Mountains Reserve, where he eliminated a large area of bunch grass and timberless land that had originally been taken in by the plan. He also eliminated areas of grazing land along the Silvies River and Bear Valley in Grant County, long a hot spot for violence against sheep. "I have drawn a line which includes as much as possible of the valuable timber and eliminates a large area of the juniper belt which is of little value for forest reserve purposes, but affords excellent grazing," he wrote. Bad news for the cattlemen of the area who needed that grass and wanted it protected.

Some cattlemen felt that they had a right to more public grazing land. They were allowed to apply for grazing allotments inside of the reserves, but that did nothing to improve the situation on the government range land outside of the reserves. A good example of that desire was the petitioning done by the Crook County Cattlemen's Association to have an area on the west end of the Blue Mountains included in the new forest reserve, an effort endorsed by Congressman Williamson. "The ardent advocacy of the stockmen in desiring to extend the reserve in this section is due to a desire on their part to have the Government protect the local range from the migratory herds of sheep from other counties," wrote Langille.

Many cattlemen felt that they had no choice but to fight back, and there was a fear that "outside sheep" would be given grazing allotments and that local cattle would be excluded as they had been in the past through collusion of corrupt rangers with sheep operators from other counties. Some cattlemen decided to stake out public land for themselves with an imaginary boundary and then to defend that claim, and so the "deadlines" came into being. A Forest Service history document explained that, in Grant County, "the Sheep Shooters was formed and blazed a 'deadline' through the woods. Any sheep, or sheep herders, found on the cattlemen's side of the line could be killed. The deadline passed just west of Bear Valley and restricted the sheep to the Izee/South Fork area. Large pine trees with deep blaze scars still mark part of this line."

Deadlines in Grant County were also referred to by early Division R ranger Cy J. Bingham, who arrived at John Day headquarters in 1907 when he was promoted to the position of supervisor. "I looked the trouble over, then I drew a line and said, 'You fellers stay on this side, and you other fellers stay on the other side.' Then I says to them, 'I want you people to understand I ain't foolin'. If there's any more shootin' up on this range, I'll get my artillery into action, too. And when I shoot, I don't shoot for pleasure!'" Bingham's account is interesting because he did not put himself above the use of deadly force in grazing disputes, and portrayed the deadline as a device invented, not by cattlemen, but by himself as a forest supervisor.

"According to the letters received by the Governor, the cattlemen have recently established new 'dead lines' to be observed this Winter," reported the *Oregonian* in December of 1904, "and have announced the intention to shoot all sheep found on the public domain in the territory which they have selected for their cattle."

Cattlemen began making public proclamations of their claims for public range. In Lake County, one of those claims was the entire area north of the road that ran from Silver Lake to Wagontire Mountain and extended into what was then Crook County. Some, like M.R. Biggs and his friends, wanted the boundaries of the reserves enlarged to include cattle grazing areas such as hillsides, valleys, and belts of juniper. They staked out their claims with blazes on trees; with the highly sensationalistic and graphic sheep kills; with warnings to herders that fled in terror; with published warning notices in local newspapers; and with cloth posters stamped with the symbol of a skull and crossbones in red ink. One deadline ran from Crooked River near Upper Falls east to Black Canyon. Along that line, which followed the Forest Reserve boundary, were blazed trees, and skull and crossbones posters with a warning printed in red ink:

"Warning to Sheep men--you are hereby ordered to keep your sheep on the north side of this plainly marked line or you will suffer the consequences. Signed, Inland Sheep Shooters."

Cloth posters with red ink had long been a tool of the the Department of the Interior's forestry branch, Division R. They used the posters on roads and trails around the forest reserves to advise travelers about forest regulations and their penalties.

The first ranger appointed anywhere in the United States was Bill Kreutzer, who in 1898 was assigned the task of single-handedly protecting the forests of the state of Colorado by the Department of the Interior. His biography, "Saga of a Forest Ranger," sheds a great deal of light on the grazing situation in the west at the time, and the relationships that existed between early rangers and stockmen.

In 1893 President Cleveland had banned all sheep from all of the proposed forest reserves, which at the time included the whole of the Cascade Mountains range in Oregon, and the Plum Creek Reserve in Colorado where Kreutzer would be stationed. This set an important precedent and created an alliance between most of the early rangers and the cattlemen. "Because of the Government order which excluded sheep from the Reserve ranges, some of the rangers had openly cast their lot with the cattlemen. Therefore, sheepmen looked on all rangers as a part of the force arrayed against them."

According to Kreutzer, early rangers were considered, by themselves and the general public, to be a police force, and most of the seasonal men were called "guards." Kreutzer was still working as a ranger in 1905 when the reserves were taken away from the Department of the Interior and put under the administration of the Department of Agriculture. "One of the inspectors took away his round, nickel-plated badge which bore the words 'Forest Reserve Ranger,' and gave him a new shield-shaped, bronze badge which pictured a coniferous tree flanked by a large U and a large S. It wasn't a symbol of police powers like the old badge, but more truly symbolized the new conception of conservation."

Kreutzer often found himself neck-deep in range squabbles, some violent, and as a result of his alliance with the cattlemen to keep sheep out of the reserves, he learned a thing or two about the methods and culture of the sheepshooters in Colorado. In 1894 the state was shocked by a violent attack on a flock of 2000 sheep that were driven over a cliff in Garfield County. The "Book Cliffs Raid" soon became famous all over the country, and the story was so often repeated that it eventually became transferred in place and in time, blurred by repetitive history and claims that it had occurred elsewhere. There are many accounts out of Oregon, all written well after the range war period, that claim that sheep were driven over a cliff here. But, careful study of the newspapers of the period, which covered all sheep kills in detail, proves that no such thing ever happened in Oregon.

The Book Cliffs Raid was investigated because of its seriousness and the large loss to the owner of the sheep, but not a single one of the estimated 200 cattlemen who had overpowered the herders on the wrong side of the deadline was ever caught. "Every one of the local cowmen had clear alibis. And as later disclosed by the supervisor before mentioned, they were true alibis, for cowmen from farther east had come in to perform the flagrant act." Trading favors in the extermination of sheep was one of the tactics of the sheepshooters, at least in Colorado.

The supervisor referred to was not named in the Kreutzer biography, but was described as a man who had once been an officer in the sheepshooters' organization, formally known as the "Stockmen's Protective Association," and later became a forest supervisor for the Reserve Service. The formal name of the Colorado sheepshooters was uncannily similar to that of the The Crook County Cattlemen's Protective Association, referred to in chapter five, that came into existence by 1901.

The area was the Grand Mesa and Plateau Valley, where cowmen had declared war against the encroachment of sheep right after the reserves were created in 1891, and claimed the high range as cattle range, complete with a deadline. Sheep were killed with guns and clubs while the herders were guarded, then released to warn other sheepmen to stay off the range. The former officer of the Association, turned forest supervisor, offered the text of the oath of secrecy taken by all of several hundred members of the Stockmen's Protective Association:

I,_____ , in the presence of Almighty God and the members of the Western Slope Protective Association here assembled, do promise and swear that I will keep inviolate and not divulge to any person or persons whomsoever any secrets or activities or names of members of the association, that I will do my utmost at all times to protect the ranges of northwestern Colorado against invasion by sheep. All this I promise and swear with a firm and steadfast resolution to perform the same without any mental reservation whatsoever, binding myself under no less a penalty than that of being shot to death should I ever in the least violate this my voluntary obligation.

"Looking back into history we find that Mary's little lamb and all the members of the genus Ovis have continually created disturbances among the peoples of the earth," begins the Kreutzer chapter on range troubles. "An early Biblical story leads one to believe that Cain, Adam's farmer son, killed his brother, Abel, because Abel's sheep got into his corn patch, or whatever he was raising. And, in turn, it might be said, sheep have raised cain ever since that time."

In a fond look back at his years with Division R as an inspector, Doug Langille wrote, "blood-red skull-and-crossbone warnings no longer mark feudal boundaries of sheep and cattle range." Langille seemed to sympathize with the plight of the cattlemen, and frowned upon the sheep. For example, when he described President Cleveland's anti-sheep order of 1893, he wrote that Cleveland had attempted "to bar from the reserve area the wooly flocks that annually swarmed over the grassy flower-decked slopes, grazed to our doorstep in clouds of dust. But the atavism and appetence of the sheepmen did not yield so readily to remote command."

"The cattlemen feel that they are entitled to the full use of certain parts of the range, but according to their statements, their requests for parts of the range have been ignored and promises made by sheep-men have been violated," wrote Langille in 1903 while investigating the proposed Heppner reserve. "Widely blazed lines have been marked by the cattlemen around several sections of land in the vicinity of Five-Mile Creek, and notices posted along the line requesting the sheepmen not to encroach upon the interior area, but these are disregarded, and in the end the cattlemen are practically driven from the range." Langille then requested that two entire townships be set aside for the exclusive use of cattle.

"All indications point plainly to the fact that there is a range war at hand, and it is probable that it will break out during the coming season," wrote Langille in 1905. "Sheep from Wasco, Crook, Sherman, Gilliam, Umatilla and Morrow Counties are driven to the mountains early each season and ranged up to the very doors of the actual settlers and cattle owners. There has been some trouble in the past resulting in bloodshed, but nothing as serious as that which threatens to come about in the near future." Langille further warned that once the Blue Mountains Forest Reserve was made permanent, guards would need to be hired to patrol boundaries, to keep the peace, and enforce the segregation of the range between sheep and cattle. Except for the formality of the language, Langille's message was very similar to that of the sheepshooter's corresponding secretary.

Langille was first an inspector for the Department of the Interior, given enormous authority to hire and fire supervisors and rangers of the department, and to "interpret in the field the law and such regulations as there were."

He was also able to adjust reserve boundaries, and was savvy enough to realize that in order to achieve anything, he had to gain public support and trust. In the winter of 1902 he met representative stockmen at Prineville and Canyon City who would be impacted by the creation of the Blue Mountains Forest Reserve.

Of his successful public relations efforts at a similar meeting in northern California in 1905, Langille wrote, "had a call for musketed volunteers been made at the conclusion of the meeting to defend the reserve, the response of the stockmen would have been unanimous."

Langille later expressed regret over his 1905 departure from Pinchot's forestry department and "early recall" which seems to have been rather sudden. "By now the Forest Service was a lusty youth. Erased was Division R, gone were the days of assessor, referee and adjudicator in the field. Unavoidably *the old order* changed, and with the change dissolved those factors which lent zest and stimulation to the blazing of new trails. I resigned."

But, was that resignation voluntary or forced? In June of 1905, while Langille was in the field working on a report of the proposed Blue Mountains Forest Reserve, he was suddenly called back to Washington, D.C. "It is to be regretted that my recall was ordered before my work in this territory was completed," he wrote in his report on the proposed reserve. "The work had been carried as far as Prineville when my recall was received." The official date of Doug Langille's resignation was November 18, 1905.

When the forest reserves were young, in the first few years of the 1900's, there were few rules in place for the management of grazing, and only a very few good men in place to enforce those rules. The balance of the field force of Division R of the Interior Department was later found to be corrupt, incompetent, or both. There were some honest rangers, "doing the best they knew in the absence of coordinative understanding," wrote Langille. "But the original type of political appointee was mostly or hopelessly unqualified."

A 1901 report by Filibert Roth, chief of Division R, attempted to lay down some of the grazing policies created by Secretary of the Interior, E.A. Hitchcock, and served as a model, or even a template, for men like Langille who were put in the uncomfortable position of sorting out the needs of competing grazing interests. The public meetings called by Langille were a part of the task assigned to him as inspector, that of reporting on the conditions found in each of the proposed forest reserves that he visited. In order to make his report, he had to collect information about current grazing needs and conditions. He had to talk to the stockmen. Langille seemed to admire Roth and his whole department, and referred to Division R as, "the praiseworthy little band," and remarked that, "no group in Washington ever strove with greater fidelity."

Roth had personally visited one of the proposed reserves that occupied part of Lake County, named The Warner Mountains Proposed Reserve, and according to Langille, "pointed the way to escape from the plague of nomadic Basque sheep." New 1901 grazing principles, announced by Hitchcock, written about by Roth, and explained by Langille, shaped the expectations of stockmen in central Oregon and superimposed a very controlled ideal upon a grazing situation that was very out of control. Those principles were to be, "the basis of all grazing regulations in the reserves" of the future. The stock associations were to take the lead in assigning grazing rights, and segregating the range between cattle and sheep. "The local associations should assign ranges to owners within the limits thus laid down," wrote Roth.

Sheep owners were to have the exclusive right to an area, separate from areas where groups of cattle owners had their range. "Local questions should be decided on local grounds, and on their own merit in each separate case," he wrote. The reserve around Mt. Raineer was used as an example, where "the range is divided into sheep and cattle ranges, the sheep range being divided into five well-defined districts, and each band of sheep receives a permit for only one of these districts. This measure has proven of great value by reducing the needless roaming of the numerous bands," explained Roth. "Though there is still considerable opposition to such a system, it may be said that nearly all of this opposition today does not come from the resident, permanent stockmen, but comes mostly from men who run stock wherever there is open range, avoiding all responsibility and owning little outside of their herds."

Roth's ideal of a range segregated between cattle and sheep was viewed as impossible, at least for the time being, by the general public and by the government officials themselves, who knew that such a system would be costly to administer and was not enforceable by the understaffed Division R. "To carry out such a system would entail considerable additional expense upon the Government," wrote Roth "and it has therefore been suggested that a per capita tax or rental should be imposed on all stock grazing in the reserves." But, who would step forward to enforce the government's policies until they became actual regulations and until funding appropriations were made or laws passed to allow the government to collect grazing fees? It seems that task was left to the cattlemen.

Sheepmen were to be penalized in the future with reduced grazing rights, a smaller permit as to the number of sheep allowed, if they willfully trespassed on the ranges of others or areas closed to grazing; entered the reserves too early or stayed too long; corralled their sheep within 500 yards of a stream or spring; bedded their sheep in the same place for more than six nights; or willfully or negligently set forest fires. These and other rules were printed on the back of every application and permit the stockmen handled. Rangers were allowed to order sheepmen to corral their bands to be counted, and to order them off of their allotment when damage was being done by the sheep.

"Extensive dry prairie country" like that found around north Lake County was considered by Roth to be cattle range. "Generally these prairie ranges are less suited as summer pasture to sheep than to cattle, since the latter stand the dry feed and intense summer heat better than do the sheep." Roth believed that cattle would find few suitable grazing areas inside of the reserves, like meadows, marshes, and areas along streams.

According to his limited view, cattle were to remain primarily on the low desert at all times of year. Hitchcock and Roth had failed to appreciate the depleted condition of the open range outside of the reserves, and the nomadic bands of sheep that would persist to overrun it at all times of the year, full knowing that the government could not enforce its own grazing policies. And, Roth's belief that the deserts of central Oregon should be cattle range ignored the fact that the desert had been and would be packed with sheep for years to come.

What were the cattlemen to do in order to survive? The early sheep kills sensationalized their plight and the need to keep foreign sheep off of the range.

"Congress, this year... failed at the last moment to appropriate funds for carrying out the work for the forestry and ranging departments," said the *Crook County Journal* in October of 1904, "but the local stock association has been assured that as soon as money for meeting the expenses of this branch is forthcoming, Crook County will be the first to receive attention."

"The grazing question is going to be a hard one to settle," wrote State Land Agent Oswald West in July of 1904. "The homesteader depends upon the few head of cattle he owns for a living for himself and family. His cattle, during the Summer, range in the hills and mountains near his home and are kept up during the winter and fed hay. If a large band of sheep come his way, they clean out the grass, and his cattle come home in the fall too poor for the market and in no condition to winter." West visited ranches around Klamath and Lake counties, and came away with the impression that the sheep kills were being done, "as a means of settling the question of grazing on the public domain." Many Lake County cattle had not been sold in the fall of 1903 due to low prices for beef.

"Reports from many points in Eastern Oregon indicate a bad Winter for cattlemen," said the Echo in September 1903. "In many places cattle are returning from the Summer range very poor, and with hay both scarce and high in price the winter will be a hard one for many cattle owners."

The new Goose Lake Forest Reserve around Lakeview was not entirely well received in 1903. "Another large tract of land has been withdrawn from settlement with the intention of creating a forest reserve which surrounds the town of Lakeview on three sides. The reason for the creation of a reserve in that district is not apparent to the ordinary mind, but it is probable that the harebrained theorists of the East who dictate the policy of the Government in forestry have discovered some valid excuse for putting Lakeview in a bottle with its mouth open to the desert."

A 1904 article in the *Prineville Review* called "Predatory Sheep" emphasized the dire nature of the problem. "Predatory sheep bands in this state constitute one of the most serious menaces to permanent prosperity of stock sections," said the article. "When grass is gone, the predatory band passes to another spot, denudes another resident's range, and repeats until a rail line is reached and shipment is made to market." Suggested remedies included passing legislation to regulate the influx of sheep, selling or leasing the range to recover damage to local ranchers, levying a tax on the transient sheep, or just excluding them completely.

The writer has concluded, after long and careful study of the subject, that representative cattlemen chose to act as a voluntary, self-appointed, enforcement arm of the reserve system. The reader will find commonality between the policies of Division R, and the tactics of the sheepshooters. What was a deadline, but a boundary segregating cattle from sheep? The Crook County Cattlemen's Association had the same organizational structure as the sheepshooters, with an executive committee, probably a president, vice-president, secretary, and treasurer. Division R and the sheepshooters shared common methods for marking range boundaries, with blazes on trees or cloth posters printed with red ink. The cattlemen had definitely been granted at least some authority by Langille, who encouraged them to delineate the range as they saw fit, and that knowledge of boundaries would have provided them with all they needed to enforce the same. Did they take that knowledge and run with it?

One cannot read Langille's memoirs without believing that he was at least cognizant of the sheepshooters as he looked back fondly on the "blood-red skull-and-crossbone warnings," and wrote with regret about how "*the old order* changed, and with the change dissolved those factors which lent zest and stimulation to the blazing of new trails." The sheepshooters, in one of their letters referred to themselves as "*our order*," and "honorary members of *the order*." The word "order" could infer a distinctive rule, a brotherhood, constitution, or even a fraternal secret society. And then, there was Langille's speedy and untimely departure from Division R.

In early 1905 the responsibility for managing the forest reserves was transferred from the Department of the Interior to the Department of Agriculture where the forests would be administered by the Bureau of Forestry under Gifford Pinchot. In July of 1905 the name of the bureau was changed to "Forest Service." One of Pinchot's early objectives was a general house cleaning and weeding out of undesirable or unfit personnel that had made the transfer to his department along with the reserves. He wanted to build a positive image of a professional department dedicated to public service and scientific forestry, and to get rid of the negative stigma attached to Division R , where personnel had been found guilty of graft, collusion in land fraud, and ineptitude. Many of the first Division R rangers had been politically appointed because of who they knew, not because of what they knew about forestry, which was often very little.

Practically every piece of literature written about the 1905 founding of the Forest Service credits that agency with having put a stop to the range wars in the west, but neglects to mention the role that the creation of the reserves played in inciting grazing conflicts, some of which appear to have been facilitated by early rangers of the Department of the Interior. Kreutzer's biography contains a look back at the range war on Battlement Mesa, and a classic example of that brand of government whitewash.

"About 10,000 sheep now graze there annually, separated from Cowland by an unfenced line, but that line is plainly marked, and both cattlemen and sheepmen respect the rights of the other. The Forest Service had solved a problem with its controlled range management which the stockmen would never have solved with their ropes, rifles, and six-shooters."

Who exactly were the sheepshooters in central Oregon? A lone pine tree on Wolf Creek in Crook County, pointed to as their meeting place, could be a clue in itself with a symbolic meaning. The Liberty Tree was an important symbol of a group called the Sons of Liberty, the same men who brought us the Boston Tea Party. The tree stood in Boston Common and was a rallying point for the growing sentiment against British tyranny. The symbol of the Liberty Tree spread throughout the colonies, with many towns adopting a tree of their own as a meeting place for satellite groups of the Sons of Liberty. In 1765 the original Liberty Tree at Boston made headlines around the world when the Sons of Liberty assembled there to protest against Britain's Stamp Act, then hung two tax collectors in effigy from the tree's branches.

Maybe not coincidentally, the symbol of protest used by the Sons of Liberty against the Stamp Act was a skull and crossbones, often printed in red. To the Sons of Liberty it symbolized "liberty or death." The Stamp Act was a tax that met with great resistance in the colonies. It taxed newspapers and other documents by requiring that a special stamp be purchased and affixed or incorporated into the paper. The Sons of Liberty believed that the Stamp Act meant death to the free press and that Britain was attempting to tax the liberty of free thought and expression. In one issue of his newspaper, The *Pennsylvania Weekly Advertiser*," Benjamin Franklin rebelliously printed a red skull and crossbones in the place where the tax stamp would be required, with the words, "An emblem of the effects of the stamp. O! The fatal stamp."

The Sons of Liberty resented and questioned the right of a distant power to tax them, and wanted to be able to vote on taxes placed upon the colonies. As with the Boston Tea Party of 1873, a protest against the Tea Act, those protesting the Stamp Act considered it to be a form of taxation without representation. The theme of rebellion against a government headquartered a great distance away by men who wanted to govern their own section was a common thread between the

Sons of Liberty and the sheepshooters. Faced with an inability to *enforce* the Stamp Act, the British Parliament repealed it in the spring of 1766.

Constitutional rights were a big concern for some who objected to the government's reserve system, described in the Kreutzer biography as "a fight born in defiance of unjust usurpation of their rights as American citizens and nurtured in bitterness at the seeming impossibility of securing justice." In the spring of 1903 the U.S. Circuit Court ruled it unconstitutional for the Secretary of the Interior to enforce his rules for grazing on the forest reserves. The court decided that the Secretary of the Interior had no authority to declare any act a crime, a power that was vested only in congress. Persons grazing on the reserves without a permit could not be charged with a crime and could not be fined.

Also created during colonial times were "committees of correspondence," comprised of members of the Sons of Liberty who disseminated information among the thirteen colonies to rally opposition and plan resistance against things like the Stamp Act. The correspondents worked to ensure that the information in official letters accurately reflected the views of the Sons of Liberty and that the letters made their way into the proper hands, a duty that was uncannily similar to the role of the sheepshooters' Corresponding Secretary.

Another fragment of colonial American culture survived in the phrase, "dead men tell no tales," found in the sheepshooter propaganda. And, there was more to be learned from that phrase than the obvious threat that it implied. It was the title of a poem from the 1790's by Haniel Long that contained symbolism common to the Vigilantes of Crook County of the 1880's, the sheepshooters, and the Sons of Liberty.

Dead Men Tell No Tales

They say that dead men tell no tales!

Except of barges with red sails
And sailors mad for nightingales;

Except of jongleurs stretched at ease
Beside old highways through the trees;

Except of dying moons that break
The hearts of lads who lie awake;

Except of fortresses in shade,
And heroes crumbled and betrayed.

But dead men tell no tales, they say!

Except old tales that burn away
The stifling tapestries of day;

Old tales of life, of love and hate,
Of time and space, and will, and fate.

In at least two of the sheep kills the attackers had blackened their faces, presumably with charcoal, and also presumably to hide their identities. One day while en route to Sparks Lake, forest rangers James R. Harvey and Cyrus J. Bingham "suddenly faced a sheepherder who held a pointed rifle." The reaction of the sheepman was due to the black charcoal on the faces of the rangers in this incident that probably happened in June of 1906.

Harvey had explained to the sheepman that he had rubbed his face with charcoal to ward off snow burn, which may not have been necessary in the month of June. True or not, the practice of rubbing the face with ashes and soot was yet another tactic of the Sons of Liberty.

In the book "The Stamp Act Crisis," which described the events leading up to the American Revolution, members of the Sons of Liberty often disguised their faces with charcoal when they performed various acts of treason, such as smuggling, piracy, destruction, and demonstrating against the Stamp Act. The practice could have been an homage to James Otis, author of "The Rights of the Colonies Vindicated" who was widely regarded as being one of the masterminds behind the Sons of Liberty. Otis was the man who first suggested the Stamp Act Congress, an assembly of representatives from most of the colonies who met for the purpose of defeating it. Otis put on the face of a penitent in "sackcloth and ashes" by the time of the Stamp Act Congress, and published a pamphlet begging the pardon of Parliament for his past treasonable acts. This was believed to have been only a ploy on the part of Otis, who continued to work covertly with the Sons of Liberty and wrote many scathing, anonymous contributions for the *Boston Gazette*.

In addition to the symbolic tree, skull and crossbones, the blackened faces, and use of a corresponding secretary, the Sons of Liberty, like the sheepshooters, referred to themselves as "The Committee." Ezra Stiles, in 1767, set down the names of men who were active in the Newport Committee of the Sons of Liberty along with a biographical sketch of each member. According to The Stamp Act Crisis, "The Committee contained some Gentlemen of the first Figure in Town for opulence, Sense, and Politeness."

There was also some symbolism in common between the Crook County Vigilantes of the early 1880's and the sheepshooters of twenty years later, and they were believed to have had some members in common. "Crook County, Oregon, is the center about which the range war revolves," wrote Arno Dosch in 1906. "This county is filled with men who love to fight, and always have. The old trouble which used to exist in that county between the Vigilantes and the Moonshiners may be dead, but many men who were in it are still living, and some of them are not too old to look for trouble. They have been there many years, and they feel as if they own the country."

In 1905 a letter from Prineville appeared in the *Oregonian*. The writer identified himself only as "Moonshiner," associated himself with the group that opposed the Vigilantes. He elaborated somewhat on the atmosphere of corruption in Crook County government at the time, and in the sheriff's department in particular. Collusion between the sheriff's department and the sheepshooters was described, at least to the extent where the sheriff was happy to look the other way when range violence occurred. That letter is reproduced here exactly and in its entirety:

Prineville, Or., Sept. 10 (1905)

To the Editor;

An editorial in last week's Crook County Journal makes the claim that the Portland papers are trying to poison the mind of the public against the defendants in the land-fraud trials and also to defame the fair name of this county. I believe this to be a mistake; perhaps through honest ignorance of the editor. Be that as it may, a brief statement of the conditions existing here at the time Crook County first came into being and which are largely responsible for conditions as they exist today, will not be altogether out of place.

In the early part of 1882 a man named Langdon killed two men, named Crook and Jory, on his homestead on Willow Creek. He was arrested and taken to Prineville and placed in charge of a deputy sheriff in the Prineville Hotel. At night a mob came in, overpowered the deputy and shot Langdon to death; it then lassoed a man named Harrison, who had formerly been employed by Langdon, and dragged him to the Crooked River bridge, about half a mile, and hanged him from the bridge, where he was found the next morning. From that time forward the mob, which was a secret organization known as the "Vigilantes," terrorized the county, and any one incurring the displeasure of its leader was either compelled to leave the country or was murdered. Al Swarts was shot, through the window of a saloon, while playing cards with a member of the mob; Sid Huston and young Lester were taken from Elisha Barnes' dwelling and hanged; Mike Mogan was murdered by "Mossy" Barnes, and Frank Mogan was shot down by Bud Thompson, the captain of the Vigilantes, and his brains beaten out with the empty revolver, without the slightest provocation. This last crime was committed in the early part of 1884.

About this time a number of law-abiding citizens got together and formed an organization known as the "Moonshiners," who ordered a lot of the Vigilantes to leave the country, which they did. In the majority of these cases nothing has ever been done, in others a farcical coroner's jury, dominated by the Vigilantes, has brought in verdicts of justifiable homicide or otherwise freeing the murderers.

A number of the original Vigilantes still remain in this county, who, together with other lawless characters, now form what is termed the Sheep-Shooters' Organization. These men are a power in county politics, and many of the law-abiding citizens of the county are afraid to report what they know, for fear of losing stock, or even their lives.

Houses and haystacks have been burned and stock killed and the losers are powerless to either prevent these outrages or secure redress. Why? One reason is that witnesses are afraid to testify to what they know, and jurors, if not already under the influence of this criminal element, are unwilling to bring in a verdict of guilty on the same ground. Violation of the law is, and has been, so common in this county that very little notice is taken of minor crimes.

Gambling is so common that a conviction could not be secured, even in the most flagrant cases.

The gambling element predominates in county politics to such an extent that it virtually controls all the offices, and it is among this element that one finds the remnants of the old Vigilantes.

This county has a jail furnished with approved steel cells, yet jail-breaks are not infrequent. Why?

Sheep killings have been frequent, but no arrests have been made, even when in at least one instance very strong circumstantial evidence was offered a certain official, said official making the statement that the party under suspicion was equally as good a citizen as the informant. That ended the matter, notwithstanding the informant lost property at the hands of the sheep-shooters.

The mysterious disappearance of "Shorty" Davis was another coup of the Sheep-Shooters' Organization, and there is yet more to come.

There are good citizens in this county who are eking out an existence in fear and trembling who would welcome a change; others, more fortunate, have sold their belongings and left for more civilized climes. How long are these conditions to obtain? A rat driven to bay will fight hard, and there are a good many of our law-abiding citizens who feel that they are now in a position where they are forced to pay taxes to protect criminals in crime and are themselves left to the mercy of sheep-shooters and barn-burners. They are afraid to speak publicly of many of the crimes known to them for fear of personal violence. It is only a question of time when these citizens will be forced to take the law into their own hands and purge the community of this undesirable element.

It is believed by many that there are but two results possible if the present conditions prevail *for any length of time, and they are mob rule or martial law.*

These conditions do not prevail to any extent in the farming districts, but the farmer is taxed to support these conditions and is therefore vitally interested in their elimination.

MOONSHINER

Two of the men who experienced the Vigilante days in Crook County and lived to write about it later were James M. Blakely and Colonel William "Bud" Thompson. Both referred to the skull and crossbones as a symbol of the Vigilantes, who were fond of boasting about their acts of terror in the local newspapers. "Some time in December (1882) a stock association was organized, with a constitution and by-laws. It was agreed that no one should ride the range without notifying the association. Copies of the by-laws were sent to every stock owner in the county and all were asked to join,"wrote Thompson, who also described the fate of a gang of alleged rustlers. " Three of the gang were hung to a juniper two miles above town, while another was shot and killed in town. The next morning notices were found posted, with skull and cross-bones attached, telling all hard characters to leave the county."

In a series of interviews for the *Oregonian* in 1939 Blakely said that the Vigilantes sent "threatening letters marked with crossbones and skulls to a good many men.... In general that crowd was in complete control. This gang formed a kind of organization in Prineville and called it a stock association. I was running cattle 14 or 15 miles from Prineville and the Barnes boys told me I'd have to get an order from them before I went out on the range." And added, "Anyone who said anything against the Vigilantes got a warning note, marked with skull and cross-bones.... John Combs... Sam Smith and I were the three men who publicly defied and fought the Vigilantes."

Elisha Barnes and his sons George W. and James M. were all very active in the protest effort against the taking of lands by the Willamette Valley and Cascade Mountain Wagon Road in the 1870's and 1880's. Elisha was said to have been the leader of the protest effort, and wrote to the Secretary of the Interior in 1878 complaining that the government was "being swindled out of a large amount of land that should be thrown open for settlement by actual settlers." The letter was signed by Elisha and George Barnes, John Luckey, and W.G. Picket. Over the course of the next few years, over twenty settlers on wagon road lands were sued for high amounts of back rent and ejected from their farms.

In 1881 A.B. Webdell wrote a complaint to senator James H. Slater asking for aid to the settlers, some of whom were being sued despite a willingness to surrender their property. Webdell even suggested that the settlers of Crook County were threatening to secede from the union with the statement, "So, you may listen to hear the sound of another Fort Sumpter gun," referring to the shot believed to have started the Civil War. "More than twenty suits have been commenced already to eject them, and all sanction by the court is refused," wrote Webdell. "Delays is death to us. All we have is gone."

Note the similarity of sentiment between Barnes, Webdell, and their friends protesting against the wagon road, to that of the Sons of Liberty. The themes of freedom, eminent domain, and rebellion against large fees that seemed unjust were common to both groups. For that reason it is the contention of the author that the use of the skull and crossbones symbol in Crook County during the 1880's was an outgrowth of the settlers protest against the wagon road. Moreover, it seems that no true organized band of Vigilantes ever existed. At least three of the men killed by the alleged Vigilantes were friends of the Barnes family (Charley Luster, Sid Huston, and Al Swarts). Are we to believe that Vigilantes were killing Vigilantes? Or, is it more likely that people protesting against the wagon road were being targeted?

By 1904 there were a few men still living in Crook County who had lived there since the vigilante period of the 1880's. Three seem to have been connected to the "Moonshiners," a political organization that had claimed to oppose the Vigilantes in those days, and the same three seem to have been connected to the sheepshooters.

Charles Samuel Smith, known as "Sam" to his friends, and usually written as "C. Sam Smith," in 1880 lived with his older brother in the household of stockman John Powell. Interestingly enough, John Powell was the grandfather of Fred Powell, one of the men who claimed to have been present at the organizing meeting of the Paulina Sheepshooters.

Smith has already been mentioned as having been a friend of James Blakely and an allie who helped him defy the Vigilantes. Like Billy Congleton and Blakely, Smith was a sheriff in Crook County, serving from 1902 until 1906. He was treasurer of the Crook County Cattlemen's Association when it was first formed in 1902 during the time that John Henry Gray was president. That spring the cattlemen met with Doug Langille to discuss ways to keep transient stock out, and to create lines to segregate the range between cattle and sheep. M.R. Biggs, then president, petitioned to have all the area around Maury Mountains set aside for the exclusive use of cattlemen. Smith and Gray were first and second vice-presidents, respectively, of the Crook County Stock Growers' Association when it was organized in 1902, and of which Roscoe Knox was also an active member.

In 1905 a seething attack on the front page of the *Bend Bulletin* was made against some sheepherders who ventured onto Smith's irrigated lands in the vicinity of Tumalo. Smith was a major stockholder in the Three Sisters Irrigation Company there, and in the article he complained of "overbearing, insolent, and defiant" herders who allowed their sheep to trample irrigation ditches and started a forest fire.

"Some of the hidden facts in regard to the long list of crimes, midnight meetings, shootings and lynchings that were so common around Prineville some 10 or 20 years ago about to be told and given the light of publicity," pronounced the *Bend Bulletin* in a shocking 1908 story that described Smith's true character. In March of 1908 a sheep camp belonging to John N. Williamson was torched, and a few days later his shearing plant and several other buildings were also destroyed by arson. In early April a mile and a half of Williamson's fence was cut on both sides of every post. "These depredations committed against the property of sheep men indicate that the bitter range war that was waged so fiercely a few years ago between cattle and sheep men has not entirely died out," said the article that went on to name none other than "C. Sam Smith, the ex-sheriff" as one of the culprits. Larkin Elliott had been arrested and claimed in his confession that Smith had hired him to help destroy the Williamson property, and that Smith and his 15 year-old son were both present and participants in the work. Smith, according to the *Bulletin* had planned to later dynamite Williamson's house while he and his family slept.

Smith was found guilty of arson on the Williamson shearing plant, and was sentenced to four years in the penitentiary. The accomplice, Elliott, also received four years. "Mr. Smith had said that Williamson was crowding us too close and that we must put him out of business," said Elliott in his testimony. He also admitted that they had poisoned some of Williamson's sheep with a mixture of squirrel poison, lye, and salt. All of those tactics were awfully reminiscent of the methods of the sheepshooters.

At the trial, Elliott's wife described an interesting encounter she had with Smith on the day of her husband's arrest. "I will go down and get him out all right, we will get the best lawyers in the state out here and I will appear on the other side against him and will get him bonds and it won't cost him anything. Don't you worry about that. The most important thing is not to mention my name," said Smith to Mrs. Elliott. After the trial, foreman of the jury John Steidl went public with a claim that two of the jurors had been tampered with in an attempt to free Smith. According to the prosecutors of the case, Smith had been bitter because Williamson had refused to buy the Smith ranch.

An editorial that appeared in the *Bulletin* in May of 1908 was written for the purpose of endorsing Frank Elkins, for the office of sheriff, who had investigated and arrested Smith. The *Bulletin* considered Elkins the exception to corruption in the sheriff's department, and contained some interesting innuendo about Smith himself connected to the case. Elkins, it said, "was bound to antagonize some who had been his friends for years. Furthermore, many believed that the successful prosecution of the guilty men would be a dangerous piece of work, and they based their judgment on what had been done by lawless cattlemen of former years.... Give us a few more sheriffs like Frank Elkins and lawlessness and 'range wars' will be stamped out of Crook County."

Elkins is believed by the author to have been the writer of the 'Moonshiner letter' of 1905. That letter contained a number of errors in fact, so was probably written by someone who was not a resident of Crook County in 1882, or who was very young at the time. The date of Frank Mogan's death was incorrectly given, and he had no head trauma; Crooks was the name of the man killed with Jory, not "Crook;" Luster was the name of the man killed with Huston, not "Lester;" Harrison was killed the day after Langdon, and not on the same night. Elkins was about 10 years old during the Vigilante days, and was a rival of Smith's for the office of sheriff from 1900 until he was elected in 1906. Elkins had the most to gain from an editorial so critical of the sheriff's department in 1905, and used the same tactic to get himself reelected in 1908 when Smith was caught red-handed in arson.

Another man mentioned by Blakely as an allie against the Vigilantes was John Combs, sheriff of Crook County from 1888 to 1890 and also 1894 to 1896. Combs had a couple of brothers in the cattle business, William J. of Crook County, and Joseph D. who lived in the Izee area of Grant County and was sheriff there from 1892 until 1896.

In 1880 Joe Combs was counted twice in the census, shown with homes in both Prineville and Grant County. In the census of 1900, Joseph Combs was listed on the same page as Carlos Bonham, the man whose "IZ" brand was the source of the town's name. Joe's daughter, Amy Combs, married W.H. "Hamp" Officer who was a member of the Officer family that told C.S. Congleton about the formation of the Izee Sheepshooters in 1896. The three Combs brothers were all engaged in the cattle business during the period, and probably traveled between the Izee and Prineville areas, so would have all been privy to the activities of the early sheepshooters.

One of Bonham's daughters, Della Keerins, in later life wrote about her experiences growing up in the Izee country.

The Bonham family ran a sort of lodging house for travelers. "We Bonham's kept every one that came along free until Joe Combs and Bill Hanley came to buy some cattle and stayed all night with us," wrote Keerins. "The next morning they asked my father how much they owed him and he said, 'not a thing...' They told him that he could not do that, and why not hang out a shingle and charge overnight guests."

In 1900 Joseph D. Combs proved up on his homestead claim in township 17 south, range 28 east, which was very close to the place where the attack on the sheep of Mrs. Welch occurred on Canyon Creek, about 15 miles south of Canyon City, in the summer of 1897. In that incident 150 sheep were shot by six masked men who held up the herder and camptender after the sheep were bedded for the night.

Since the pioneer days the Combs brothers had been friends of the family of Frank Menefee, who was district attorney of Crook and Wasco Counties from 1900 through 1904. The Combs family originally settled on Ochoco Creek, north of Combs Flat. John Combs was, in addition to being a cattleman and sheriff, a butcher, realtor, and very involved in local politics. He was a member of the Republican Party and had close ties to John N. Williamson who, like Smith, Blakely, Congleton, and Combs was a onetime sheriff of Crook County. Williamson served as sheriff immediately after Blakely and before Combs, from 1886 to 1888.

In 1902, John Combs was a delegate to the Oregon State Republican Convention from Crook County. At the county convention where he was elected to that spot, the Republicans drafted and passed a resolution on grazing that stated, "We demand that the stockmen of Crook County be given the preference of ranging their flocks in that part of the Cascade Forest Reserve situated in Crook County over the stock owners of other counties."

On March 2, 1904, through some political maneuvering with Williamson, John Combs was recommended for appointment as the new supervisor of the northern division of the Cascade Forest Reserve. It was likely that Combs also had some help from Menefee, who had been a law partner of E.B. Dufur, brother of W.H.H. Dufur who held the supervisor's job from 1898 through 1902. "John Combs of Prineville had been recommended to the president for the appointment by Williamson and Fulton," reported the Deschutes Echo of April 16, 1904. "It now appears that some Prineville Republicans have been 'knocking' Combs to the Interior Department, until it is doubtful whether he will get the place."

John Combs had no forestry training, but he did have at least one friend who was a ranger for Division R, Fred P. Claypool, who was also a deputy sheriff in 1903 and 1904, and a family friend of Williamson. Whatever was contained in those letters or reported about Combs, the appointment putting Combs in charge of a bunch of forest rangers fell through.

Combs was mentioned in a couple of places in tales from the vigilante period. The Vigilantes were supposedly formed at the end of 1881 in the Prineville area when a group of men decided that they did not agree with the way that the law had been administered, particularly after the murders of Stephen J. Jory and Aaron H. Crooks in the spring of 1882. The original purpose of the Vigilantes was supposed to have been to protect the county from outlaws and horse thieves. "It is recorded that a horse thief was never captured or punished by this organization, although a number of suspects were ordered to quit the range and leave the country," according to "An Illustrated History of Central Oregon."

The Vigilantes fell out of favor with the few people who condoned their acting outside of the law when their tactics were taken to extremes and men were shot, hung, and dragged to death and the Vigilantes claimed credit for the crimes. "Few were punished legally, although evidence was overwhelming. Grand juries were hampered in their actions by active sympathizers of the Vigilantes who were picked upon for jurymen." Combs was mentioned in one of those killings, when Al Swarts was shot through a window during a card game on December 21, 1882. The next night two young men, Charles Luster and Sidney Huston were shot and hung.

Those two young men, according to Blakely, had been staying at the Swarts ranch, which leaves the reader to wonder if they might have had some information bearing on the Swarts murder. "Somebody wrote a boastful account to the newspapers, claiming credit for the Vigilantes, glorying in the performance and saying that Schwartz and the boys were part of a gang that had been running stolen livestock out of the country," said Blakely.

When the dead are defamed and turned into villains, then and only then can the murderers become heroes. They become Vigilantes, on the side of good. That clever tactic would also allow the killers to push the guilt off on a mythic band of men who took the law into their own hands, a band of men that never existed. And a mythic band of men is much easier to drive out of the country than an actual band of outlaws. How convenient. A similar tactic was later employed by the sheepshooters, who wrote boastful accounts and portrayed themselves as heroes protecting the range from predatory sheep.

James M. Blakely claimed that all of the men appointed by the governor for the new county of Crook and put into office in January of 1883 were allies of the Vigilantes.

They were S.G. Thompson, judge; S.T. Richardson, county clerk; George H. Churchill, sheriff; S.J. Newsom, assessor; H.A. Dillard school superintendent; G.A. Winckler, treasurer; Richard Graham, coroner; and commissioners B.F. Allen and C.M. Cartwright. "The Vigilantes boasted about cleaning up the range, and maybe they did scare away a few stock thieves, but they also killed a number of law-abiding men. There isn't a single record of them having caught or killed a rustler," said Blakely, who may have jumped to the conclusion that the new county officials were connected to the Vigilantes because of some posters that appeared at the same time they did. Those were the same posters that Thompson described as having "skull and cross-bones attached, telling all hard characters to leave the county."

"The 'Moonshiners organized in the winter of 1883-4 for the purpose of putting a stop to the rather too industrious work of the Vigilantes," said Blakely. "And incidentally to gain political control of the county.... the 'Moonshiners' were successful at the polls and elected nearly their whole ticket." The real name of their group was "The Citizen's Protective Union," but they were referred to as the Moonshiners. One of the Moonshiners elected was Mark D. Powell, who got the spot of tax assessor, and incidentally was an uncle of Fred Powell, the man who attended the sheepshooter's planning meeting. Those named by Blakely as members of the Moonshiners included John Combs, C. Sam Smith, Al Lyle, and interestingly enough, Til Glaze. "Another good friend I had in those vigilante days was Til Glaze, the saloon man, said Blakely. "Til never joined our bunch against the Vigilantes, but he was with us and not them."

The saloon man must have been a very popular fellow, because Thompson, alleged leader of the Vigilantes, also considered him a strong allie and selected him as a member of his posse, all "men of unquestioned courage and discretion," wrote Thompson. Glaze's saloon was supposed to have been a favorite meeting place of the Vigilantes.

In his "Reminiscences," Bud Thompson named a few of the men who worked with him outside of the law in fighting crime. Til Glaze, Sam Richardson, George W. Barnes, and Charley Long were selected by Thompson to help him hunt down the killers of Crooks and Jory. Thompson always denied having been a member of the Vigilantes, although his memoirs made it pretty clear that he did not have much respect for sheriff Storrs and his deputy. "I did not, for reasons of my own, mainly that he talked too much, tell the Deputy of my plans," wrote Thompson. Thompson's brother Samuel was appointed as judge for the new county in 1882 and served in that capacity until the first election was held in 1884.

Blakely was adamant that the Moonshiners broke up the Vigilantes with a display of force, although he only described three specific incidents in his "Juniper Trees" story. One in which he pointed his gun at the county treasurer, then later refused to buy the poor man a drink; another when "Sam Smith, John Combs and the Wagner boys and I went to the saloon where the Vigilantes had been meeting, but they were gone;" and a third when supposedly 75 or 80 men (that being the approximate population of Prineville at the time) calling themselves Moonshiners paraded down the street together on horseback, with Blakely in the lead, and got only as far as the Til Glaze saloon. That last event apparently happened immediately before the election in which Blakely became sheriff.

Was there ever a real gang of Vigilantes operating in Crook County? There was a lot of violent crime there in 1882 and 1883, but all of the victims seem to have been law-abiding citizens, not rustlers and outlaws. Maybe the Vigilantes were a mythic band, created by the real killers in order to avoid capture? Or, were they just a byproduct of the Moonshiner's long association with saloon man Til Glaze, a whisky-induced fantasy that allowed them to bad-mouth the incumbents, stand on a 'reform' platform, and get themselves elected?

George Harkleroad, who lived and worked around Prineville in 1882 said, "Probably the Moonshiners were more interested in wresting political control of the county from the Vigilantes than in bringing some of their members to justice. At that time the voters in Crook County were not Republicans or Democrats -- they were Vigilantes or Moonshiners."

The family of Amos Dunham moved to Crook County in 1884, just after the Vigilante troubles, and his son Claude seemed to believe that the Vigilantes and the Moonshiners shared some members. An account by Dunham in the book "Jefferson County Reminiscences," expressed his opinion. "Right or wrong, the Vigilantes stopped cattle stealing in a country with law no closer than the Dalles," he said. "Some of them were heady with their success and were also feared. They organized, calling themselves Moonshiners."

John Combs was present at one of the shooting deaths that happened in the Prineville area in 1882. The victim, Al C. Swarts was shot with a shotgun through a closed window while playing cards at the Nickelson and Burmeister Saloon on the night of December 22, 1882. Combs was a witness who gave a statement to the coroner's jury. "Some gentlemen were playing cards, one of them was Mr. Swarts," testified Combs. "Sat down by the table and watched them a while. Someone from the outside fired a gun through the window. Mr. Swarts says, 'Jesus Christ, what's up!' I then left the room. Did not know that anyone was shot. Saw no one on the outside. Have no knowledge of who the person was who did the shooting."

Another witness, W.H. Kinder, gave the opinion that Swarts could not have been shot by someone standing on the ground, but had to have been shot by someone standing on the porch, which was built up above street level. That cast some doubt on the statement of Combs, the first man on the porch, who could have easily slipped out the door when no one was paying attention. Or, was it his job to watch the door until the deed was done?

For the discussion of the third man, we must turn ahead to the account of the organizing meeting at the Sheepshooter Tree, supposed to have happened in 1898. The Billy Congleton mentioned in the story of the Sheepshooters' Tree, presented in chapter five, was a first cousin of ranger Charles S. Congleton, who told the story. Billy had been sheriff of Crook County from 1900 to 1902.

According to Charles Congleton, his cousin Billy had told him the same story about the meeting at that tree as had Fred Powell, but on a separate occasion. Despite that corroboration, there were a couple of holes in the account.

The speaker, Henry Snodgrass, was supposedly from far away Izee in Grant County. If that was so, then how was that man able to identify by name an estimated twenty-five to forty Crook County men, and by fire light, no less? Also, a careful check of public records for the period shows that no one by the name of Henry Snodgrass lived in Grant County. No Henry Snodgrass ever paid taxes, was married, divorced, or died in Grant County. He never purchased a homestead or other land from the U.S. Government in Grant County, and he was not in the U.S. Census for 1880 or 1900 in Grant County. The preponderance of the evidence shows that there was no such person. The only Snodgrass found in Grant County was a produce merchant, not a cattleman, by the name of James H. Snodgrass who lived at Canyon City around 1900.

However, there was a different lone pine tree in Crook County that was also said to have been the meeting place of the sheepshooters, pointed to by a separate source. It was located in township 16 south, range 21 east, section four, next to Committee Spring, the source of Committee Creek. That stream supposedly got its name from the sheep shooting committee, and joins with Gray Creek near the site of the famous tree. The spot was pointed to by Ralph Elder, who was a ranger for the Ochoco National Forest in the 1920's, and a friend of Doug Langille, the two of them having served together in the 20th Engineers in France in 1919.

The Gray family was very prominent in the cattle business in Crook County for many years, and had a large ranch at the confluence of Horse Heaven Creek and Crooked

River called Bonnieview Ranch. John Henry Gray, known as 'Henry' to his friends, was the head of that family, and served as sheriff of Crook County during the time of the alleged planning meeting of the sheepshooters, from 1896 to 1900. He was succeeded by Billy Congleton, who claimed to have been present at the meeting. Was the meeting of cattlemen called by Henry Gray, who knew each of them by name and who, in his role as sheriff, was attempting to find a way to deal with growing range tensions? Congleton too, would probably have been present, working as a deputy sheriff under Gray.

Otto and Bruce Gray, sons of J.H. Gray, were mentioned previously as having been named in a family history as proprietors of the store that supplied ammunition to the sheepshooters. The Grays were also very friendly with the family of Roscoe Knox, named as the man associated with sheepshooter propaganda, who lived in the same area. Knox and Henry Gray were both members of the Crook County Stock Growers' Association. Gray and Sam Smith were both founding members and officers of the Crook County Cattlemen's Association. Gray was the first president of that group, and became vice-president in December of 1902. It seems probable that the man named 'Henry' who spoke at the planning meeting of the sheepshooters was John Henry Gray. How Powell came up with the name 'Snodgrass' is a mystery, although he would have known Henry Gray and may have been attempting to shield the Gray family.

The three men named as having had possible ties to the sheepshooters were also all connected to the Crook County Sheriff's Department, and there were additional clues in the newspapers of the period that cast suspicion on the sheriff's office. "There is no man above the law, and no man beneath it," wrote Oscar Metzker in a fiery editorial after the discovery of Conn's body. Sam Smith was Crook County sheriff during the time of the sheep kills in north Lake County, and since he was running for reelection in 1904, may have chosen to strike outside of his own county to avoid criticism from voters who might say that the sheriff wasn't doing his job properly. At about this time, Smith was severely upbraided by an editorial accusing him of dereliction of duty.

"The Conn tragedy became a living issue in Southeastern Oregon politics, and led to the defeat at the polls of public officers who appeared to have taken the side of the criminals or to have hesitated to procure their arrest and conviction," wrote Oscar Metzker. "Now thousands of sheep have been slain in Crook County as a consequence of the same conspiracy to expel the sheepmen from the range... the operation of law has completely broken down."

Excuses were offered by the newspapers. "It would be extremely dangerous for the sheriff and his posse to follow the mountain trails after men whom he could not identify," said the *Prineville Review.* "He might arrest on suspicion; but he could be taking his life in his hands to enter the mountain fastness after the supposed criminals."

And what about the governor's offer of a substantial reward for the arrest of Conn's killers? Wasn't that an unusual course to take in the pursuit of ordinary ruffians? The reward was supposed to have been offered because some prominent residents of Lake County, probably Conn's brothers, had convinced the governor to do so. After the reward offer failed to bring results, the governor explored the equally extreme idea of sending Secret Service men to east Oregon to seek out the fiends who had traveled sixty miles into Lake County to kill sheep, and also, presumably, to kill Creed Conn.

"Since the last session of the Legislature, range difficulties in Lake and Crook counties have reached an acute stage, resulting in the willful killing of many hundred sheep, and it is charged, in the loss of one human life in the former county," said Governor Chamberlain in his annual address for 1905. "A few men bent upon the ruthless destruction of personal property might travel by night a distance of sixty miles from one county into another, apply the torch, perform their nefarious mission of slaughter and return to the point of departure before the setting of another sun. Under such circumstances it is exceedingly difficult to procure evidence sufficient to convict."

"But even if the local authorities showed a disposition to neglect their duty, the Executive has no authority to do more than appeal to them. The power of removal from office, a most potent one in such cases, is not conferred upon him in this, as in some other states. If vested with this power, those officials who from selfish, political, or other reasons refuse to do their duty could be replaced by others who would not be deterred therefrom by any considerations." Chamberlain's message made a plea for an appropriation of funds for the employment of "skilled and fearless secret service men" and made obvious the governor's suspicion that the authorities in Crook County were in collusion with the sheepshooters. Congress answered the Governor's plea with an appropriation of $10,000 to be used in apprehending and punishing persons guilty of maliciously killing stock.

Then there was Lafe Conn's only witness for the sheep kill at Reid Rock, a Basque by the name of Julius Escallier. Around 1900 there were very few Basque people living in Crook County, and none in Lake County. There were eight Basque sheepmen living in the vicinity of Suplee and Paulina, and one of them was Alex Escallier. Did Lafe Conn pick a Crook County man to act as his witness because the man would be able to identify other Crook County men he had seen in the area of the sheep kill?

Perhaps the most telling of all was a move to stop range fights made by Congressman Lee Steiner, a close personal friend of District Attorney Conn. Steiner introduced a bill at the start of 1905 that would make the counties of Crook, Lake, Klamath, and Grant financially responsible to sheepmen who were victims of the sheepshooters. "Communities that have to pay for damage once or twice rarely do so again, because they require their peace officers to enforce the law," said Steiner. Sheep owners were to be reimbursed for their losses by the county in which the killing occurred. "The residents of these counties will sit up and notice things if the losses of sheep killing come out of the county funds, and the depredations will be stopped."

In 1899, during John Henry Gray's term as sheriff, there occurred at Prineville the alleged suicide of an affluent merchant by the name of James O'Farrell, and that suspicious death would be alluded to exactly five years later by the man who placed the body of John Creed Conn on the Sandy Knoll.

SOURCES:

Editorial, Deschutes Echo, October 17, 1903.

Editorial, *Deschutes Echo*, August 29, 1903.

"Placing the Responsibility," *Deschutes Echo*, October 10, 1903.

"Elect the Old Officers," *Oregonian*, September 17, 1903.

"Losing its Land," *Oregonian*, September 7, 1903.

"About the Reserve," *Lake County Examiner*, June 18, 1903.

Message of George E. Chamberlain Governor of Oregon, to the Twenty-third Legislative Assembly of 1905. Oregon Messages and Documents, 1905, Governor's Regular Session Message, Salem, Oregon, J.R. Whitney, State Printer, 1905. Available on the web site of the Oregon State Archives at: http://arcweb.sos.state.or.us/governors/chamberlain/message1905.html

"Of Interest to Stockmen," *Lake County Examiner*, April 7, 1904.

"No Funds at His Disposal," *Oregonian*, December 13, 1904.

http://www.fs.fed.us/r6/malheur/ecology/hist-conquest.shtml. Web page includes history of the Malheur National Forest in Region 6.

"Shelves in Grant County Too Small for Cy Bingham," *Oregonian*, December 9, 1932.

"Blazes on the Skyline," by Robert Hall Cox, 1988, Pacific House Books, Eugene Oregon, p 27. Bingham and Harvey were at nearby Middle Horse Lake together on June 20, 1906.

"Central Oregon Place Names," vol. 1, Crook County, by Steve Lent, 2001, Maverick, Bend, Oregon, p 49.

"Report on the Proposed Blue Mountains Forest Reserve," by H.D. Langille, 1906, Department of the Interior, General Land Office, p 9-11, 12, 15- 18.

"Saga of a Forest Ranger," by Len Shoemaker, 1958, University of Colorado Press, Boulder, Colorado, p 1, 55, 82, 92-96, 98, 101.

"Mostly Division 'R' Days," Harold D. Langille, December 1956, Oregon Historical Quarterly, p 301-313, Abbott, Kerns & Bell, Portland, Oregon.

"Timber-Lines, Thirty-year Club," region six, U.S. Forest Service, vol. XIV, June 1960, p 42.

The Proposed, Heppner Forest Reserve, Oregon," 1903, by H.D. Langille, Agent and Expert, Bureau of Forestry, U.S. Department of Agriculture, p 11-13.

"Grazing in the Forest Reserves," by Filibert Roth, 1901, U.S. Government Printing Office, Washington D.C. Reprinted in the "Yearbook of Department of Agriculture for 1901," p 337, 340, 343, 347-348.

"Cattlemen Hold Annual Meeting," *Crook County Journal*, October 20, 1904.

"Life Safe in County," *Lake County Examiner*, July 28, 1904.

Editorial, *Deschutes Echo*, September 12, 1903.

Editorial, *Deschutes Echo*, May 30, 1903.

"Predatory Sheep," *Prineville Review*, October 20, 1904. Originally published in the Portland Journal.

"Mostly Division 'R' Days," Harold D. Langille, December 1956, Oregon Historical Quarterly, p 301-313, Abbott, Kerns & Bell, Portland, Oregon.

Wikipedia offers several good articles on the Liberty Tree, the Stamp Act, and the Sons of Liberty, available at: http://en.wikipedia.org/wiki/Liberty_Tree

"Lone Woods Guard of Old Days Tells of Work," *Bend Bulletin*, September 21, 1934.

"The Stamp Act Crisis," by Edmund S. Morgan and Helen M. Morgan, 1953, University of North Carolina Press, Chapel Hill, North Carolina, p42, 46, 109, 127, 128, 188, 192.

Untitled article, *Deschutes Echo*, March 21, 1903.

Franklin's skull and crossbones stamp appeared in issue no. 1195 of his paper. An article and image of the stamp are available at: http://bushlibrary.tamu.edu/pastexhibits/free_jour.php

"When the Juniper Trees Bore Fruit," Oregonian, March 12, 19, and 26, 1939. Stories of James M. Blakely, as told by Herbert Lundy.

"Reminiscences of a Pioneer," by Colonel William Thompson, 1912, San Francisco, California. The book is now available as an ebook through Project Gutenberg at: www.gutenberg.net

"The War for Range," by Arno Dosch, *Pacific Monthly*, vol 15, February 1906.

"How the Law is Broken," *Oregonian*, September 14, 1905

"History of the Willamette Valley and Cascade Mountain Wagon Road," by Cleon L. Clark, 1987, Deschutes County Historical Society, Bend, Oregon, p 59-65.

"C. Sam Smith Dies Suddenly," *Crook County Journal*, May 31, 1920.

U.S. Census Bureau, Tenth Census of the United States, 1880, Prineville, Crook County, Oregon.

"An Illustrated History of Central Oregon," Western Historical Publishing, 1905, Spokane, WA, p 219, 710-712, 776, 790-791, 828.

"Our Stockmen Meet," *Crook County Journal*, December 4, 1902.

"Stockmen Meet," *Crook County Journal*, March 13, 1902.

"Cattlemen Organize," *Crook County Journal*, December 4, 1902.

"Damage by Sheepmen," *Bend Bulletin*, July 21, 1905.

"A Startling Story," *Bend Bulletin*, April 24, 1908.

"Smith Found Guilty," *Bend Bulletin*, May 15, 1908.

"Denies it in Toto," *Bend Bulletin*, May 15, 1908.

Editorial, *Bend Bulletin*, May 22, 1908.

Grant County Biographies, http:// www.oregongenealogy .com/grant/bios2.htm.

U.S. Census Bureau, Twelfth Census of the United States, 1900, Rosebud Precinct, Grant County, Oregon.

U.S. Census Bureau, Tenth Census of the United States, 1880, Middle Precinct, Grant County, Oregon.

"Della Bonham Keerins Reminiscences," March 17, 1964. Reprinted in "Izee Country Historical Tour," Crook County Historical Society, 2007, Prineville, Oregon.

"Combs Family Came to Crook County With First Pioneers," *Crook County News*, August 4, 1939.

Combs Family History File, Bowman Museum, Prineville, Oregon.

"Killed a Woman's Sheep," *Oregonian*, July 9, 1897.

"Portland, its History and Builders," vol. 3, by Joseph Gaston, 1911, S.J. Clarke, Chicago, p 726-729.

"History of the Willamette National Forest," available on the web site of the Forest History Society at: http://www.foresthistory.org/ASPNET/Publications/region/6/willamette/chap2.htm. Claypool's name appears incorrectly as "T.P. Claypool," and is listed in Chapter 2 with other early Division R rangers.

Local Items, *Deschutes Echo*, July 4, 1903. Refers to deputy Claypool.

Local News, *Crook County Journal*, July 7, 1904. Claypool was a deputy sheriff until mid-July of 1904.

"Prineville Man Named for Place," *Oregonian*, March 3, 1904.

"A Party Feud," *Deschutes Echo*, April 16, 1904.

"Williamson Wins," *Prineville Review*, March 27, 1902.

"The Six-shooter in Old Oregon," *Oregonian*, June 16, 1934.

"Bullwhackers, Muleskinners, Pioneers, Prospectors, '49ers, Indian Fighters, Trappers, Ex-Barkeepers, Authors, Preachers, Poets, & Near Poets, & All Sorts & Conditions of Men," by Fred Lockley, 1981, Rainy Day Press, Eugene, Oregon, p 255.

"Jefferson County Reminiscences," by Many Hands, 1957, Binfords & Mort, Portland, Oregon, p 24-25. In 1885 what is now Jefferson County was a part of Crook County.

Coroner's inquest testimony and verdict in the death of Al C. Swartz, December 22, 1882, Coroner and Inquest Records, Clerk's Vault, Crook County Courthouse, Prineville, Oregon.

Coroner's inquest verdict in the death of Sid Huston and Charles Luster, December 23, 1882, Coroner and Inquest Records, Clerk's Vault, Crook County Courthouse, Prineville, Oregon.

"Central Oregon Place Names," vol. 1, Crook County, by Steve Lent, 2001, Maverick, Bend, Oregon, p 147-149.

U.S. Census Bureau, Tenth Census of the United States, 1800, Prineville, Crook County, Oregon. Gray gives his name as "Henry" to the census taker. Sons Otto and Bruce are at home.

"A History of the Oregon Sheriffs, 1841-1991," by Linda McCarthy, 1992, Oregon State Sheriff's Association, Portland, Oregon.

"Oregon Geographic Names," by Lewis A. McArthur and Lewis L. McArthur, seventh edition, 2003, Oregon Historical Society Press, Portland, Oregon, p 223, 866.

"Oregon Atlas & Gazetteer," 1998, third edition, second printing, Delorme, Yarmouth, Maine. Both Committee Creek and Gray Creek are south of Big Summit Prairie in the lower right corner of page 80.

"A History of the Fremont National Forest," by Melva Bach, 1990, Forest Service, USDA, Pacific Northwest Region, Fremont National Forest, p 70.

"Across Oregon's 'Desert' by Buckboard," Harold D. Langille, December 1958, Oregon Historical Quarterly, Abbott, Kerns & Bell, Portland, Oregon, p 326.

"The Crook County Journal's Annual Number," 1901, *Crook County Journal*, Prineville, Oregon. Special Edition contains a biography of John Henry Gray.

"A Hundred and Sixty Acres in the Sage," 1984, by Beverly A. Wolverton, self published, p57-59.

"Sheep Killing Again Unearthed," *Lake County Examiner*, December 22, 1904.

"Should be Punished," *Lake County Examiner*, May 5, 1904.

Editorial, *Ashwood Prospector*, May 24, 1904.

Editorial, *Prineville Review*, June 2, 1904.

"Ban on Range Feuds," *Oregonian*, January 4, 1905.

"Much Interest Taken in Sheep Killing Law," *Crook County Journal*, January 19, 1905.

This small news item, taken from the *Lake County Examiner*
of March 9, 1899 links the murder of John Creed Conn to the
suspicious death of James E. O'Farrell, which occurred almost
exactly five years earlier.

Chapter Seven

James

Around the year 1900, it was the custom of local
newspapers all over Oregon to print a section of small tidbits
of news and gossip contributed by readers. On March 9, 1899
one of those local news contributions to the *Lake County
Examiner* came from none other than John Creed Conn.

> *J.C. Conn, the wide-awake merchant of Silver
> Lake, arrived on Tuesday's stage. He reports
> everything flourishing and good prospects for
> stockmen in his section. Mr. Conn says there
> is no truth in the report that James O'Farrell
> had committed suicide at Prineville; that he
> was alive in Silver Lake last Sunday.*

When that message from Creed Conn is broken down
into its component parts, it has a tremendous bearing upon the
investigation of his homicide, and is as important today as it
was in the spring of 1904.

Conn claimed to have seen James O'Farrell on the
streets of Silver Lake on Sunday, March 5, almost exactly 5
years to the day before the date that Conn himself vanished
from the streets of Silver Lake on March 4, 1904.

O'Farrell was a man who was presumed to have met
his death by suicide at Prineville, a claim that was inexplicably
refuted by Conn. Creed Conn mysteriously disappeared from

Silver Lake, and was immediately, inexplicably, presumed to have committed suicide.

Both Conn and O'Farrell were affluent merchants in their respective small towns, O'Farrell being a leading citizen of Gale, near present day Merrill, Oregon.

The *Examiner*, a Republican paper, paid Conn a compliment by referring to him as "wide-awake." It meant that he was on top of things, and took a progressive view favoring the upbuilding of the state and the economy. The crime scene at the Sandy Knoll was organized and the body positioned to deliberately make Conn appear to be asleep. One newspaper article even used in its headline the words "as if in repose" to describe the position of the body. Conn's hands were up at the top of his head, as if he was taking a nap on that knoll. In his pocket was found an intact bottle of laudanum, which was not only a common turn-of-the-century aid for insomnia, but was also often used metaphorically to disparage a political moderate.

That O'Farrell died an untimely death while visiting Prineville is suspicious in light of the widely held belief that Conn was killed by the men from the Prineville area who had perpetrated the sheep kill at Reid Rock, and possibly also the slaughter at Benjamin Lake.

All of the information extracted from that short "Local News" item would have played heavily on the mind of District Attorney Lafe Conn as he worked to solve the murder. Creed and Lafe Conn were close, in age and in many other ways. They trusted one another, they went to college together, and whatever one believed, the other was privy to. Lafe Conn would have known about Creed's declaration that O'Farrell was alive, and may even have investigated it to some extent. So the clues deliberately left by the killer or killers would not have escaped the notice of the highly intelligent young district attorney. The simple fact that O'Farrell died at Prineville, and the evidence that the sheepshooters came from that same area, combined with the timing of Conn's disappearance on nearly the same date, and smack in between two sheep kills, could easily have steered the homicide investigation toward the sheepshooters.

Word of the course of the investigation was leaked to the *Deschutes Echo* first, probably by William Holder, who at the time was editor of the *Chewaucan Post* at Paisley, located inside of Virgil Conn's store building. Holder also owned the plant where the *Deschutes Echo* was printed and was a friend of editor George Schlect. And because of the mocking nature of the deliberate clues, it was assumed that the killing was done out of spite. If Conn was killed by the sheepshooters, as was soon rumored, then they must have had some reason for killing him.

So, who was James O'Farrell, and how did he come to figure so prominently in the death of John Creed Conn five years later? Conn would certainly have known O'Farrell, and practically declared as much when he told the newspaper that he had seen the man alive. They may have been acquainted in the mercantile trade, but would have known each other long before they opened their respective stores.

In 1880 the O'Farrell family lived in Lake County near Christmas Lake. The father, William, was 44 years old, an Irish immigrant, and a blacksmith. His wife Octavia, also a native of Ireland, was 39. The father had omitted the "O" from his name when questioned by the census taker that year, and probably did so in his daily life to hide his nationality amidst the strong anti-Irish sentiment of the period. Later in life, his children would reintroduce the "O" to its proper place at the front of the family name. Creed Conn had worked as a clerk in the store of his brothers George and Virgil at Paisley from 1886 to 1892, and since it was the only mercantile store within many miles, would have been acquainted with all the members of the O'Farrell family. One of the O'Farrell boys obtained local celebrity to such a degree that his story has become a legend to rival that of the sheepshooters.

Edward O'Farrell, who was about six years younger than his brother James, is believed by some to have been the heroic rider of the Silver Lake Fire. That holocaust, which occurred on Christmas eve in 1894, claimed the lives of 43 people who had gathered for a holiday party. Many of the victims were children, and every resident of the town of Silver Lake was scarred, either emotionally or physically, by the blaze that took members of nearly every family. O'Farrell's role was to ride. He bolted off into the frozen blackness toward the south in search of a doctor, because Silver Lake had no doctor at the time. He rode without resting, and ruined the horse he had under him, knowing that his friends and neighbors lay dying from their injuries.

In 1900 Ed still lived in Lake County, near Summer Lake with his father, William. In January 1903 he married Anna Martin, a Silver Lake girl, and the happy couple moved into a small cabin on his ranch near the site of present day Ana Reservoir. Tragically, Ed O'Farrell too met an untimely death. Only three and a half months after his wedding, he died of a fracture of the skull that was said to have come from a hard knock against a post that happened while he was corralling some horses.

The sons of William and Octavia O'Farrell were: William Jr., born 1864; James E. born 1866; Christopher C., also known as Charles C., born 1867; Timothy born 1873; and Edward, the youngest, born 1877. There was also a girl, Mary, who was born in 1870 and who used the nickname "Mannie."

Besides the celebrity of Ed, and the mysterious death of James, the family could claim yet another interesting historical footnote. They were the prior owners of the ranch of Alonzo Long, father of Anna Long Linebaugh and Reub Long, the latter being one of the co-authors of the popular book "The Oregon Desert." In an unpublished oral history, Anna Linebaugh recalled that her father had purchased a place known as the Jackson Homestead on the southwest edge of Christmas Lake from a man named Thomas Farrell in 1900. Government records from the period do partially agree with Linebaugh's statement.

When the 1880 census was taken, the entire O'Farrell family, minus the "O", was recorded on the same census page as John Jackson, who Linebaugh referred to as having been the prior owner of the ranch. The term "owner" is used loosely here because the land would not be surveyed until 1882, so whoever lived on it really only owned the improvements, such as the big barn, the broken down fences, and the log cabin described by both Long and Linebaugh as being there when they arrived. Jackson did not have title to the land itself, and neither did the man that he bought the ranch from, Peter Chrisman, or Christman, the man for whom Christmas Lake and Peter's Creek were named. Christman was one of the earliest pioneers of the area and a cattle rancher, and the name "Christmas Lake" was a corruption of "Christman Lake" which was the original name of the place. In 1882 Christman sold his ranching enterprise to Fred Cox and John Jackson.

In 1891 William O'Farrell patented a homestead claim of 160 acres at township 26 south, range 18 east, section 32, which embraced the entire west shore of Christmas Lake. In 1893 John P. O'Farrell, who seems to have been a brother of William, patented an adjoining claim to the north in section 29 of the same township. At the time William acquired title to his claim, he relinquished it to his son James. The land was passed through the family, first sold to sister Mannie in 1897, and on March 26, 1900 to brother Ed, who at the same time bought the homestead of his uncle John. On April 23, 1900 Ed sold the whole 320 acres to Alonzo Long, whose daughter Anna was only slightly off in her recollection by naming Thomas Farrell, instead of Ed Farrell, or O'Farrell the purported hero of the Christmas Eve Fire. In 1912 and 1913 Alonzo Long proved up on homestead claims totaling 320 acres adjoining the land he bought from O'Farrell.

By April of 1901 Octavia, Christopher, Tim, and Ed O'Farrell were living in Moyie, British Columbia where the brothers worked as quartz miners. Their uncle John lived nearby in east Kootenay. By 1891 William, the father of the family, was living in San Francisco, and seems to have become permanently estranged from the rest of the family.

James O'Farrell, the man that Conn said had not committed suicide, still paid taxes in Lake County in 1890 and 1895. Around that time, James built a new mercantile store in the vicinity of Gale, which also had a post office, a school, and a blacksmith shop. The town of Merrill was platted my Nathan S. Merrill in 1894, and the town of Gale, which was a few years older and less than two miles to the northeast, merged into it. O'Farrell was living at Gale with his wife and operating his store there by May of 1895. He also seems to have gotten into some trouble there. That same year he was indicted for disturbing a religious meeting and giving liquor to a minor all in one day, then about a month later he charged the county sheriff with conversion.

In June of 1892, James O'Farrell married Lillie Vanderpool at the Silver Lake home of Warren Duncan, who had previously married her sister, Ida Vanderpool Anderson.

Witnesses were George Cooley and Effie Anderson. The Vanderpool girls were daughters of James W. and Mary E. Vanderpool of Prineville. A third Vanderpool girl, Nellie, married John Klippel, brother of Lanis Klippel, who was very well known around Paisley. James O'Farrell was a witness at the 1891 Silver Lake wedding of Nellie to John Klippel.

From this information it seems probable that Creed Conn would have been familiar with the O'Farrells, and also that James O'Farrell had been visiting his wife's family at Prineville when he allegedly committed suicide. Unfortunately, no newspaper accounts detailing the circumstances of his death have survived. Conversely, the author was not able to, after a most thorough search of all public records for the period, prove that James O'Farrell was alive after 1899.

His brother, Christopher, was one year younger than James, and was probably the man that Creed Conn saw on the streets of Silver Lake around the time of the funeral for James. Chris had immigrated to Canada first, in 1892, followed by Tim in 1897, Mannie and Octavia in 1899, and Ed in 1900. So, Conn would not have seen Christopher for about seven years. Chris could have returned from British Columbia to attend the funeral with brother Ed, who was still living in Lake County. It seems that Creed Conn mistook Christopher for James, an error that was probably doubly embarrassing because it was printed in the county paper, an error that the killer chose to exploit when he placed Conn's body on the Sandy Knoll.

During the intervening years, another man has been offered up as a suspect in the deaths of Conn and O'Farrell. Writer Teressa Foster in her authoritative history, "Settlers in Summer Lake Valley," referred to this when she wrote, "The truth is that Conn was murdered by a Silver Lake rancher. (The same gentleman shot off the thumb of sheepherder Bert McKune, who tried vainly to protect the Reid band in a range battle...). Foster referred to the 'thumb shooting' incident again when she wrote, "Guy and his brother, Bert, went to work for Lola's father, John Reid, who ran sheep north of Christmas Valley and around Silver Lake for part of the year. The brothers were herding sheep near Christmas Valley when masked men rode up and said they were going to kill their sheep. When the herders attempted to make a defense, Bert's thumb was shot off."

Foster, who arrived in Lake County in 1943, seems to have drawn the above conclusions from recollections of others about an article that appeared in the *Crook County Journal* on February 2, 1905. The article, which was picked up from the previous week's issue of the *Central Oregonian* at Silver Lake, described how Bert McKune's thumb was torn off at the first joint by the third of three shots fired by a man that was too far away for McKune to identify. The shooting occurred near Cougar Mountain, about 30 miles northeast of Silver Lake and near Benjamin Lake. The place appears as "Cougar Butte" on some modern maps. According to the 1905 article, after McKune made his way to Silver Lake, Warren Duncan delivered the injured man to Paisley, probably to see a doctor. It should be noted here that the attack on McKune's sheep at Reid Rock occurred one year before the 'thumb shooting' incident, and that whatever Foster was told regarding the identity of the shooter was pure conjecture because even Bert McKune did not know who the man was. Since only two men were named in the article, it seems likely that Foster was left with the impression that Duncan was the shooter.

Teressa Foster was not the only person who had a funny feeling about Warren Duncan, and Duncan did have some pretty interesting connections to both the Conn murder and the death of James O'Farrell. Duncan had been a brother-in-law of O'Farrell's, and so would have known many of the details about his alleged suicide. He had been a trusted friend of Conn's and was involved in a timber deal with him on Dead Indian. He also was the man who hauled Creed Conn's body into town for the inquest, and who the next day hauled it to the cemetery for burial. As such, he probably would have seen Conn's injuries, and also may have remembered the comments that the murdered man had made about seeing O'Farrell alive on the streets of Silver Lake.

On October 12, 1904, Warren Duncan went to Paisley with 'ear witness' George S. Parker to call on Virgil Conn. Duncan wanted to be paid from the estate for his services in transporting the body and for an old debt for a buggy rental to Creed Conn. Parker was also paid for some work he had done for the estate. Whether or not the men were discussing any probable connections to the prior death of James O'Farrell is not known, but Virgil Conn did have a definite intense reaction to whatever was being said. When he wrote his name at the top of Duncan's receipt, his handwriting became very garbled, then, when he got to the bottom of the form, he accidentally began to sign his own name in the space where Duncan was supposed to sign. When he got to Parker's receipt he forgot what year it was, and wrote in 1903. Duncan had not been a witness at the inquest or a member of the jury, and perhaps he felt that this was his chance to speak his peace about the glaring similarities and the uncanny connections between the two deaths.

If during his lifetime Warren Duncan continued talking to friends and family about his insights about Conn and O'Farrell, or any inside information about Creed Conn's life, or the injuries to the body, he could have very well left the impression one or two generations later that he was somehow connected to the Conn murder. And he was, but not in the way that the real killer was. After a tremendous amount of reading, digging, and obsessive researching, the author has concluded that Warren Duncan was not a killer.

The body was positioned to communicate, and that communication was an integral part of the act for the killer, who felt compelled to do more than just dump the body, but to share some part of the homicidal experience with those who would later view it. The crime scene was organized and ritualized. He may have wanted to taunt investigators with deliberate clues about his identity.

Much of what was done was unnecessary, that is to say, it went beyond what was needed to murder Conn. The easiest thing the killer could have done, probably, would have been to shoot him and walk away. It was not necessary to hold onto the body for seven weeks and then display it prominently on that knoll. The trauma to the head was done after Conn was already dead, and was not even considered as a contributory cause of death. The second gun shot was also not needed because the first shot went through his heart. Taking Conn's journal did not help to achieve murder. Planting his gun and a bottle of laudanum at the scene were of no help at all. And, the positioning of the body, "as if in repose," was of no use whatsoever. None of these things done by the killer served to make Conn any 'more dead' than he already was. These were the killer's signature behaviors, and some of them were things he felt compelled to do to satisfy emotional or psychological needs. They were his way of expressing himself, and revealed clues about his identity.

The murderer's modus operandi may change... but his distinctive trademark does not. These are the killer's calling card. This man leaves his mark on his work, like a painter leaves his signature on a canvas."

-Sherlock Holmes in
the Case of the Silk Stocking

Lafe Conn used the O'Farrell news item to frame his investigation, and tried to nail down a motive, little knowing that the person he searched for had no motive, at least not in the usual sense. He killed for psychological gratification. And because the body was stored for a period of time, and the head was mutilated before it was returned, it was likely that the killer would kill again. That behavior was the organized work of a hedonistic killer.

SOURCES:

"Local News," *Lake County Examiner*, March 9, 1899.

"Local News," *Lake County Examiner*, April 9, 1903. Item describes sale of the *Paisley Post* to William Holder.

"The Growth of Lake County, Oregon," by Georgie Ellen Boydstun Stephenson, 1994, Bookpartners, Wilsonville, Oregon, p 104. In 1902 the *Post* moved into the brick store building of Virgil Conn.

Editorial, *Deschutes Echo*, July 4, 1903. Names George Schlect as the new owner and editor of the *Echo*.

"Echo Office Destroyed by Fire," *Deschutes Echo*, August 1, 1903. Article states that the Echo would be issued from the office of the *Prineville Review* until further notice.

U.S. Census Bureau, Tenth Census of the United States, 1880, Lake County, Oregon.

"Silver Lake's Most Tragic Christmas," by G. Sellers, Old West magazine, vol. 6, no. 2, Winter 1969. Article names Ed O'Farrell as the heroic rider.

U.S. Census Bureau, Twelfth Census of the United States, 1900, Summer Lake, Lake County, Oregon.

"Remarks," Anna Linebaugh, unpublished ms., October 28, 1981, p 1.

"Homesteading the High Desert," by Barbara Allen, University of Utah Press, Salt Lake City, Utah, p 28.

"The Oregon Desert," E.R. Jackman and R.A. Long, 1969, Caxton, Caldwell, Idaho, p 30-32.

"Death of Ed O'Farrell," *Lake County Examiner*, April 23, 1903.

"High Desert Roses, Significant Stories from Central Oregon," vol. 1, by Melany Tupper, p 27-40. This section of the author's earlier book details the naming of Christmas Lake.

Peter Chrisman to Fred Cox and John Jackson, Index Volume 3, Grantors, Lake County deed and title records, Lake County Clerk's Office, Lake County Courthouse, Lakeview, Oregon.
Bureau of Land Management, records of the General Land Office, land patents of William O'Farrell serial #ORLAA 068663 and John P. O'Farrell serial # ORLAA 068664 , http://www.glorecords.blm.gov/PatentSearch

From William O'Farrell to James E. O'Farrell, April 5, 1891. Deed and title records, vol 7, p 528, Lake County Courthouse, County Clerk's Office, Lakeview, Oregon.

From James O'Farrall and Lillie O'Farrall to Mannie O'Farrall, May 1, 1897. Deed and title records, vol 10, p 133, Lake County Courthouse, County Clerk's Office, Lakeview, Oregon.

From Mannie O'Farrell to Edward O'Farrell, March 26, 1900. Deed and title records, vol 13, p 435, Lake County Courthouse, County Clerk's Office, Lakeview, Oregon.

From John P. O'Farrell to Edward O'Farrell, March 26, 1900. Deed and title records, vol 13, p 433, Lake County Courthouse, County Clerk's Office, Lakeview, Oregon.

From Ed O'Farrell to A.W. Long, April 23, 1900. Deed and title records, vol 10, p 469, Lake County Courthouse, County Clerk's Office, Lakeview, Oregon.

Bureau of Land Management, records of the General Land Office, land patents of Alonzo Long serial #301876 and 365142, http://www.glorecords.blm.gov/ PatentSearch

Tax Roll for Silver Lake, Lake County, Oregon and Gale, Klamath County, Oregon, for the years 1890 and 1895, Oregon State Archives, Salem, Oregon.

Provincial Summary, 1901 Census records for British Columbia, Yale and Cariboo, Moyie. Available online at: http://automatedgenealogy.com/ census/Province.jsp? province=BC

"An Illustrated History of Central Oregon," Western Historical Publishing, 1905, Spokane, WA, p 980-981.

"Oregon Geographic Names," by Lewis A. McArthur and Lewis L. McArthur, sixth edition, 1992, Oregon Historical Society Press, Portland, Oregon, p 344.

"Local News," *The Klamath Star*, May 30, 1895.

The State of Oregon vs James O. Farrell, June 14, 1895, Klamath County Circuit Court, Book No. 2, 1892-1899, p 229, Klamath County Museum, Klamath Falls, Oregon.

The State of Oregon vs James O. Farrell, May 18, 1895, Klamath County Circuit Court, Book No. 2, 1892-1899, p 214, Klamath County Museum, Klamath Falls, Oregon.

"Marriage Records, vol. 1, 1875-1895, County of Lake, Lakeview, Oregon," 1995, Oregon Youth Conservation Corps, Lakeview, Oregon, p 44, 47.

Obituary of Lillie O'Farrell, *Prineville Review*, February 22, 1912.

This photo of Ole Hamilton was printed in the *Oregonian* and submitted by someone at Silver Lake, with the caption, "Ole Hamilton, the supposed murderer of Julius Wallende, who is now a fugitive from justice. A large reward is offered for the arrest of the murderer."

Chapter Eight

Julius

The killer of Creed Conn wanted to, had a psychological need to, communicate with the people investigating the murder. For him the killing was the supreme game, and he delighted in the murder as the ultimate 'win.' Being able to subsequently fool and toy with people like Lafe Conn who persistently worked to solve the crime was great sport for him, and it allowed him to prolong the fantasy, to relive the crime. He took such delight in that particular murder, and was so obsessed with reliving it, that he began to plot a reenactment. He planned to kill again.

On Friday, the 13th of March, 1908, citizens of Silver Lake were forced into reliving the horrible tragedy of Creed Conn's murder when the body of a young man was pulled from Silver Creek. Julius Wallende had mysteriously disappeared from the streets of town eleven weeks before. The victim's "head had been frightfully battered and his skull fractured in numerous places," reported the *Oregonian*.

Wallende came to Oregon from Edmunds County, South Dakota, and seems to have arrived in Silver Lake in the Fall of 1907. In early October of that year he had a filed on a homestead claim seven miles east of the present day center of the town of Christmas Valley. He was very young, only 17 at the time of his death, and was living at one of the hotels in Silver Lake when he disappeared. "He was murdered at Silver Lake, Oregon about December 27, 1907," said Henry H. Hach, who had a homestead near Wallende. "He had the lumber purchased for his house when he was murdered."

The afternoon of the murder Wallende collected his pay of $90, then spent the evening at the hotel in Silver Lake where he was staying until such time as he could finish building his cabin on the homestead. "From Wallende's nature it is concluded that he was not a man who would leave the hotel as he did at 9:30 unless he had an engagement with someone," said a report from Silver Lake written three days after the discovery of the body. After his inexplicable absence, relatives and friends suspected foul play, and had made inquiries and notified county Sheriff Albert Dent.

Several people were at the scene when Wallende's body was pulled from under the ice of Silver Creek, which had begun to come off of the creek about a week before. The first was Ethel Billings, who was the wife of Forest Service Ranger Nelson "Jay" Billings. The Billingses lived in the original Silver Lake ranger station, which was a small house the government had purchased from Mrs. Elizabeth Ward on the east side of Silver Creek. The current, much more modern quarters of the

Silver Lake Ranger District now sit on the same property. The story of the discovery of the body was told to Beth Billings Olin, daughter of Jay and Ethel, and related by Teressa Foster in her book, "Settlers in Summer Lake Valley."

> *"One evening in the late fall, Mrs. Billings heard the dog making a great commotion near Silver Creek close to the station. She grabbed a lantern and hurried out to see what was upsetting Pedro. To her horror, she saw a man frozen under the ice. She quickly put on her riding clothes, strapped on her six-shooter, and leaving a note for Jay, rode off to the Chrisman Hotel in Silver Lake. There she remained until Jay returned and the mystery of the dead man was cleared up."*

A separate account credited the discovery to a man who had been a close personal friend of Creed Conn's in the Republican Party, James H. "Bert" Gowdy. The report came out of Silver Lake on March 16.

> *"The body was found by Bert Gowdy who overheard some boys talking about an old coat they had seen in the water of the creek and which they had been unable to pull to land. He and the men with him secured a long pole and managed to get the body up to the bank, where it was tied with ropes."*

One of the men who claimed to have helped to pull the body to shore was a ranger by the name of Gilbert Brown. Brown had been assigned to the Fremont National Forest in the spring of 1907 when the reserves near Silver Lake had been put under administration. He was from Crystal in Klamath County, and had worked as a teacher in the area around 1903. Memoirs of Brown's seem to indicate that he worked as a fire guard before he was appointed as a ranger for the Forest Service in the south Cascades in 1906. During the early 1900's the Forest Service hired many male school teachers to work as summer guards, partly because they were well educated enough to pass the civil service exam. "On several occasions Gilbert Brown assisted the sheriff in arresting criminals for crimes committed on or near the national forest," wrote Melva Bach in "History of the Fremont National Forest," and she credited Brown with having located Wallende's body, "where it had been found in Silver Creek."

What is interesting about this account is that Brown received orders at Lakeview sometime in December of 1907, probably just before Wallende's disappearance, to assume the duties of Deputy Supervisor at Lakeview. Brown said, "which title I received effective January 1, 1908, and served in this capacity until October 1, 1910." Since Brown was working at Lakeview at the time the body was discovered in March of 1908, it seems unlikely that he was one of the men who found it. Jay Billings was probably detailed as "acting" supervisor at the time of the disappearance and working in Brown's absence because he later inherited Brown's old job as ranger.

The killer, some time before depositing the body, sent a letter to Silver Lake from Portland with information on where to look for the body. The recipient of the letter was not named, but it may have been Ranger Billings. "After searching parties had been started out in all directions, the body of Julius Wallende... was found in Silver Creek. It was learned by the local police that the information which led to discovery of the body last Friday was sent out from Portland in the form of an unsigned letter," said the *Oregonian*. "An effort will be made by local private detectives to learn the identity of the writer of the letter." The killer had held onto the body deliberately so that he could write that letter, go to the stream one night and plant the body, and thereby stage a reenactment of the frantic search of Silver Creek that had occurred in March of 1904.

The recovery site of the Wallende murder, like the Sandy Knoll, provided a number of clues as to the identity and motivations of the killer. The body had probably been placed in the stream the night before, when everything was frozen and the killer would leave no tracks. Ethel Billings said she heard her dog Pedro making a "great commotion," which was not the usual canine reaction to dead things. There had been someone moving about down by the stream. The water would have been high, and the killer would have needed to spends some time there in order to secure the body in such a way that it would not wash downstream and would stay in the visible place where he wanted it to be. It seems unlikely that the body of Wallende could have remained near town during two and a half months of torrential water flow.

The earliest surviving account of the find appeared in the *Oregonian* on March 15. "The body was discovered lying in the bed of a creek, where it had evidently been thrown *to ward on suspicion*," said the article, which was written at Silver Lake the day after the discovery. The writer of that article made it plain that he believed the body had been placed in the creek for a specific reason, to cast suspicion upon a certain party or parties. The killer had chosen that site to communicate a connection to the Conn murder, and possibly also to taunt investigators, because that site had originally been assumed to be the location where Conn lost his life. In Wallende's case, circumstances at first seemed to suggest that he had fallen into the stream from the bridge. "No motive for the crime can be discovered and there is a possibility that Wallende lost his way in the dark, fell into the creek, and was drowned. The current of the creek might have battered the skull." A follow up story the next day described the area. "The spot was in plain sight of the bridge, which has to be crossed by anyone going north from town."

A coroner's jury was assembled on Saturday by John S. Martin who, as Justice of the Peace for the town, acted as coroner. Martin, like Gowdy, had been a close friend of Creed Conn's in the Republican Party. The jury described the injuries and condition of the corpse. "The body was in an excellent state of preservation, but upon the head were found ten gashes that looked as though they might have been made with the but of a revolver." Two of the blows had caused fractures to the skull, one of which was on the top of the head. His nose had been broken, and his arms were badly bruised. "The right arm was raised in the position a man would have if he were trying to ward off a blow. There was also a bruise on the arm. The neck and face were swollen which might indicate that he had been choked."

As in the Conn inquest, the jury examined the body and focused on the history of the victim immediately prior to his death. They interviewed everyone known to have had contact with the victim on the day of the disappearance, and learned that the money Wallende had been paid and his gold watch and chain were missing. He had been seen leaving the hotel at 9:30 P.M., presumably to meet someone. Wallende's parents lived in South Dakota, he had relatives in Portland, where he belonged to an Oddfellows lodge. His family was informed of the discovery by telegraph. The manner of death decided upon was homicide, and the jury recommended that the county court offer a reward for the apprehension of the killer. Immediately after the inquest, the body was buried at Silver Lake Cemetery.

Rewards were soon offered for the arrest and conviction of the killer. The first was an offer of $350 made on March 17 by the citizens of Silver Lake, and a major contributor was Charles W. Embody, one of the partners in the local sawmill, who may have been Wallende's employer. The cash was put on deposit in the safe of Francis Chrisman, who also chaired the town meeting where the reward was raised. The Silver Lake people petitioned Governor Chamberlain and Judge Daly requesting that the state and the county offer rewards as well. The commonalities between the Conn and

Wallende cases did not escape the notice of the crowd of people who gathered to appeal to Governor Chamberlain. They remembered that he had become involved in the attempts to solve the Conn murder in 1904.

After two days of investigation at Silver Lake, the sheriff and the district attorney came up with a suspect. "Allie" or "Ole" Hamilton was named in a warrant issued for his arrest, and his description was broadcast around the state by telegraph. "He is described as about five feet nine inches in height, mouth very drawn, bulldog face, nose slightly roman, very reserved and makes no friends, smooth shaven, shoulders rather broad, stature very straight, round head and face, blue eyes, weight 175 pounds, age about 28." The reward put up by Silver Lake people had increased to $450 by this time, and the Governor had offered an additional $4,000.

Hamilton was picked out as a suspect because he was an acquaintance of Wallende's, had been questioned at the inquest, but had left Silver Lake five days afterwards. "Fugitive in Mountains" was the dramatic headline in the *Oregonian* on March 24. An unnamed source had phoned Portland, supposedly from Silver Lake, and informed the *Oregonian* that Hamilton had been "heard of near Odell" where he had abandoned his horse and gone off on foot and was assumed to be heading into Lane County via the old military road. What was interesting about that report was that it completely contradicted another account that came out of Silver Lake on the same day, on or around March 23.

"A letter from Silver Lake brings the news that one Ole Hamilton is suspected of being the murderer. He has an unsavory reputation and since the finding of Wallende's body has skipped out, going by way of Klamath Falls and registering there under an assumed name," said the *Bulletin* of March 27. "Hamilton is the man who threatened a lady who was making the trip from Rosland to Bend on the stage with him last summer. He was intoxicated and the stage driver was compelled to tie him hand and foot to prevent trouble."

"Hamilton's answers at the inquest were not entirely satisfactory, and he is the only man who knew that Wallende had any considerable sum of money just before his disappearance last December," continued the information from the letter. "It is suspected that Hamilton has more than one murder to his credit, as he is known to have left Silver Lake last summer with Gregory Messner, who intended to file on a homestead and who has not been heard of since although he has $100 on deposit in the safe of a Silver Lake merchant. Messner had $200 or $300 in cash when he left and it is now believed that Hamilton murdered him."

The author is of the opinion that the person who contacted the *Oregonian* on March 23 stating that Hamilton had gone to Odell was the killer, working behind the scenes to pin the crime on someone else. Even in 1908 the authorities would have had enough sophistication to know that it was unwise to reveal too much about the investigation to the press, and certainly would not have told the area where they planned to search for the killer. To do so would provide all the tools needed to fabricate alibis, cover tracks, and avoid capture.

In comparison, the earlier statement made to the press that named Hamilton as a suspect was much more basic, containing only his description and a photograph, and seems to have come from the sheriff the day after Hamilton left Silver Lake. The killer had already shown a propensity, a desire to communicate with the arrangement of the body and the crime scene, and another letter telling where he had left the body. It was very possible that he could have written to the *Oregonian* as well.

Hamilton does not seem to have ever been arrested, or to have lived in Lake County again, so was probably eliminated as a suspect early in 1908. A final article on the murder, published in the *Central Oregon* at Silver Lake in late March claimed, "It is the general belief at Silver Lake that robbery was not the only motive that prompted the heartless murderer to commit the terrible deed."

Certain factors in the Wallende homicide rang a bell with many of the friends of Creed Conn, who still lived in Silver Lake and still held his murder fresh in their minds. The blunt force trauma to the head and face; the gold watch that figured prominently in both cases; the riderless horse abandoned by the main suspect; the alleged 'death plunge' into Silver Creek and the way that that stream was the focus of the search. The murder weapon was assumed to be a revolver in both cases, although it was used in different ways. Both men disappeared on a Friday, shortly after leaving their hotels. Both bodies were returned in an excellent state of preservation and left in a place where they would be visible from the main highway.

Given the obvious connections between the two murders, it seems very curious that the press did not pick up on the idea. The newspapers did not mention Creed Conn even once in the Wallende murder, and they never even suggested that the sheepshooters could have been involved in the young man's death. But, the killer himself did mention Creed Conn, and did make reference to the sheepshooters, by using the victim's body and the staged crime scene as a communication medium. By arranging for the body to be found on Friday, the 13th, the killer invoked the image of the skull and crossbones.

Instead of keeping Wallende's body for seven weeks, as he had in Conn's case, the killer hung onto it for an additional four weeks, just so that it could be found on Friday the 13th, according to superstition, an unlucky day. That superstition, which began circulating in the U.S. in the 1800's, seems to have its origins in Norse mythology, and was later magnified in the legendary arrest of the Knights Templar in France in 1307.

> *"The Knights Templar were a monastic military order founded in Jerusalem in 1118 C.E., whose mission was to protect Christian pilgrims during the Crusades. Over the next two centuries, the Knights Templar became extraordinarily powerful and wealthy. Threatened by that power and eager to acquire their wealth, King Philip secretly ordered the mass arrest of all the Knights Templar in France on Friday, October 13, 1307."*

The red skull and crossbones, before it was a symbol of the sheepshooters, and before it was a symbol of the Vigilantes, was a symbol of the Knights Templar. The Joli Rouge, invoked by Haniel Long in his 1888 poem "Dead Men Tell No Tales," as "barges with red sails," later became known in the vernacular as the "Jolly Roger." According to the article, "History of the Jolly Roger," the flag was first used by a French order of militant monks known as the 'Poor Soldiers of Christ and the Temple of Solomon,' commonly known as the Knights Templar." The same article described the battlefield tactics of the Templars. "They fought like men possessed, either prevailing in their cause, or suffering death under the banner of Gol gotha, the place of the skull, where their Christ died." At the time of their arrest, the Templars had the largest sailing fleet and the most successful banking system in Europe. "On the eve of the arrests, the entire Templar fleet mysteriously vanished from the port of LaRochelle carrying with it a vast fortune, the fate of which remains a mystery down to this day."

By giving up the body of Wallende on Friday the 13th, and putting it in the stream that had figured so prominently in the Conn murder, just opposite of the ranger station, the killer was saying, "We are the sheepshooters. We killed Creed Conn, and we killed this boy, too." An elaborate ruse, or "Rouge," as it were.

And, who was Greg Messner, the other young man who had disappeared from Lake County in 1907? Could he have been another victim of the same killer? Was all of the talk about Hamilton just a ploy to throw the investigators off track? There was a 19 year-old man with an unusual first name,

Annick G. (possibly "G" for Gregory) Messner, who lived in the Valley Falls area of Lake County in 1900. He was the son of Jacob and Maggie Messner, and the author has been unable to find any trace of him in public records beyond the year 1900, which has left her to suspect that he went missing and his body was never recovered.

In the first few years of the 20th century, not much was known or understood about multiple murderers. Their signature behavior, what was done beyond what was necessary to kill a person, baffled investigators. News accounts describing the investigations into the murders of Conn and Wallende make it plain that the authorities searched in vain for a motive in both cases, and for that reason had led themselves astray. Their investigations had fallen apart.

SOURCES:

"Mute Evidence of Crime," *Oregonian*, March 15, 1908.

Homestead patent application file of Julius Wallende, serial #424854, Bureau of Land Management, records of the General Land Office, National Archives and Records Administration, Washington, D.C. Patent was issued to Wallende's mother, Lena Samson, in 1913 with the help of Governor Chamberlain.

"Settlers in Summer Lake Valley," by Teresa Foster, 1989, Maverick, Bend, Oregon, Appendix p. 2.

"Republicans Hold Their Primaries," *Lake County Examiner*, March 13, 1902.

"Republicans Hold Their County Convention," *Lake County Examiner*, March 27, 1902.

"Found With Ugly Gashes," *Oregonian*, March 19, 1908.

"A History of the Fremont National Forest," by Melva Bach, 1990, Forest Service, USDA, Pacific Northwest Region, Fremont National Forest, p 19, 21, 24, 29, 33, 35.

"Register of Teachers," *Lake County Examiner*, July 23, 1903. Brown is teaching at Warner Lake School.

"Lake County Teachers," *Lake County Examiner*, October 22, 1903.

"An Illustrated History of Central Oregon," Western Historical Publishing, 1905, Spokane, WA, p 1001. Gilbert D. Brown is named as a teacher in 1903 at Crystal in Klamath County.

Timberlines, Thirty-year Club, Region Six, U.S. forest Service, vol XIV, June 1960, p 49-53. A short sketch of the career of Gilbert Brown.

"Silver Lake Aroused," *Oregonian*, March 18, 1908.

"Found with Ugly Gashes," *Oregonian* March 19, 1908. Dateline is Silver Lake, March 16.

"Silver Lake Murder," *Bend Bulletin*, March 20, 1908.

"Suspect Allie Hamilton," *Oregonian*, March 21, 1908.

"Seek Slayer of Wallende," *Oregonian*, March 22, 1908.

"Suspected of the Murder of Julius Wallende," *Oregonian*, March 25, 1908. Photo

"Fugitive in Mountains," *Oregonian*, March 24, 1908.

"More Particulars Given," *Bend Bulletin*, March 27, 1908. Cites the *Central Oregonian* at Silver Lake as the source of this article.

Julius Wallende is incorrectly listed in the cemetery index for the Silver Lake Cemetery, which gives his name as "Julius Wallmade." Date of death is also incorrectly given as March 8, 1908. Wallende was believed to have died on the night he disappeared, December 27, 1907. Available online at:http:// files.usgwarchives.org/or/lake/cemeteries/ silverlakecem.txt

"Dr. Bernard Daly Dies," *Lake County Examiner and Lakeview Herald*, January 8, 1920.

The author visited the graves of John Creed Conn and other members of the Conn family at the old masonic section of the Roseburg Memorial Gardens in 2003. Creed Conn's grave is in space 5, row 1 of block 2, lot 24.

"13: The Story of the World's Most Popular Superstition," by Nathaniel Lachenmaeyer, 2005, Plume, New York, New York, Available online at: http://books.google.com/books.

"Extaordinary Origins of Everyday Things," by Charles Panati, 1987, Perennial Library, New York, New York, p 13.

"History of the Jolly Roger," by unknown author. Available online at skullandcrossbones. org/articles/jolly-roger.htm

"The Facts on File Encyclopedia of Word and Phrase Origins," by Robert Hendrickson, 1997, Checkmark Books, New York, New York, p 347.

Editorial, *Roseburg Review*, November 22, 1910.

U.S. Census Bureau, Twelfth Census of the United States, 1900, South Warner Precinct, Lake County, Oregon.

THREE DEFENDANTS IN THE LAND-FRAUD TRIAL

An artist for the *Oregonian* created this drawing of the Crook County defendants, from left, Dr. Van Gesner, John N. Williamson, and Marion R. Biggs. The three men were tried and convicted for defrauding the government of federal lands in 1905.

Chapter Nine

A Makeshift

In an editorial for the *Lake County Examiner* of May 5, 1904, Oscar Metzker, a close friend of the Conn brothers, wrote insightfully about what he believed was behind the sheep kills and other range violence.

"There is a band of lawless desperadoes somewhere in the country whose depredations are unbearable and should be run down at any cost. The people of Lake county pay taxes to have their property protected and to tolerate such dastardly work as the wholesale destruction of a county's wealth will surely bring our county to shame and disgrace. Because the owners of property destroyed have lost all they had and are not able to prosecute the case, is no reason why parties guilty of the crime should go unpunished. Neither should the fact that prominent men are engaged in breaking the laws be used to stimulate crime."

The *Central Oregonian* at Silver Lake, after the attack at Reid Rock, told readers, "While only a meager account of the killing can be had at this time, enough has been learned that the killing was done by five masked men, and certain parties are suspected and startling disclosures are expected to take place in the near future." Startling? Really? The public was to be startled when they learned the identities of the sheepshooters.

It was stated early in this work that clues to the identity of the sheepshooters could be traced through the newspaper stories of the time. Probably the most important of those stories was a series of four articles, published in the *Oregonian* from May through December, 1904 (see Appendix A). A careful study of those articles and all that was ever written about the Conn murder and the sheepshooters has led the author to the conclusion that the Series of Four was written by Alfred S. Bennett, defense attorney for John N. Williamson, his business partner Dr. Van Gesner, and Marion R. Biggs of Prineville. The firm of "Williamson and Gesner," had important, large and covert business dealings with Biggs, and the three were found to be partners in crime. They also seem to be the source of the infamous C.B.W. editorial, the last in the Series of Four, where the small serif inside the letter "G" was missing. The text seems to have arrived without the serif at the *Oregonian*, whose editors misread a defective "G" as a "C" when they subscribed responsibility to the authors of the inflammatory piece that contained an interview with a sheepshooter.

A careful study of the Series of Four reveals several things about the writer. It shows that all four articles were written by the same person; that the writer was either an attorney or had a strong background in trial law; that he was keenly interested in the details of the Conn murder; that the writer knew very little about the three major sheep kills of 1904, so was probably not a resident of Crook or Lake Counties, did not research the sheep kills, and was not himself a participant; that he was very conscious of the audience that he was 'playing to,' the readers of Portland; that he was not a friend of the Conn brothers because he did not know certain details about the family, like the number of siblings and that Creed's first name was John; that he was determined to blame the Lake County sheep kills on Lake County cattlemen, despite evidence to the contrary; that he was interested in blaming the Conn murder on the sheepshooters; that he wanted readers to believe there was a vast conspiracy and a network of sheepshooters operating in east Oregon; and that he was not a sheepman himself, although obviously an allie of someone who was. Alfred S. Bennett was all of the above.

The first in the Series of Four was published on May 10, with a dateline of "May 6 Lakeview," and had the sensational headline, "Reign of Terror." It contained numerous helpful references to the coroner's inquest records that since that time have been misplaced by the personnel of the Lake County Clerk's Office. Bennett seems to have traveled to Lake County for the purpose of reading the findings of the inquest, and interviewed the coroner, some members of the coroner's jury, and the examining doctors while he was there. He seems to have drawn all that he knew about the Benjamin Lake sheep kill from the *Examiner* of May 5.

The May 10 article contained at least three misstatements of fact that were pretty obvious attempts to sensationalize the sheep kills, to incriminate Conn, and to protect Bennett's clients. He strongly suggested that Conn provided the ammunition to the sheepshooters and was a conspirator, a notion that was later dismantled by other writers. He greatly exaggerated the number of sheep that were killed in Lake County in the spring of 1904. And, Bennett mistakenly claimed that the two Lake County raids were done by two different groups of men, even though the accounts of the herders and other local people described the methods of those sheepshooters as having been extremely similar.

In another attempt to turn attention away from his clients, Bennett claimed that residents of Lake County had done both sheep kills and had also murdered Conn. It should be remembered here that the very first suggestion that the sheepshooters killed Conn appeared in the *Deschutes Echo* on March 19, and the source of that suggestion will be shown to have been an allie of the sheepshooters who desired to credit them with the murder.

On June 9, Bennett provided another article for the front page of the *Oregonian*. It contained a wealth of detail describing what was found at the Sandy Knoll, the condition and position of the body, and an abundance of evidence to show that Conn could not have died at his own hand. He blatantly blamed the Conn murder on the sheepshooters of Reid Rock with, "it was the men that did that slaughtering that murdered Conn." Bennett also expounded upon a bunch of circumstantial evidence in a very poor attempt to tie the murder to the Lake County sheep kills, probably because they occurred during the same season as the murder. This article claimed Conn was considered an enemy of the sheepshooters because of his relationship to the district attorney, a loose association at best. If Lafe Conn had been considered the true enemy, then why hadn't the sheepshooters gone after him instead? This article continued to paint a picture of a vast conspiracy of sheepshooters.

The third of the Series of Four, printed on July 14, was Bennett's reaction to the published letter of Ervin K. Henderson (see Appendix B), a member of the coroner's jury. Bennett again made numerous revelations about the circumstances of the murder, refuting the suicide verdict and denouncing the jury. He revealed that he had been to Lakeview and Paisley recently because of his intimate familiarity with the inquest findings, which would have been on file at the county clerk's office, and because he had evidently interviewed the coroner, some members of the jury, and the inquest doctors, Witham and Hall.

The sheepshooters were only vaguely referred to in the third article, which reminded readers that the members of the jury were all Lake County cattlemen, and his remarks could be summarized as an attack on the jury based upon the physical evidence in the case. He tried to implicate employees of the ZX Ranch in the Conn murder by pointing out that the company's secretary had been on the jury that delivered the unsatisfactory verdict of suicide. Bennett also cast aspersions on William D. West, a close associate of the ZX, by insinuating that he won the post of assessor in the recent election because he seemed to take the side of the sheepshooters.

The final, and perhaps most telling of the four was written at Ashland, after the Morrow and Keenan sheep kill, published on December 12, attributed to "C.B.W.," and titled "Drive Out Sheep." That article and its patently fictitious interview with a sheepshooter contained at least six factual errors. Here Bennett twice exaggerated the number of dead sheep, did not know the number of sheepshooters present at the attack on the band of Morrow and Keenan, as was testified to by the camptender, and allowed his mythic sheepshooter to claim that the herder had been alone, when in fact, young Keenan was also present. Those errors show that the writer was not personally involved in the sheep kills, although he persisted in a portrayal of a conspiracy of sheep shooting associations spread across Crook, Lake, and Grant Counties.

The sheepshooter that Bennett pretended to interview claimed that he and his friends had moved the sheep onto 'deeded land' in a deliberate attempt to push the blame onto the rancher who owned or leased that property. That one statement spoke volumes. Although attributed to a fictional character, it was absolutely true that the sheep of Morrow and Keenan had been moved before killed, and the sheepshooters had moved them onto the range that was leased by Williamson and Gesner.

> "The band of sheep was then driven to a corral on deeded land, which was done for a double purpose, as we could then shoot without their scattering, and we could also point to the carcasses and say: 'Well, they were on deeded land, and whoever killed them did so merely as an act protecting their own property.'"

The claim of self-defense was particularly telling, because that was the foundation of all the work done by Bennett in defending Williamson, Gesner and Biggs in the land fraud trials of 1905. The defendants in those trials would repeatedly claim that they had no choice but to illegally lay claim to government land, that they had been forced to do so to protect their range because of the "reign of terror" taking place at the time and the treats of the sheepshooters. Bennett took the side of the sheepmen in that final article, which should come as no surprise since Williamson and Gesner were in the sheep ranching business.

Another error was to double the actual distance between Prineville and the Lake County sheep kills, an error that could be expected from a man who did not live in central Oregon. The finding of cartridge boxes with a Prineville firm's cost mark on them at Benjamin Lake was explained by the attorney as having been delivered by friends of the Lake

County sheepshooters from Prineville. And in his final article, Bennett again credited the sheepshooters with the Conn murder, stating that the two Lake County sheep kills "were probably also responsible for the death of Creed Conn."

Bennett lived at The Dalles in 1904, and so may have missed some of the detailed local accounts about the sheep kills, like the one that appeared in the *Ashwood Prospector* as the result of testimony from Keenan, an eyewitness. The attorney tried to impress upon the reader that nearly all cattlemen were sheepshooters and part of a vast conspiracy to destroy the sheep industry.

> *"At different times in the past the cattle interests have been accused of having an organization which has been responsible for these depredations, but each time the answer would come back: 'We are not guilty, and cannot possibly furnish you a clew, unless it is some irresponsible parties who have wantonly killed your stock without cause.' This answer has been a makeshift to herald to the outside world, in lieu of anything more definite."*

The author believes that the two Lake County sheep kills, and possibly also the attack on the sheep of Bill Brown, were perpetrated by allies and associates of Williamson and Gesner, and that the word "makeshift" was not only a favorite expression of attorney Bennett's, his whole defense was a makeshift. The sheep kills were a makeshift and a smoke screen, done after the fact of the land fraud and during the federal investigation that began in January of 1903. The attacks on the sheep and the Series of Four were a graphic propaganda tool designed to manipulate popular opinion around Portland, the place where the jury would be drawn from, and to create the illusion of a full-scale range war in east Oregon that made it necessary for Williamson, Gesner, and Biggs to commit land fraud for the purpose of self protection. Furthermore, Bennett exploited the high-profile murder of John Creed Conn to advance his own agenda. The Conn murder was 'shoplifted' by the defense team to make the sheepshooters seem even more ominous; to make them into more than killers of sheep, but killers of men in the minds of potential jurors.

Later in 1904, ranching neighbors of Williamson and Gesner, incensed by the fraudulent taking of government land that infringed on their range, who knew by familiarity that the firm had been behind the sheep kills in Lake County, drove the sheep of Morrow and Keenan into one of Williamson's corrals and killed them. The methods and number of men involved clearly differentiated them from the sheepshooters at Reid Rock and Benjamin Lake.

There seems to have been a long history of spite between the ranches of Gray and Williamson-Gesner going back to at least 1902 when there was so much interest in removing private fences from public lands. During the third trial of Gesner, Biggs, and Williamson, John S. Watkins was placed upon the witness stand by the government. Watkins had played a small part in the scheme of Williamson and Gesner to obtain government land by fraud in 1902. According to Watkins, the reason that the plan was foiled and the men landed in court was that the government had received a 'tip' from "Henry" Gray and his brother-in-law, Dick Breese, and that it had been "spite work on their part" because Williamson and Gesner had previously complained about Gray having fenced off part of the public domain. "I heard it talked of among us witnesses, that we thought Henry Gray and Dick Breese sprung it a long time ago," said Watkins, who complained about having lost a whole summer's work on account of being dragged back and forth to court at Portland. "Henry Gray and Dick Breese were the sons of bitches that started it."

As the result of the complaint, Gray had been forced to pull down the fences that enclosed both the odd numbered sections of wagon road land he had under lease, as well as the even numbered government sections that were in between. The rancher had saved a lot of money on fencing material by simply running a continuous line along the border of the wagon road, rather than encircling each individual odd section, and had benefited from the additional grass as well. Destruction of the fence had worked a hardship on Gray, which was what prompted him to pay a threatening visit to Williamson and Gesner in June of 1902, warning them to keep their sheep off of the land that he had previously had under fence.

Soon after Gray's 'visit,' Williamson and Gesner began enacting their plan to expand their range and illegally acquire title to the even numbered sections in the area, some of which had previously been used by Gray. The author is of the opinion that Gray's men attacked the sheep of Morrow and Keenan on the range of Williamson and Gesner out of spite, and were probably never tried for the crime because Gray agreed to testify for the government in the fraud trials.

Timeline:

-Early June, 1902 John H. Gray was appointed temporary President of the Crook County Cattlemen's Association.

-June 16, 1902 Gray met with Gesner, Williamson, and probably also Erwin N. Wakefield who was at that time a partner in the firm. Gray allegedly threatened that they would suffer if they did not remove their sheep from the range that he wanted.

-June 30, 1902 The first bunch of Williamson and Gesner's entrymen file on their claims. One of these men is Erwin N. Wakefield.

-July 1902 Williamson and Gesner file applications for a large amount of school lands lying just outside of the western edge of the proposed Blue Mountains reserve. James A. Boggs acts as their agent and pays entrymen $10 each to transfer title. Their plan is to have the western boundary of the reserve extended to cover their school sections, then exchange their school lands for valuable lieu scrip.

-July 28, 1902 Lands are set aside for the proposed Blue Mountains Forest Reserve and closed to entry.

-Fall 1902 A band of sheep belonging to Joe Lister, a friend of Gray, are shot into in Grant County near Izee.

-Early December, 1902 Crook County Cattlemen's Association elects its first permanent officers: M.R. Biggs, President; A. Thompson, Vice-president; J.H. Gray, Secretary; C. Sam Smith, Treasurer.

-January 1903 investigation into the claims of Williamson and Gesner's Crook County entrymen begins when the General Land Office becomes suspicious because most of the entrymen have gotten their money from the same source.

-January 3, 1903 Erwin N. Wakefield quits the firm of Williamson and Gesner.

-Late February 1903 Bill Brown sheep kill at Riddle Canyon, 487 dead. Owner was a resident of the county in which the sheep were killed.

-Early April 1903 Edwin Z. Wakefield sheep kill at undisclosed location in Crook County, 150 dead. Wakefield was the twin brother of Erwin N. Wakefield, who had been a partner of Williamson and Gesner. Owner was resident of the county in which the sheep were killed, and his brother was a witness for the prosecution.

-Late May 1903 Gesner is questioned by a Special Agent of the General Land Office.

-June 5, 1903 Williamson is questioned by a Special Agent of the General Land Office.

-September 1903 Williamson is no longer a partner in the school lands deal, having sold his share to Portland merchant Sig Sichel and Portland doctor Andrew C. Smith. Van Gesner remains a partner of Smith and Sichel.

-October 22, 1903 M.R. Biggs' ranch on the Ochoco Creek lost 170 tons of hay to arson.

-December 1903 through January 1904 fraudulent claims of Williamson and Gesner are suspended pending investiga-tion by the General Land Office.

-February 2, 1904 McKune and Benham sheep kill at Reid Rock, 900 dead. Owners were residents of the county in which the sheep were killed.

-April 28, 1904 sheep kill at Benjamin Lake. The animals belonged to several men. Newspapers of the time give the number dead as 2,300, although that number was probably an exaggeration. Owners were residents of the county in which the sheep were killed.

-August 19, 1904 sheep of Morrow and Keenan were driven into a corral on the range of Williamson and Gesner and slaughtered, 600 dead. Owners were residents of the county in which the sheep were killed.

-June of 1905, while Inspector Langille was in the field near Prineville working on a report of the proposed Blue Mountains Forest Reserve, he was suddenly called back to Washington, D.C.

-July through September, 1905 Williamson, Gesner, and Biggs are tried three times on a charge of conspiracy to suborn perjury for frauds on lands near the Williamson shearing corrals in Crook County.

-November 18, 1905 Langille's resignation made official.

-March 15, 1906 Blue Mountains Forest Reserve was permanently established.

-September 1906 the school lands fraud trial takes place at Portland. Those involved were Binger Hermann, Franklin P. Mays, Willard N. Jones, James A. Boggs, John N. Williamson, Van Gesner, John Mitchell, and George Sorenson. Mays and Jones were convicted on September 13, 1906.

***

The allies of Gray knew that a primary reason that Williamson and Gesner had been able to get away with their sheep kills was that they had been committed far away, where it was unlikely that the sheepshooters would be recognized, and it would be difficult to trace them to their homes. Then there was the tale, according to folk history, that the sons of Henry Gray had supplied ammunition to the sheepshooters, and the report that a large amount of ammo with a Prineville firm's cost mark had been found at one of the sheep kills, probably Benjamin Lake. Of course, Lake County Sheriff Horace Dunlap would have attempted to trace the source of that ammunition, and would have contacted the store that it came from to discover who had made such a large purchase. One of the few entities that could justify such a large stockpile of ammo was the Crook County Sheriff's Department under Sam Smith. Even though Smith does not seem to have ever been formally named in connection with the sheep kills, if Gray's sons really did name Smith, that could help to explain the rift between the ranches of Gray and Williamson-Gesner.

Williamson and Gesner had no real motive for an attack on Morrow and Keenan because they had already employed their land fraud device to dominate the area of range that they wanted. With ownership of all of the even numbered sections going to Williamson and Gesner, Morrow and Keenan would be essentially forced out. James Keenan himself admitted during the third trial that an amicable arrangement had been made between the two firms in which he was to move from the vicinity of the Williamson range in exchange for a grazing allotment in the Cascade Forest Reserve. Williamson and Gesner probably would not have ordered a sheep kill on their own land. Nothing could have been, or was, more damning to their interests. For during the land fraud trials of 1905 they were repeatedly accused by the government prosecutor, Francis J. Heney, of having killed the sheep that were found on their range. Finally, if Williamson and Gesner had instigated the attack on Morrow and Keenan, then the C.B.W. article would probably have been far more accurate.

There was also some anecdotal information tying the Grays to the attack on the sheep of Morrow and Keenan. In her book, "One Hundred and Sixty Acres in the Sage," Beverly Wolverton wrote that Otto Gray, son of John Henry, "bought Grace Prairie, which at that time they called little summit." Although Wolverton mistakenly referred to Gray Prairie as "Grace," and was mistaken about that place being known as "little summit," which name has been attached to the real Little Summit Prairie since at least 1904, it is interesting to note that she associated the Gray family with the location of the Morrow and Keenan sheep kill.

Another anecdote came from Lorene Winnek, who at age 85 was interviewed by writer Gale Ontko. Winnek recalled a sheep kill, which she referred to as the first in Crook County, that had happened in the month of August. Other particulars of her account were incorrect, although she did seem to be describing the attack on the sheep of Morrow and Keenan. She claimed the year of the attack was 1902, when it was really 1904. And, she said some of the sheep, plus the herder himself and his dogs, were all driven off a cliff and plummeted to their deaths, which certainly never happened. The place where Winnek believe the sheep kill occurred was near her parent's timber claim at Gray Prairie, named for John Henry Gray, when in reality it occurred at Little Summit on the eastern edge of the county.

One detail of the Winnek account that seems very credible is that she remembered that one of the young men involved in that sheep kill, the Morrow and Keenan sheep kill, was "an older teenager who was dating a girl in the next block and I had a crush on him because he was nice to me." By 1905 John Henry Gray, his wife Rebecca, and son Roy, age 17, had moved to Prineville, and the census of 1910 showed the Winneks living on 2nd Street, and the Gray's living on 3rd. Roy Gray would have been 19 in 1904. So, more than one longtime resident of Crook County associated the Gray family with the Morrow and Keenan sheep kill.

In the summer of 1902, Williamson and Gesner had induced about 100 of their employees and neighbors to file under the Timber and Stone Act on lands that adjoined their sheep range, with the understanding that the friends would later sell their claims to the firm. Williamson and Gesner carefully selected even numbered sections from amongst the odd numbered sections of Willamette Valley and Cascade Mountain Wagon Road land that they already had under lease as summer pasture in township 15 south, ranges 18 and 19 east. Biggs, who was working as commissioner at the local government land office, greased the skids for the firm by supplying them with some of the entrymen that they needed, and in his dual role as attorney for the firm, falsely advised all involved that what they proposed was, in fact, legal. The three men were indicted for subornation of perjury on February 11,

1905 because the government investigators had reason to believe that they had persuaded the entrymen to swear falsely that they were acquiring the land for their own exclusive use and benefit, when their real intention was to obtain it for the firm of Williamson and Gesner. Their illegal proceedings were an attempt to defraud the government of federal lands.

The pervasiveness of timber fraud in Oregon in the early 1900's was best summed up by federal judge Charles B. Bellinger, who presided over several important land fraud trials of the time.

"Our investigations of frauds which have been committed against the United States lead us to the irresistible conclusion that there has been a growing tendency in this state during the past five years to disregard the obligation of an oath in matters relating to the securing of title to public lands, and that this tendency has been fostered and encouraged by public land officers of the United States, whose duty it was to check and prevent the same. We regret to report that our investigations lead us to the conclusion that the public conscience has become dulled by constant and frequent infractions of the laws relating to public lands on the part of timber and land speculators and their more or less ignorant or guilty victims."

Special agents of the Department of the Interior had begun land fraud investigations in Oregon on a grand scale in 1902. In late 1903, Attorney General Knox selected Francis J. Heney, a personal friend, to come to Oregon and act as an assistant to District Attorney John H. Hall of Portland.

Heney was a force to be reckoned with. Not just because he had the firm backing of the Attorney General, but also because he was a shrewd and ruthless prosecutor. One author who described Heney wrote, "If the evidence was strong, Heney would properly present it. If it was not so strong, then he would argue brilliantly to make it appear conclusive. If it was weak, then he would argue at length until it seemed at least persuasive. Under no circumstance would he capitulate." This was the man that Gesner, Biggs, and Williamson would face in open court, in not one, but three trials that were bitter, excruciating, and exhausting. By the end of the second trial, defense attorney Bennett was literally reduced to tears. Heney was soon granted absolute power by Knox, who saw to it that he displaced Hall as District Attorney and that all special agents and Secret Service operatives working the land fraud cases were at his disposal. The trials ripped apart the lives and alliances of the three men, and caused deep divisions in Williamson's Republican constituency.

"Prosecutions of land fraud offenders in Oregon in 1904-08, by Francis J. Heney, revolutionized political affairs in the state," wrote Harvey Scott. "It turned many holders of Federal office out of power and broke up the Mitchell faction, which had been dominant in Oregon during the larger part of thirty-five years."

Several other prominent Republicans were investigated, and tried. Some were convicted. Notable among those were Binger Hermann and Senator John H. Mitchell who were both personal friends of the Conn family. So many prominent republicans were singled out, that the party begged President Roosevelt to remove Heney, claiming that the California Democrat was trying to wreck republicanism in the state of Oregon.

On December 2, 1902, Secretary of the Interior Ethan Allen Hitchcock made a public declaration to stop land frauds. Hitchcock called for sweeping reforms to the timber land laws, but what really got the attention of Williamson and Gesner was a statement that people of small means, like their own entrymen, were to be singled out. That statement became the bugaboo of the three partners in fraud.

> "As many as five members of a family who, it can be readily shown, never had $2075 in their lives, walk up cheerfully and pay the price of the land and the commissions. Under such circumstances, there is only one conclusion to be drawn, and that is where a whole carload of people make entry under that act, the unanimity of sentiment and the cash to exploit it must have originated in some other source than themselves. In all such cases a rigid inquiry will be instituted to determine the bona fides of the entry."

It was found that in mid-June of 1902, Williamson, Gesner, and Biggs had induced people to file on lands in townships 15 south, ranges 18 and 19 east in order to obtain title for the Williamson-Gesner Sheep Company. The three men went to great lengths to accommodate their entrymen. They took them on a tour of the lands that included a picnic supper, pointed out which parcels they should file on, and supplied them with money for all necessary and associated fees. Williamson himself, although he was a state senator at the time, made room in his busy schedule to personally survey the boundaries of the tracts and write down the legal descriptions of the claims for some of the entrymen so that they could file on the even numbered sections desired by the firm. Entrymen included Williamson and his wife, Gesner, two nephews of Williamson, Biggs, and a number of sheepherders in the employ of the firm.

When the government men followed up on the tip from Gray, they read the cross-examination statements that the entrymen had been required to make when they filed. They found that Dr. Gesner had furnished most of the entrymen with the money for their claims, and that most were people of small means who could not have raised the $426 needed.

When Williamson and Gesner read about Hitchcock's mission to end land fraud on the front page of the *Oregonian*, they reacted in a number of ways. Some of the entrymen of small means received letters from Gesner warning them to relinquish their claims and then to destroy the warning letter. To some of those entrymen who came into Biggs' office to relinquish, Williamson himself read aloud a portion of Hitchcock's proclamation to end frauds.

It was at that point, about the middle of December, 1902, that Gesner, Biggs, and Williamson came up with their defense. A need, they would claim, to protect themselves that had necessitated the taking of the lands that they had no legal right to. They would claim self-defense, but instead of laying the blame off on that old master of temptation--Satan--the personification of evil, as ludicrous as it might have seemed, they laid the blame for their behavior on the sheepshooters. The sheepshooters had made them do it.

When Dr. Van Gesner was first placed upon the witness stand by defense attorney Alfred S. Bennett and his partner H.S. Wilson, he offered the following elaborate tale, as reported by the *Oregonian*:

> "The witness gave a history of the war between the sheep and cattlemen, in which the now famous '30-30 men' played such an important part in the Horse Heaven country. The entrymen, he testified, had first approached him and asked him to lend them money with which to file on the claims. He stated that he agreed to furnish them the money, providing they would give him the use of the land for a range for his sheep. For the use of the range he had agreed not to charge them interest on the loans. He said that the Sheepshooters had established a deadline, and in order to protect his property he was

*forced to secure more range, and thought that
he had gone the right way about it, when he
made the loans to the entrymen who came to
him and asked for financial help."*

Gesner then described how a cattleman had come into
his office in July of 1902 and asked to use a tract of the wagon
road land that was leased by the firm. Gesner refused. "The
cattleman had told him then that he could not use the land and
had posted notices on the tract warning the sheep away. The
cattlemen in that locality were known as 'sheepshooters....' The
witness stated that he had consulted two attorneys about the
matter of taking up timber claims in order to find out if he
could not do something to protect himself from the outrages of
the cattlemen without breaking the law of the Government in
taking land." The attorneys that Gesner consulted were George
W. Barnes and Marion R. Biggs. The threatening cattlemen,
who Gesner and Williamson would name in the second trial,
were John Henry Gray and Joe Lister. The meeting actually
occurred on June 16, 1902.

Lister seems to have been more of a general stockman
than Gray because he also owned at least one flock of sheep.
He lived about four miles northwest of Paulina, and in the fall
of 1902 his sheep had been fired into while they were out on
the range in Grant County near Izee. Lister's ownership of
sheep was one of many small details that made it seem that the
range war difficulties were not simply a matter of cattlemen
hating sheepmen, and vice versa.

"If these leases of the wagon road company didn't
protect your property how would the timber filings protect
you?" Asked prosecutor Heney during his cross-examination
of Gesner.

"Well they thought that the road company got title to
their lands in a corrupt manner and do not respect their title,"
said Gesner, who went on to explain that he made it known
that he "would lend money to anyone who would take up
timber in that belt where I wanted range," and that "it was
worth $500 to me." The careful reader will note here that in
1902 stockmen put up posters on the boundary of the wagon
road lands, just as had been done in the early 1880's by settlers
who protested with skull and cross bones signs to the wagon
road's acquisition of lands.

Heney asked, "What was your object in wanting to lend
money on mortgages given on timber land?"

"I wanted to protect my own property. There was a
reign of terror in that country then and to protect myself I lent
the money," said Gesner, employing once again the
sensationalism that the defense had pinned its hopes upon.

The Words "reign of terror," had been used in the headline and in the lead of the their first article in the Series of Four.

It was brought out that Gray, like Marion R. Biggs, was a member of the Crook County Cattlemen's Association and that the visit of Gray who, according to the prosecution "threatened" Gesner, occurred before the firm began lending money to entrymen. Gesner repeated his story of the sheepshooters to the prosecutor, describing how the cattlemen had met in the Horseheaven country and warned the sheepmen out of the range, and that sheep had been killed in large numbers. It is worth noting here that one of the two sheepshooter trees, the one described in chapter six and identified by Ralph Elder on Committee Creek, was on the eastern edge of the Horseheaven area, being within a few miles of Horse Prairie, Horse Spring, and Little Horseheaven Creek. Contained within the same range was Gray Prairie, named for the family of John Henry Gray, who had a timber claim of his own on the south side of Gray Prairie.

During the second trial, Heney drew an emphatic denial from Gesner when he asked him "if Morrow & Keenan's sheep had not been killed on the Williamson range at the instigation of Gesner?" In answer Gesner said "that the sheep had been run over onto the range (of Williamson and Gesner) and killed by the cattlemen."

One of the entrymen the firm had lent money to was Henry Hudson, who claimed that Marion R. Biggs told him to destroy the promissory notes and mortgage papers for the money lent him by the firm in case an investigator put in an appearance. "Biggs admitted having once told Hudson just before the coming trial, that *'if they cinched one, they would cinch us all.'*"

The word "cinch," or "sinch" appears conspicuously elsewhere, in Bennett's fourth article where a sheepshooter was allegedly interviewed. "That sheepman will never get within miles of our range again, that's a *sinch*," said the fictional character. The use of that word could be a coincidence, but it certainly leaves us to wonder if the alleged sheepshooter was none other than M.R. Biggs.

During his testimony, Biggs described how, even though he had been U.S. Commissioner of the land office at Prineville, sworn to uphold the law, he had allowed Dr. Van Gesner to provide him with an illegal timber claim of his own, and that he had even asked Gesner for the legal description of the tract. During the time that the entrymen were filing in the summer of 1902, Biggs kept at his office a list of the 160-acre parcels wanted by Williamson and Gesner.

When John N. Williamson was placed upon the stand, he at first claimed that he could not remember having been in Prineville during the time that the entrymen filed, and both

Gesner and Biggs attempted to shield him by claiming that Williamson had not been there. Prosecutor Heney then produced the register book of the Poindexter Hotel at Prineville, showing that the senator had checked in on June 15. Williamson attempted to deny that the handwriting was his own, in answer to which Heney supplied eye witnesses that had seen Williamson, not only at the hotel, but also out in the timber when they went out to inspect their claims. Some had seen him working with a surveyor, and others stated that the senator had written down the legal descriptions of their claims for them to take to the land office.

The defense attorneys entertained for a while Williamson's own rendition of the sheepshooter tale. "We had some road lands that we wanted to run a line over," said Williamson. "Some of it was land that we had leased, and other was what we wanted to lease. I also wanted to survey out my timber claim. There was a fight on at the time between the cattlemen and the sheepmen, and we also wanted to survey out the boundaries." Williamson admitted that the firm was interested in leasing additional land from the wagon road company, and given the confrontation that was had between Gesner and the Gray, it seems likely that up until that time Gray had grazed his stock on the land, and adjoining sections of government land, without the benefit of a lease. Williamson and Gesner had moved to infringe upon Gray's territory. During the cross-examination Williamson, admitted that he and Gesner had borrowed a total of $9,000 from two different banks in order to loan it to the entrymen for taking claims. "Do you remember having had a talk with Gesner and a cattleman about ranging cattle and sheep?" Asked Heney.

"Yes, if I was there, then, perhaps I had a conversation."

"Who was the man?"

Do you really want to know his name?"

"Yes, I would like to."

"Well, it was J.H. Gray," said Williamson.

"He has a claim close to the shearing camp?"

"Yes, sir."

Toward the end of the second trial, when the defense rested its case, Heney called as a witness John Henry Gray, who was referred to by the *Oregonian* as, "the man who Gesner testified had warned the firm of Williamson & Gesner to keep off the range or they would suffer."

"The witness stated that he did not tell Dr. Gesner that the sheep would have to be taken off the range or that the cattlemen had appointed him as a spokesman to warn the firm of Williamson & Gesner to give up the land desired by the cattlemen." Heney then reminded the jury that one of the defendants, Marion R. Biggs, had been president of the Crook County Cattlemen's Association in 1902, but overlooked the fact that, at the time of the meeting, Gray himself had just been appointed as temporary president of the newly formed cattlemen's association. Biggs was not elected to the spot until December of 1902. Gray's opinion was that, as of 1902, there had been no war between the cattlemen and the sheepmen of Crook County, and that "whenever any disputes arose, they were settled by being referred to committees."

The author has to concur with Gray's observation. Newspapers of the early 1900's offered good coverage of all incidents of range violence, large and small, usually on the front page. A study of those papers makes it clear that there were only minor incidents in Crook and Lake Counties prior to 1903. The first sheep kill of any consequence happened in February of 1903 when Bill Brown's flock was attacked near Hampton Buttes on the southern edge of Crook County. Next were the sheep kills at Reid Rock and Benjamin Lake in the spring of 1904, and the attack on the sheep of Morrow and Keenan, after they were moved onto the range of Williamson and Gesner, did not occur until August 26, 1904.

In the third fraud trial in September of 1905, William F. Elliott, father of Larkin, was called to the witness stand. "The witness did not remember of there being a 'dead line' established in the country around Prineville," reported the *Oregonian* about the 1902 grazing season. "He said that in 1904 Morrow and Keenan had 600 head of sheep killed upon the land at that time in dispute between them and Williamson and Gesner, and the first firm, as a consequence had abandoned that part of the country.... Elliott further testified that the cattlemen of the country were on friendly terms with the firm of Williamson & Gesner, and that they paid as much attention to the binding force of a lease to road land as to the title gained from the Government for timber claims."

Elliott was probably the source from which Heney drew the conclusion that Gesner, Biggs, and Williamson were behind the Morrow and Keenan sheep kill, but was he a reliable source? In 1902 Elliott was a cattleman living in the Mill Creek area, and not an employee of either firm. He did not claim to have been a witness to the sheep kill, which had occurred in the northeast corner of the county, and so his claim against Williamson and Gesner should have been considered conjecture or hearsay. But, it was entirely possible that the elder Elliott had gotten the idea that friends of the firm were killing sheep from the recent threatening encounters his son Larkin had with Sam Smith.

Heney attempted to show the jury that Gesner, Biggs, and Williamson had propagandized and sensationalized the sheep kills after the investigation into their frauds had begun, and had done so as a smokescreen, a makeshift, and a defense for their actions after the fact to give the appearance that there had been some legitimate excuse for their frauds. Moreover, the shrewd prosecutor, repeatedly and openly accused the three men of having orchestrated the killing of sheep.

> *"The attorney charged that the firm of Williamson & Gesner had been behind the sheep-killing in which Morrow and Keenan had lost 600 head of sheep and had been forced out of business, while the first firm took the lands leased by the misfortunate ones,"* said the *Oregonian* of August 1.

> *"It was also argued that the defendants Biggs and Gesner had seemingly agreed in the plan of the defense to do all in their power to shield Williamson, who was in fact, the brains of the conspiracy and the most guilty of all."*

Defense attorney Bennett denied the accusation regarding the killing of Morrow and Keenan's sheep, and called it "ridiculous and absurd" in his closing remarks at the second trial. Gesner, during cross-examination, said that the herders of his firm and of the firm of Morrow and Keenan had agreed upon a boundary line between their respective ranges, and did not think there had been any difficulty between the sheepmen in 1904. James Keenan, during the second trial, testified that there had been some difficulty between the two firms, but that it had happened in 1902 and in the vicinity of the old Cadle Ranch, and not near the scene of the sheep kill that happened in 1904 at Little Summit Prairie, about 27 miles away.

If the main focus of the trials had been sheep shooting, rather than land fraud, the full truth about the major sheep kills would surely have been brought to light. However, as he made his closing remarks, summing up all of the important points of his case, the attorney for the defense tipped his hand several times by employing some of the favorite turns of phrase that had also been used in the Series of Four articles that sensationalized the sheep kills and exploited the murder of John Creed Conn. A murder that was shoplifted by the defense to add weight to its argument that Gesner, Biggs, and Williamson had no choice but to commit land fraud. Conn's murder made the sheepshooters seem even more ominous, and the need to defend oneself even greater.

In speaking to the jury, Bennett said, "Your duty gentlemen, seems, perhaps, a *perfunctory* duty to you." His use of the word *perfunctory* was unusual and was probably a 'pet word' of the attorney. In all of the many news articles and editorials for the years 1904 and 1905 that were carefully studied by the author, the word "perfunctory" only occurred twice. In the closing remarks of Albert S. Bennett, and in the June 9 article where he criticized the coroner's jury, writing that, "The inquest seems to have been only *perfunctory.*"

"Throughout the case of the Government ran a thread of corroboration which, when it was put together in one story, *vindicated* the defense," argued Bennett. The word *vindicated,* although slightly more common in the vernacular of the day, also appeared in the June 9 editorial where Bennett wrote, "Governor Chamberlain, in offering rewards has inspired the people to *vindicate* the law." And also that the killers of John Creed Conn, "could easily have spirited Conn's body away and buried it in the mountains, but they wanted *vindication.*"

In a rather odd comparison of his clients to scarce albino animals found in the wild, Bennett said, "that it would be as probable that they were guilty when they had held such untainted reputations from boyhood to the present as that three white deer should be found *in one band numbering* no more than the population of Prineville." Bennett used the same expression in the last article in the Series of Four, the sensational interview in which the alleged sheepshooter had been quoted as saying, *"The band of sheep numbering* about 2000 was then driven to a corral on deeded land," and *"our party, numbering some dozen men."*

All through the year 1904 the government prosecutors were busy with their investigation, collecting evidence against Gesner, Biggs, and Williamson. Is it any coincidence that all of the major sheep kills happened, all of the sheepshooter letters were written, and four editorials crediting the sheepshooters with the Conn murder appeared during the same year? Of course, these few selections from Bennett's 'garden of words' do not prove that he was the writer of the Series of Four, but those editorials did contain a large amount of legal jargon and seem to have come from the mind of someone who had spent considerable time in court.

"Reign of Terror," *Oregonian*, May 10, 1904 contained the following:
- "circumstantial evidence"
- "would have observed him"
- "the testimony of the physicians"
- "after hearing the evidence, a verdict of suicide was returned"
- "bring the parties to justice"
- "in consultation"
- "his brother as Prosecuting Attorney" (note caps)
- "another consultation"

"Was Not Suicide," *Oregonian*, June 9, 1904 contained:
- "as to the clothing"
- "influenced the jury most strongly for a verdict of suicide"
- "bore damaging evidence against the perpetrators"
- "still in evidence"
- "vindicate the law"
- "under the constitution they could not again be placed in jeopardy of their lives"
- "sustain the theory of suicide"

"First in Heart," *Oregonian*, July 14, 1904 contained:
- "another case on record"
- "these details are immaterial"
- "summing up the case"
- "arraign the living"
- "is it at all material"
- "reasonable doubt"
- "the Judge who is anxious" (note cap)
- "present one side of the case"
- "every material point"
- "point is immaterial"
- "is this point material"
- "It is the custom in all important cases to give the occupation of the jurors."
- "drew no inference"
- "they want vindication"
- "the testimony of the two examining physicians, which is a matter of record, will show"

"Drive Out Sheep," *Oregonian*, December 12, 1904, contained the following:
- "full protection of the law"
- "criminal operations"
- "wantonly killed your stock"
- "are implicated in these affairs"

- "the scene of the shooting"
- "the fact that it was unsolicited"
- "qualms of consonance"

The word "consonance" has probably never been a part of the vernacular of the town of Prineville, the place where the sheepshooter interview allegedly took place, but is a term used in law to describe a consistency or agreement of the parts of a defense case and witness testimonies. The writer, assumed to be Bennett, used the phrase to say that he was publishing the sheepshooter's account without the outlaw's express permission. *"The fact that it was unsolicited enables him to give it without any qualms of consonance."*

The writer's capitalization of the word "Judge" was interesting because it was an error to capitalize the word used outside of a person's formal title of address. Bennett himself was a former judge of Wasco County, and had begun his career as a defense attorney after retiring from the bench. Throughout the many pages of articles about the land fraud trials of 1905, the *Oregonian* repeatedly referred to him as "Judge Bennett."

Though Gesner, Biggs, and Williamson probably did not personally participate in the act of killing sheep, the three men had close ties to some others who seemed capable of it. One of those men was Charles S. "Sam" Smith, who was described in chapter six as an 1880's friend of James Blakely's in the Citizen's Protective Union, also known as the Moonshiners. Smith was also the man convicted in 1908 of torching Williamson's shearing plant and was suspected in other smaller crimes in which the property of stockmen was destroyed. In 1908 Smith and Williamson were definitely at odds, but from 1902 though 1905 Smith was a devoted allie of Williamson and Biggs.

In September of 1905, Gesner, and Smith, who had been sheriff of Crook County since 1902, were indicted by the federal grand jury for "conspiring to intimidate government witnesses," and thereby preventing them from testifying in the third trial of Williamson, Gesner, and Biggs.

The witnesses who were the object of the intimidation were John S. Watkins and Larkin Elliott, who both testified during the second trial. Threats and persuasion were used by Smith and Gesner to induce the witnesses to not give damaging testimony. Elliott, who would later be an accomplice of Smith's in arson, was awaiting trial in Crook County in 1905 for the larceny of a calf and a horse. Smith, as sheriff, had Elliott over a barrel, and told Elliott that if he wanted a happy outcome on the larceny charge, he would have to cooperate. "If you don't go down there (to Portland) and do the right thing, they'll cinch you surer than hell up here," Smith said.

Gesner was alleged to have also coerced Elliott with the statement, "You do the right thing, and I'll see that you get out of your trouble."

"It is claimed that Sheriff Smith has been exceedingly active in the defense of the three men in the pending land fraud trials," reported the *Oregonian*, "and that in furtherance of the alleged conspiracy he came to Portland about August 24 and remained here until September 7, employing his time principally in the attempt to intimidate and coerce Government witnesses."

John S. Watkins was told that if he testified against the defendants, Smith and Gesner would destroy his reputation for veracity, injure him in business, and "get even with him." The threats against Elliott and Watkins were made on August 17 at the Perkins Hotel in Portland in the presence of others.

When the Crook County Cattlemen's Association was first formed in September of 1902, Smith and Biggs had both been decided upon as temporary officers of the association, which shows that the two men were well acquainted. Biggs was president, and Smith was treasurer. In 1904 Biggs was still a member of the association, and pushing for a definite segregation of the sheep and cattle ranges. During that year, Smith was Crook County Sheriff, and Biggs was Crook County Judge, having been appointed the year before by Governor Chamberlain. Is it any wonder that no sheepshooters were ever brought to trial?

Wilford J. Crain, another Prineville entryman for Gesner, Biggs, and Williamson, was badly abused for having appeared as a witness against them in 1905. Robert Harrington, Marshal of Prineville, brutally assaulted Crain and threw him in jail for having testified, and his barn containing a large amount of valuable hay was burned while he was at Portland in attendance at the trial. Marshal Harrington was another close associate of Sam Smith's. Before becoming Marshal, Harrington lived in Smith's house and worked for him on his ranch.

Aside from the coercion of witnesses, Smith and Williamson seem to have been connected in another respect. On April 2, 1904 Williamson, who was then serving in the U.S. House of Representatives, wrote a letter to Commissioner William Richards asking that 50 timber claims be expedited. The congressman acted on the behalf of Mason E. Brink, whose letter he enclosed with his own. "I will again add my earnest desire that these claims shall proceed at once to patent," wrote Williamson. The 50 claims had been held up for investigation by the General Land Office because they were believed to be fraudulent. Brink was eventually indicted for land fraud on May 5, 1906. Also named in the indictment were Charles M. Elkins, John Combs (another close friend of

Williamson's), the Gilchrists of Gilchrist Timber, and a number of other men in what came to be known as the "Michigan Case." Brink and Williamson were both members of the A.F.&A.M. lodge at Prineville and were both active in Republican politics. Brink was on the committee in 1902 that took time out from regular business of the party to draft a resolution demanding that Crook County stockmen receive first shot at grazing allotments on the forest reserves.

Since at least 1900, Brink had been a partner of C. Sam Smith in an irrigation enterprise. The Three Sisters Irrigation Company drew water from the Tumalo River at the foot of the mountains, and Brink was responsible for selling their lands to settlers. Both men were major stockholders. Theirs was the first irrigation company in the Bend area, and it was taken over by the Columbia Southern Irrigation Company in 1905. Brink was president of the Crook County Irrigation Association in 1902, and was also county judge at that time, so would have worked closely with Sheriff Smith in legal matters around Prineville.

Other partners of Smith's in irrigation matters were Sam J. Newsom and James B. Cartwright. Newsom himself was accused of having been a Vigilante by Blakely, and Cartwright was the son of another alleged Vigilante, Charles M. Cartwright, according to Blakely. Those men, both supposed to be avowed enemies of the Moonshiners, by 1901 were very tight with Moonshiner Sam Smith, leaving historians again to ponder whether or not the Vigilantes ever actually existed.

One associate of Brink's stands out as the person most likely to have been the Corresponding Secretary of the sheepshooters, the man responsible for at least two inflammatory letters in which he pretended to be a member of the gang. William H. Holder, known as "Billholder" by his rivals, was publisher and/or editor of the *Prineville Review*, the *Paisley Post*, and for a time in 1903, the *Silver Lake Bulletin*. Don P. Rea of the *Bend Bulletin* described Holder as "a mental scavenger," whose education in newspaper etiquette had been neglected, and "whose associations in recent years do not seem to have improved him."

The very first suggestion that the sheepshooters were responsible for Conn's murder was printed on the press of Holder's *Prineville Review*, and Holder could easily have been the 'source' for that information. Holder had a penchant for printing fantastic claims based upon nothing. One glaring example being an article in the *Review* on June 30, 1904 in which he claimed that a suspect in the Conn murder had been arrested at Portland and would be brought back to Lake County for trial. In reality, a man had been arrested there on a completely separate charge, and had no connection whatever to the Conn murder.

Holder's writing style could be described as long-winded and rambling. Throughout his articles, like the writer of the sheepshooter letters, he searched for an ending, but seemed unable to settle on one. He was instrumental with Brink in forming the Crook County Irrigation Association, and was named as its secretary when it was formed in late 1902. An article describing the association's first session was 'classic Holder,' replete with resolutions and 'whereases.'

> *"And be it Further Resolved that the secretary of this Association is herby directed to communicate with the Secretary of the Interior tendering the hearty co-operation of this Association to the department...."*

> *"Be it Further Resolved, that the secretary of the Crook County Irrigation Association is hereby directed to convey to the Secretary of the Interior Department a copy of these resolutions and urge by letter and otherwise upon the Secretary of the Interior the momentous importance...."*

These two resolutions make it clear that Holder was a 'corresponding secretary' of the irrigation association. And, as luck would have it, the half-page sample of his writing contained a few phrases that were also found in the sheepshooters' official correspondence. The Corresponding Secretary of the irrigation association was also fond of the antiquated expression, "viz." He wrote, "suggested by the worthy committee having the matter in charge, *viz*, $500,000." In April of 1903, the "notice to stockmen" published "by order of committee" contained the phrase, "We the citizens of Ochoco respectfully request the sheepmen to respect the range enclosed by the following described boundary lines, *viz:*" And then went on to warn stockmen to keep off of about two townships along Ochoco Creek. Holder was also the man who, in 1910 when Conn's body was exhumed, wrote that, "The belief was so strong at the time that Conn knew who the sheep killers were and was murdered by some of the gang, that the Governor offered a reward of $2,000." And Leander Liggett, who was Holder's editor at the *Silver Lake Bulletin*, was also a deputy sheriff under Sam Smith.

Another man close to the conspiracy of Gesner, Biggs and Williamson was Prineville attorney George W. Barnes. During the third trial Barnes testified that he "had been employed by Dr. Gesner soon after his indictment to interview witnesses and find out what they had testified to before the grand jury." The witnesses referred to were entrymen of Williamson and Gesner, and Barnes was hired to help plan a defense by finding out what had already been confessed.

Biggs had a close association with Barnes and the two men had been law partners in the late 1880's. Gesner was related to Barnes by marriage. The Barnes family were accused, probably falsely, of being members of the Vigilantes by Blakely in his "Juniper Trees" memoir, and in a biography of George W. Barnes written in 1968. It was the Barnes home that Charles Luster and Sid Huston were taken from and lynched in 1882. Bud Thompson, who never admitted to being a Vigilante, did describe George W. Barnes as a close ally in those days. Elisha Barnes and his sons were all bitterly opposed to the Willamette Valley and Cascade Mountain Wagon Road which had taken some of their valuable range lands, and were instrumental in the formation of the early "stock association" referred to by Blakely. Because the skull and crossbones used in the 1880's seems to have been a symbol of protest used by settlers against the taking of their lands by the wagon road company, and the Barnes family were squarely on the side of the protest, it seems likely that Biggs, Smith, Gesner and friends inherited that symbol from George W. Barnes. Additionally, Barnes, Smith, and Biggs were all friends in the Democratic party in Crook County.

In his closing remarks at the third trial, in which Gesner, Biggs and Williamson were convicted, Heney accused Williamson of being the head and the front of a conspiracy in which the "ignorant and trusting men and women of Prineville and vicinity" committed perjury. "But if a Congressman enters into a scheme to influence a lot of poor and ignorant men and women to disobey the law, then the community begins to lose its fear and shame. They say, 'How can any one point the finger of shame at me when I am only doing what our Congressman is doing?'" asked Heney. Was that what Oscar Metzker meant in 1904 when he wrote that "Neither should the fact that prominent men are engaged in breaking the laws be used to stimulate crime"?

In chapter three it was mentioned that Philip S. Barry, was out on bail for having shot a man and awaiting trial at the time of the slaughter on February 2, 1904. One of Barry's defense attorneys was James A. Boggs, who was yet another partner of Gesner, Williamson, and Biggs in a separate, massive fraud.

Despite the probable confusion between their two names, Marion R. Biggs and James A. Boggs had shared an office in Prineville in 1902. Boggs served as a clerk for Biggs in the processing of paperwork related to timber claims, and also acted as an agent in the fraudulent acquisition of school lands. "Mr. Heney brought out the fact that Boggs was employed by Williamson and Gesner in getting something like 13,000 acres in the Blue Mountain reserve," said the *Oregonian* of the school lands deal. "Wasn't he engaged in selecting school lands for you and Williamson in the Blue Mountain reserve?" Heney asked Gesner during the first trial.

"No, sir." replied Gesner

"Wasn't he interested with Williamson and Gesner in taking up these lands?"

"Yes, he was interested."

"How long was he there?"

"Six months or a year."

"Do you remember hearing of the creation of the Blue Mountain forest reserve on July 28, 1902?"

"I can't remember the date, but I remember that the lands were withdrawn."

"Don't you remember that Boggs started to Salem on July 26 before the withdrawal had been announced to file on lands in the reserve?" Asked Heney, revealing a separate conspiracy in which the men had filed fraudulent claims on school lands with phony entrymen. The state school lands, which consisted of the 16th and 36th sections of each township, were located just outside of the western end of the proposed reserve. The plan of Gesner, Williamson, and Boggs was to have the western boundary extended to encompass their fraudulent claims, and then to exchange the school sections for valuable lieu scrip certificates which they could sell at a huge profit.

Williamson sold his share of the deal early to two Portland men, merchant Sig Sichel and Dr. Andrew C. Smith, and was no longer financially at risk by October of 1903. But Dr. Van Gesner remained a partner in the scam, and had considerable money invested. In his report on the proposed reserve, H.D. Langille described what the men had been up to:

The stockmen of Crook County have petitioned for the inclusion of several townships surrounding the western end of the western extension, and Congressman Williamson has endorsed the petition in part, but an examination of the tract books shows a large amount of alienated land in these townships and the publicity given the matter by the Stockmen's Association has caused many locations to be made, presumably for the purpose of creating base for lieu selections, hence I cannot approve the recommendation. The ardent advocacy of the stockmen in desiring to extend the reserve in this section is due to a desire on their part to have the Government protect the local range from the migratory herds of sheep from other counties.

Langille, who always displayed a respect for the exact meaning of words in all of his writing, described those generating "publicity" as "the Stockmen's Association," so it is important to note here that there was no such group. Crook County at the time had a "Stock Growers' Association," and a "Cattlemen's Association," and some were members of the "Oregon Woolgrowers' Association," but there was no "Stockmen's Association," so Langille seemed to be trying to say that those generating the propaganda were not restricted to one particular organization, but were members of some of those groups.

The "alienated" land that Langille referred to was the school sections fraudulently filed upon by Williamson and Gesner. And Langille's last sentence in reference to the matter practically spelled out what was going on. The men interested in the school lands were creating propaganda about range wars in order to hasten the final approval of the reserve. Their claim was that the creation of the reserve would end the horrible range tensions, which incidentally, they themselves had helped to create, and the sheep kills were their favorite, most graphic, propaganda tool. Once the reserve was made permanent, Dr. Van Gesner could get his lieu scrip and cash in.

Fortunately for residents of the commonwealth of Oregon, the officials of the General Land Office took Langille's advice and did not include the Williamson and Gesner school sections in the reserve, the boundaries of which were made permanent on March 15, 1906. Of course, the reputation of Gesner had been pretty well trashed during the fraud trials of the year before, so no one in the government was listening to his plea that the reserve be extended.

The first two fraud trials in the summer of 1905, for the men having induced dummy entrymen to file on land adjacent to the shearing plant of Williamson and Gesner resulted in 'hung' juries, meaning that the twelve jurors in both trials could not reach an agreement as to the guilt or innocence of Gesner, Biggs, and Williamson. Heney asked to retry the case twice, and during the third trial, in September of 1905, he was able to convict all three men.

In 1906 Gesner and his new partners in the school lands deal, Smith and Sichel, were left holding the bag and lost a great deal of money. Sichel complained bitterly in court that Williamson had swindled him out of $2200, and Smith got buncoed for $2207 on 'the lieu scrip that never was.' Williamson was indicted on a charge in connection with the school land frauds on February 13, 1905, along with Binger Hermann, Franklin P. Mays, Willard N. Jones, and George Sorenson. Williamson and Boggs, who seems to have vanished before 1905, were never tried on that indictment. Mays and Jones were convicted on September 13, 1906.

Philip S. Barry, was first tried for the murder of Timothy Ahern in May of 1904 with James A. Boggs and Eldon M. Brattain as his attorneys. Just before the trial, "attorney Edwin Mays of Portland," the brother of Franklin P. Mays, spent a few days in Lakeview. The jury could not agree as to Barry's guilt or innocence, with one juror standing for acquittal.

Had Williamson, Gesner, Boggs, and Biggs made a similar offer to the Barrys as had been made to Larkin Elliott? Phil S. Barry found himself in deep trouble in late 1903 when he shot Ahern, and the Barrys had been made somewhat famous by the *Examiner* article as men who were effective at herding, shooting, and clubbing jackrabbits. Was Barry offered his freedom on the murder charge in exchange for an 'inside job' at the Reid Rock sheep kill? Or, are his choice of Prineville attorney Boggs, and the appearance of Mays at the time of his trial just remarkable coincidences? The Barry case was retried in October of 1904, after Lafe Conn was no longer district attorney, and Barry was found "not guilty."

The taking of timber claims with the unspoken intention of later selling to a major timber concern was very commonly done during the period from 1900 to 1905, and the Crook County people were certainly not alone in that respect. The majority of the people of the town of Silver Lake seem to have taken up timber claims too, as had Creed Conn, and a number of his friends.

SOURCES:

"Masked Men Kill Sheep," *Lake County Examiner*, February 11, 1904. Article was reprinted from the *Central Oregonian* at Silver Lake.

Testimony of John S. Watkins in the land fraud case of Marion Biggs, Van Gesner, and J.N. Williamson, September 12, 1905, manuscript collection of the Oregon Historical Society, U.S. District Attorney records, #1704-3, file 11.

"Heney Lets Fall Scathing Words," *Oregonian*, August 1, 1905.

"Witnesses Admit Their Perjury," *Oregonian*, July 25, 1905.

"Reign of Terror," *Oregonian*, May 10, 1904.

"Was Not Suicide," *Oregonian*, June 9, 1904.

"First in Heart," *Oregonian*, July 14, 1904.

"Drive Out Sheep," *Oregonian*, December 12, 1904.

"Local Notes," *Deschutes Echo,* October 24, 1903.

" Range War Still Continues," *Lake County Examiner*, September 1, 1904. Describes the location of the attack on the sheep of Morrow and Keenan as taking place at Little Summit Prairie and 40 miles east of Prineville, which matches the present day location of Little Summit Prairie.

"Thunder Over the Ochoco," by Gale Ontko, Maverick, Bend, Oregon, vol 5, p 235-238.

U.S. Census Bureau, Thirteenth Census of the United States, 1910, Prineville, Crook County, Oregon.

Timber and stone cash entry for Anna L. Winnek, patented May 21, 1907, serial #ORTDAA 070825, township 15 south, range 20 east, section 22. http://www.glorecords.blm .gov/ PatentSearch/ The claim of Anna L. Winnek, mother of Lorene, adjoins that of John Henry Gray.

"Public Lands, Politics, and Progressives: The Oregon Land Fraud Trials, 1903-1910," by John Messing, *Pacific Historical Review,* February 1966, vol. XXXV, no. 1, p 35, 53, 43-49, 54, 59.

"History of the Oregon Country," by Harvey W. Scott, 1924, Riverside Press, Cambridge, vol. 1, p 346.

"Hitchcock's Report," *Crook County Journal*, December 11, 1902.

"Other Side of Stock War," *Oregonian*, March 18, 1903. A letter to the editor by John Luce of John Day who described several small sheep kills in Grant County.

"A Hundred and Sixty Acres in the Sage," 1984, by Beverly A. Wolverton, self published, p 8, 12, 58. On January 3, 1903 Wakefield sold his share of two parcels of land to Williamson and Gesner.

"Indicted by Jury," *Oregonian*, February 12, 1905.

"Heney Flays J.N. Williamson," *Oregonian*, September 24, 1905.

"Jury finds all Three Guilty," Oregonian, September 28, 1905. Article contains a timeline of events in the case. Williamson borrowed $6,000 from a bank at The Dalles on December 15, 1902.

"Indicted by Jury," *Oregonian*, February 12, 1905. The entrymen began making final proof on their fraudulent claims in December 1902 and January 1903 before M.R. Biggs. The statements of the entrymen saying that they had borrowed money from the same firm was what aroused suspicions and started the investigation when those statements were received by the General Land Office.

"Its Work is Done," *Oregonian*, April 9, 1905.

"Biggs and Gesner Deny Conspiracy," and "Defense Opens its Case," *Oregonian*, July 15, 1905.

"Biggs Testifies for Defense," *Oregonian*, July 16, 1905.

"Williamson Says He is Innocent," *Oregonian*, July 18, 1905.

Bureau of Land Management, records of the General Land Office, land patent of John H. Gray, serial #ORTDAA 070792. Land is in T15S R20E, sections 21 and 22, patented October 3, 1904. http://www.glorecords.blm.gov/PatentSearch

"Central Oregon Place Names," vol. 1, Crook County, by Steve Lent, 2001, Maverick, Bend, Oregon, p 73. This book claims that Gray Prairie was named for Roy Gray, son of John Henry Gray.

"Defense Waives its Argument," *Oregonian* July 19, 1905.

"Witnesses Admit Their Perjury," *Oregonian*, July 25, 1905.

"Defense Closes its Case Today," *Oregonian*, July 29, 1905.

"Starr Will Take Stand Monday," *Oregonian*, July 30, 1905.

"First Day of the Defense," *Oregonian*, September 20, 1905.

"Heney Rests His Case Now," Oregonian, September 19, 1905.

Biggs Family History book #H-2, undated article from 1944 describing the Golden Anniversary of Marion R. Biggs and wife, Bowman Museum, Prineville, Oregon.

"When the Juniper Trees Bore Fruit," Oregonian, March 12, 19, and 26, 1939. Stories of James M. Blakely, as told by Herbert Lundy.

"Reminiscences of a Pioneer," by Colonel William Thompson, 1912, San Francisco, California. The book is now available as an ebook through Project Gutenberg at: www.gutenberg.net

"George Barnes" (biography), *Central Oregonian*, Centennial Edition 1968, p 11.

"History of the Willamette Valley and Cascade Mountain Wagon Road," by Cleon L. Clark, 1987, Deschutes County Historical Society, Bend, Oregon, p 59-65.

"The Mogans," by Mae L. Smith, p 1, family history file, Bowman Museum, Prineville, Oregon.

"Trial is Near to its Close," *Oregonian*, September 16, 1905.

"Heney Lets Fall Scathing Words," *Oregonian*, August 1, 1905. In this article defense attorney Wilson said that the defendants were surrounded by "a cloud" of Secret Service agents.

"Bennett's Reply is Most Caustic," *Oregonian*, August 2, 1905.

The Free Legal Dictionary, by Farflex, definition of consonance,http://legal-dictionary.thefreedictionary .com/ consonance

"Williamson Not a Party," *Oregonian* July 16, 1905.

"Defense Closes its Case Today, *Oregonian* July 29, 1905.

"Preliminary Examination," *Lake County Examiner*, December 3, 1903.

"Phil Barry Out on Bail," *Lake County Examiner*, December 10, 1903.

"Local News," *Lake County Examiner*, May 10, 1904.

"Jury Disagrees in Barry Case," *Lake County Examiner*, May 26, 1904.

"Jury Acquits Barry," *Lake County Examiner*, October 27, 1904.

"More Crook County People Under Ban," *Crook County Journal*, September 14, 1905.

"Both are Indicted," *Oregonian*, September 9, 1905.

"Damaging Story Told by Sichel," *Oregonian,* September 8, 1906.

U.S. Census Bureau, Twelfth Census of the United States, 1900, Prineville, Crook County, Oregon.

"Cattlemen Organize," *Crook County Journal*, December 4, 1902.

"Cattlemen Hold Annual Meeting," *Crook County Journal*, October 20, 1904.

"Looters of the Public Domain," by S.A.D. Puter and Horace Stevens, 1908, The Portland Printing House, Portland, Oregon, p 445, 450-454.

"The Crook County Journal's Annual Number," 1901, *Crook County Journal*, Prineville, Oregon.

"Pioneer spirits of Bend," by Joyce Gribskov, 1980, self-published,   Bend, Oregon, p 84.

"Resolutions of Condolence," Prineville Lodge #76 A.F.&A.M. to the family of James Parker Combs, April 14, 1900, obituary book #1, page 1, Bowman Museum, Prineville, Oregon.

"Williamson Wins," *Prineville Review*, March 27, 1902.

"Irrigation Again," *Crook County Journal*, December 11, 1902.

Editorial, *Bend Bulletin*, May 8, 1903.

"May Have Man Who Killed Conn," *Prineville Review*, June 30, 1904.

"Grim Reminder of 1904 Range War," *Lake County Examiner*, November 24, 1910. Story was picked up from the *Silver Lake Leader*, of which Holder was editor at the time.

"An Illustrated History of Central Oregon," Western Historical Publishing, 1905, Spokane, WA, p 787.

"The Growth of Lake County, Oregon," by G.E.B. Stephenson, 1994, Book Partners, Inc, Wilsonville, Oregon, p 105.

"Mitchell's Part in Conspiracy,"*Oregonian*, September 5, 1906

"Fight Centers on Williamson," *Oregonian*, September 6, 1906

"Puter Exposes Land Fraud Ring,"*Oregonian*, September 7, 1906

"Damaging Story Told by Sichel," *Oregonian*, September 8, 1906.

"Witness Hopkins Cast into Cell," *Oregonian,* September 8, 1906.

"Report on the Proposed Blue Mountains Forest Reserve," by H.D. Langille, 1906, Department of the Interior, General Land Office, p 16.

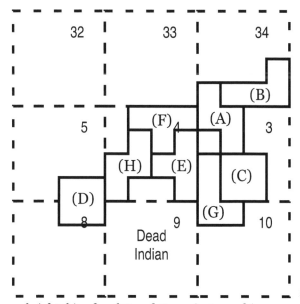

Claims of eight friends of Creed Conn in townships 29 and 30 south, range 16 east. (A) James R. Horning patented 10/28/04; (B) Elizabeth P. Horning 10/28/04; (C) Thomas J. LaBrie 10/28/04; (D) Lulu C. LaBrie 10/28/04; (E) Warren M. Duncan 10/28/04; (F) Ida A. Duncan 12/01/04; (G) Augustus B. Schroder 12/29/04; (H) Ida Schroder 12/29/04.

Chapter Ten

Dead Indian

The story of the murder of John Creed Conn has endured for over one hundred years because it was sensational, and there were three things that made it so. The *Oregonian's* front page articles that credited the murder to the sheepshooters were one reason; the peculiar circum-stances surrounding the case were another; and Conn's celebrity was the third.

Creed Conn was an astute and insightful business-man. The Conn freight team was a symbol to the community of Silver Lake, and Creed Conn knew it. It symbolized greatness and prosperity. The team became a promotional tool for the business as it traveled to The Dalles and Shaniko. Everyone in the north end of the county looked forward to the return of the team that was not only showy, but carried with it an immense load of new merchandise. As the team passed, the few people who owned cameras would run out into the street to take pictures of it.

Creed Conn and his best friend from childhood, Thomas J. LaBrie, moved to Paisley in Lake County from the Roseburg area in the mid-1880's when both men were in their twenties. LaBrie was well known throughout Oregon for his horsemanship and his ability to handle a big freight outfit. It is not known exactly when Tommy LaBrie began driving for Conn, but a short biography of LaBrie says that he was employed for Conn in the early days, hauling freight back and forth from The Dalles, before Shaniko became a shipping point. It is possible that LaBrie and his team worked for the Conn Brothers' store at Paisley even before that, because Creed Conn himself worked there.

By 1900, LaBrie was no longer driving for Conn, and had settled into a life of farming and ranching. It was at that time that Creed Conn moved to purchase the magnificently trained freight team of Tommy LaBrie. On July 23, 1900 Conn borrowed $1,000 from Louisa Gilfry, a family friend, to finance the purchase of the team. It was a major investment, and the cost of feeding and maintaining 14 large animals, along with 10 percent interest on the loan every year, were major expenses for a businessman of 1900. But, Conn recognized the importance of the team. He knew that it symbolized his company name, and that it was the means for him to finance the expensive trips to Shaniko for merchandise by hauling out wool from the sheep camps.

The Conn brothers' business at Paisley seems to have come apart around 1889 when Virgil Conn bought out the interest of his brother George in their mercantile store there, and Creed bought a town lot for himself in Silver Lake. In 1892 George sued Virgil in what became a nitpicking and embarrassingly drawn out dispute over petty financial matters. That was the year that Creed Conn went to establish a new store in Silver Lake, although his brother Virgil maintained a partnership interest in the new store for at least three more years.

In 1895, Creed Conn made another smart business move when he purchased a second, highly visible town lot, lot 4 in block "F" on the western edge of Silver Lake. On that lot he would build a new store building between 1897 and 1899, a store with a sign that anyone coming in from the north would see as they entered town, and before they saw the sign of Chrisman's, or of any other merchant for that matter. To guarantee high visibility for his business, Conn also bought the whole west end of block "F," and the lots across the street as well. In 1897 Conn was joined at Silver Lake by his old friend Tommy LaBrie, who left Paisley when Virgil Conn went off to join the state legislature. By 1900 the big and powerful freight team, the new store building, a prominent family, the right clothes, a leadership position in local politics, and his handsome good looks made Creed Conn an object of admiration and envy.

And, because Conn was a highly visible figure, and a local celebrity, a major controversy erupted when LaBrie retired from freighting and Conn purchased the team. Each animal in that team was so smart, so highly specialized, that people all over the county argued and placed bets as to whether or not another man could drive them. LaBrie himself had raised and trained each animal, and the 10 mules, and the two brainy lead horses moved together like clockwork, with LaBrie himself as an integral part of the team. In the little town of Silver Lake in 1900, Conn trying to break in a new driver was the equivalent of the Portland Trailblazers replacement of coach Jack Ramsay. Could another man do the job?

"One freight team that used to come here had twelve mules, belonged to a fellow named Creed Conn," recalled Russell Emery in a 1978 interview. "He run a store down here, one of the stores. And he couldn't find a driver." Emery, who was not born until more than a year after Conn replaced LaBrie, misidentified the man who got the job as Ed Henderson, who actually was the driver for Chrisman. "Well, I'll take your team and if I can't drive them, the trip won't cost you anything," was the version of the story of the new driver that Emery had heard. "So they let him take this team and drive them. He was an old muleskinner." Despite the inaccuracy of the name, Emery's account is interesting in that the replacement of Conn's driver was such a big deal that the story was still remembered in the community 78 years later.

The name of Conn's driver from 1900 to 1904 has been lost to history, but it may have been Elmer D. Lutz, a teamster who lived in Silver Lake from 1887 through 1910, and boarded at the home of another friend of Conn's from Douglas County, Walter Buick. Lutz, like Conn, was very active in the Republican Party in Lake County, and during the time that Conn was missing was elected constable for the town of Silver Lake.

Around 1901, Conn moved out of the single room in the house of Al Dunning where he had been boarding, and moved into the Silver Lake Hotel where he lived in relative luxury and sent his laundry out. That summer he expanded his business with the addition of the young clerk Frank W. Payne, who had just graduated from business college.

In 1902 Creed Conn borrowed money again, this time $580 from George Gilfry, husband of Louisa. A portion of this loan probably went for the purchase of his flashy new team and buggy, and an excellent saddle horse. By the middle of the year, Conn had acquired many of the external symbols of wealth and status, and more debt and expenses than he could easily handle. That year, for the first time, he was unable to pay cash for the new stock of merchandise for his store from Murphy, Grant and Company of San Francisco, and had to buy on credit. Then there was the cost of feeding, shoeing, and boarding the team, and he had to pay $100 to Louisa Gilfry in interest on the loan. By the fall Conn began to look for new investments to increase his income. In October he purchased, on credit, one of the early horse-powered combines made by the McCormick Harvesting Machine Company for $323, probably to put his team to work in harvesting grain when they were not hauling freight.

By the spring of 1903, Conn had become painfully aware of his mounting bills. Property taxes were due, another interest payment to Louisa Gilfry was coming up in July, the debt to George Gilfry would be due in November, he had to charge more groceries for his store, and the team was eating him out of house and home. The wages of new employee Frank Payne became a difficulty, and he began underpaying the clerk by September, then laid him off for the month of December. Looking ahead, all that he could see was debt. By the same time the next year, he would have to come up with more than $2,500 to pay all that he owed. The alternative would be to admit failure and sell out to pay his creditors, some of whom would surely sue him for recovery.

Early 1903 saw the arrival in Silver Lake of ever increasing numbers of "timber seekers," who were mostly hired to purchase inexpensive timber land from the government, and then to immediately sell it to major timber concerns. Although that purpose was never stated, it was commonly known that they, like the entrymen used by Gesner, Biggs, and Williamson, were not acquiring the land for their own use and benefit. By the use of these "dummy entrymen" timber companies could acquire many 160 acre parcels for about $425 each, when the timber that they contained was worth more than twice that figure, sometimes a lot more.

During the month of February 1903, two groups of newspaper men put their sights on Silver Lake as a place to make a quick killing in advertising dollars. Under the law, the dummy entrymen were required to advertise their intentions to take certain claims under the Timber and Stone Act, and for each ad there was a fee. It is clear that Creed Conn and some of his neighbors were caught up in the excitement.

Silver Lake on the Eve of a Big Boom
Silver Lake, Oregon, Feb. 20, 1903

Ed. Lakeview Examiner:

For the last week I have heard that the little town of Silver Lake was crowded with strangers and that it was impossible to get accommodations for all. I had also heard that a newspaper would be published next week by a stranger whose name is Bailey. Today I went up to town, and I found the half had not been told. Twenty-six men and one woman, all strangers; are here locating timber land. Today, Creed Conn introduced two men to me, one by the name of Baldwin, the other I have forgotten. They are also going to start another newspaper as soon as they can get a building erected. Think of it; two newspapers in this one time considered out of the way place, and the extreme settlement in northern Lake county. And you might say almost surrounded by a desert country. They tell us that there will be four hundred emigrants looking for homes and locations on the desert, and that Silver Lake will be the centralized point of Lake county. A man was hired to haul out a load of hay to the McCarthy ranch about 12 miles from town, and he was given twenty dollars per ton.

There is undoubtedly a "niger in the woodpile," and these parties are on a hot track. There is lots of room for homes on the Silver Lake desert. I did not travel over three hundred miles this summer not to see them. In many places, water will be found near the surface. Will say there is considerable excitement among the present population. My name might be "Scar Faced Charlie," but it ain't. I guess I won't change my name for a while, but sail under the old nom de plume.

More Anon, Lone Pine

The account above was probably written by George Duncan Sr., who was a regular correspondent to the *Examiner*. The first newspaper man named was doubtless Samuel M. "Mart" Bailey, who came to town with Clarence Black, Leslie N. Kelsay, and writer Sidney D. Percival from the *Crook County Journal* and started the *Central Oregonian*.

The other man, Baldwin, described as an associate of Conn's, would have been Prineville banker Thomas M.

Baldwin. He was connected to the other paper that started that spring, the *Silver Lake Bulletin*, owned by William Holder and Wells A. Bell, with Leander Liggett as editor and William Wagner as foreman. Baldwin, who could be described as a bit of a "dandy," was mayor of Prineville in 1903, and associated with Holder in attempts to induce a railroad to build to there. Holder was probably the second man, whose name Duncan could not remember, because he was identified in a separate article in the *Examiner*. Baldwin may have known Conn through fraternal circles, as both men were members of the Ancient Free and Accepted Masons, or "AF&AM." Both papers began publishing in March of 1903, although by November the *Central Oregonian* had bought out the *Bulletin*, with Holder retaining an ownership interest in the new joint venture.

The Big Boom timber deal did not actually pan out. The *Deschutes Echo* reported in early March that the group of 27 was from West Superior, Wisconsin, and that "From a private source we learn that twenty-six timber filings recently made at this place for lands in the Lakeview district have been rejected for conflict with former entries." The timber claims of the 27 people were never advertised.

Creed Conn did have a good reputation in the community, and was regarded as a generous man, perhaps too generous. He allowed a number of people to buy items on credit from his store, and by 1903 was owed $3,000 in bad debt by people who were either unwilling or unable to pay. That reputation for generosity may have been what made his continued borrowing possible.

Like many other small town mercantiles of the time, the J.C. Conn General Merchandise Store served as a bank of sorts for the community. Most of those stores had safes, and enough cash flow to handle deposits and withdrawals for a few people. With the nearest real bank about a hundred miles away in Lakeview, the Conn mercantile was the next best and most secure option. Local people would sometimes deposit a sum of cash with Conn for a particular future use, such as payment to the government for a homestead or timber claim. Conn would record the transaction in his pocket journal, the same journal that disappeared when he did, then write the depositor a promissory note that would guarantee the return of their money at some future time. The pocket journal was more of a transaction register than it was a diary, something like a check register or savings passbook in which Conn would also record orders for customers, his own personal banking transactions, and deposits and payments of all kinds.

On June 17, 1903, Martha S. Lane deposited $3,270 with Creed Conn, for which Conn wrote her the customary promissory note and promised to pay that sum back to her one year later at a rate of eight percent interest. Three thousand dollars was a very large amount of money in 1903, roughly equivalent to about four and a half year's pay to a skilled worker. The amount $3,270 was not a round number, as would normally be the result of a personal loan, but it was the exact amount of money needed to purchase eight timber claims from the federal government at $400 each, plus the filing fees of $10 each for seven of those claims. Having Conn act as banker in the transaction would have served the dual purposes of convenience and concealing the source of the money.

There was a set of eight timber claims filed upon in early June of 1903 near Dead Indian Mountain, just south of Silver Lake. The entrymen were four married couples: Tommy LaBrie and his wife Lulu; Warren Duncan and his wife Ida; Gus and Ida Schroder; and Robert J. and Elizabeth Horning. One of the entrymen, Gus Schroder, paid his own filing fee of $10. The eight claims were all contiguous and covered about two sections in township 30 south, range 16 east. All of the eight named Byron Cady and/or Robert M. Patterson as the men who located them on their claims. All of the eight had personal ties to Creed Conn.

The Bureau of Land Management still maintains a database of homestead and timber and stone claims in the form of a public web site that makes it relatively easy to study timber claims made during the early 1900's. By looking for claims with similar dates, locations, and document (receipt) numbers issued by the land office where the claims were filed, it is often very simple to identify a group of timber seekers working together on a deal. When the filings are made at the same time, on contiguous pieces of land, when patents are issued on the same date, and when a prior friendly association of those people can be shown, it is pretty nearly a sure thing that they were working in collusion to acquire timber land. When several people worked together to file on contiguous claims, the value of each was increased because they could be logged as one uninterrupted block.

Martha Lane and her deceased husband, Andrew, had been, along with the Duncans, some of the earliest cattle ranching residents of Silver Lake. When the Christmas Eve Fire of 1894 took the life of her widowed sister, Malinda J. Payne, Martha's 12 year-old nephew Frank was brought into her household. George Payne, who is often described as the one responsible for starting that accidental fire, was the older brother of Frank. In 1896, when Andrew died, Martha Lane and the children retained ownership of their 1,700 acre ranch northwest of Silver Lake, but around 1899 moved to Harrisburg, Oregon where the children could benefit from higher education.

Creed Conn had been a friend of Martha Lane's family for a long time. Her maiden name was Small, and Conn was particularly friendly with her brother, George H. Small. The two men were avid hunters, and Conn always kept a stock of sporting goods in his store with a variety of guns and ammunition. When Conn set up his first store at Silver Lake in 1892, there were still a few grizzly bears in the country. One of those bears, known as "Old Yank" was notorious for terrorizing livestock and so, in the spring of 1899, a party of men that included George Small and his son, Earl, Creed Conn, Jefferson Howard, and William P. Vandevert and his bear dogs, set out after the mighty bruin. "After a chase of many miles through the snowdrifts, the bear took refuge in a small cave on the north slope of Yamsay Mountain where he defied smoking out and harassment by the hounds. A rancher, Jeff Howard, boldly but foolishly moved in and prodded the bear out with a pole to the waiting riflemen. Earl recalls that the bear's roars were most awesome to a boy of 12. The hide was given to J.C. Conn, the Silver Lake merchant and member of the hunting party," was the story told by Earl Small to the *Bulletin*.

One interesting feature of the timber deal on Dead Indian was the role played by Tommy LaBrie, who was a member of the Booth family. Booth, as in "Booth-Kelly Timber Company." After Tommy's father Ferdinand LaBrie died in 1866, his widowed mother Ann married John O. Booth. John Booth's brother, Robert A. Booth Jr., founded the company at Springfield in 1889. Dealing in timber lands was something that everyone was doing around 1903, or so it seemed, and Tommy LaBrie acted as a witness for all of the other seven entrymen in the deal on Dead Indian.

Booth-Kelly, which was affiliated with Oregon Land and Livestock Co., Ochoco Lumber Co., California and Oregon Land Co., and Weyerhaeuser, got into several 'scrapes' with the federal government over their dealings in timber lands. James H. Booth, an uncle of LaBrie's, was let go from his job as receiver at the U.S. Land Office at Roseburg in 1903 because of grave concerns about his conduct, but was reinstated, probably because of the political pull of another uncle, Senator Robert A. Booth, one of the most influential members of the Mitchell-Fulton wing of the Republican Party. In early 1904 James H. Booth was forced by President Roosevelt to dispose of all of his interest in the Booth-Kelly Company, of which he was secretary, in order to keep his position with the land office.

On April 8, 1905, James H. Booth was indicted for accepting money in exchange for advance information about the availability of timber lands while he was receiver at Roseburg. At the end of the year, the Secretary of the Interior still suspected Booth of using his position in the land office to work deals for Booth-Kelly, and employees of the General

Land Office were prohibited from becoming interested in any way in the purchase of public lands.

James H. Booth and Robert A. Booth were both indicted in 1905 for conspiracy to defraud the federal government of public lands through the use of false affidavits and proofs of homestead entry. Robert Booth was vice-president of the Booth-Kelly Company and a senator in the state legislature at the time. Again, in 1915, Robert A. Booth, manager of the company, and John F. Kelly, vice-president, were convicted for frauds dating back to 1902 with members of the LaRaut family, who were cousins of the LaBries and arrived with them in the Roseburg area from Montreal in 1852.

Warren Duncan owned the livery and blacksmith shop where Creed Conn's team was shod and repairs were made to his wagons around the time of his death, a fact that was well documented in the probate records. Duncan also was responsible for delivering Conn's remains to the inquest and then to the Silver Lake Cemetery. Gus Schroder was related to Duncan by marriage to his first wife, and also related to clerk Frank Payne by marriage because both had married daughters of James Martin.

J.R. Horning seems to have been the intended beneficiary of the deal on Dead Indian. He had been a next door neighbor of the Lanes for many years, and raised cattle on a section of land he owned northwest of Silver Lake. Horning was the first to visit the site of the claims, on June 1, with a timber operator by the name of Robert M. Patterson. The three other couples followed on June 6 to inspect and file on their claims. Horning and his wife returned on June 9 and filed on June 10. On February 8, 1904 Horning went to the Lakeview land office to pay for his claim and that of his wife, accompanied by Creed Conn, who probably had the needed funds wired from his bank in San Francisco.

James Horning was a trusted friend of Conn's, and his ranch was where Conn relocated his valuable freight team after the barn containing his wagons had been destroyed, presumably by arson. Horning cared for the team after the fire, and continued boarding them until they were sold in May. Both men were members of the First Baptist Church, and of which Horning was church clerk.

The LaBries and Duncans went to Lakeview on February 24, 1904 to pay for their claims, at which point they became legal owners of the timber lands. Two days later, Creed Conn appeared at Lakeview and paid the bank $450 to cover a note of his that the bank had already paid, probably to the six entrymen who would receive $75 each as payment for their help in securing the claims for Horning. Horning's wife did not collect $75.

By 1905, Horning had given up ranching and had gone into the real estate business full time at Linkville in Klamath County. He and Mark L. Burns, who sold insurance, established the partnership of "Burns and Horning" there. At the time of the 1910 census, Horning and wife were living in Portland on the corner of Yamhill and Morrison streets, and Horning gave his occupation as "real estate salesman."

James R. Horning made some interesting testimony during the application process for his timber claim. Entrymen were required to make several sworn and signed statements, as were their witnesses, as to the veracity of their claims and intentions. When Special Agent Horace T. Jones asked Horning, "From what source did you obtain the money with which to take this claim?" Horning answered, "I had part from the profits of my business, and part I borrowed from by brother-in-law Walter C. Buick, and part from Mrs. Lane, a neighbor of mine," and added. "My reason for borrowing that money is, that I happened to be a little short of cash at the time."

When agent Jones questioned LaBrie regarding the Warren Duncan claim, he asked, "Has he ever been connected with any mill or timber men or corporation?" LaBrie answered, "Not that I know of. I think not." A rather comical answer, considering LaBrie's family ties to the Booth-Kelly company. LaBrie was asked the same question when he acted as witness on Schroder's claim, and answered "no." Concerning his own timber claim, Jones asked LaBrie, "Have you ever been connected with any mill or timber business?" To which LaBrie also answered, "no."

On June 17, 1903, the day that Creed Conn accepted the funds of Martha Lane, there was no evidence that the woman was in Lake County, but several members of the Booth family were, including Judge William A. Booth of Prineville; Senator Robert A. Booth and his son Floyd; and James H. Booth, receiver of the Roseburg land office. The Booths would have passed through Silver Lake on the stage on their way to Lakeview, and Conn may have accompanied them to receive the cash.

There is no evidence that Creed Conn played any role in the timber deal on Dead Indian beyond acting as a banker for the others. Although, because of his obvious close ties to Martha Lane, Horning, LaBrie, and Duncan, it is entirely possible that he was to receive a portion of the profits from the sale of the land or timber. But, Conn already had a timber claim of his own, far to the north near Mush Spring, in township 27 south, range 12 east, section 11. Mush Spring was a very prolific source of water in those days, and Conn's claim was about two miles south of the place where John Embody would relocated the sawmill of Sam Porter around 1907.

When Conn saw all of the previously tied-up Government land passing into private hands at a great profit, he recognized an opportunity to relieve his fears of drowning in debt. So, on the third of April, 1903, Conn and his friend, Ray Jackson, went out to inspect two claims near the spring with locator John Bloss, and sawmill man George F. "Frank" Scott. Both Bloss and Scott were from the Sisters area, and it is possible that Scott was looking for some people to take claims around the spring so that he could locate a sawmill there.

Conn owed money to almost everyone, but he banked on his reputation for generosity again when he borrowed $1,500 from friend Al Geyer in October of 1903. That loan was a short term one that he promised to repay in two months, but that increased his total debt load to $4,000. Conn probably hoped that he would be able to sell the two claims and pay Geyer back by the middle of December. Since late 1902 it had become increasing difficult to get timber claims passed to patent due to the government's investigation and a large backlog of cases, so Conn may have, in his desperation, attempted to sell the two claims even though they were not yet patented.

There is some evidence that Conn wanted to do just that. In the first week of December, 1903, he took an unexpected trip to Prineville, even though the weather was horrible and the condition of the roads was even worse. He did not have enough money for stage fare, so took his own team and buggy, broke a wheel cap on the return trip, and had to have someone haul the buggy home for him with a promise to pay for the transportation later. Also in December, on the 13th and the 19th, Conn trudged out in the deep snow on successive trips to the timber claims, probably to show them to prospective buyers. A single inspection of one's claim was all that was required by law, and showing the claim to others seems to be the only reason that Conn would have gone out into the woods twice in one week under awful weather conditions.

Conn originally partnered with Jackson on the twin claims near the spring, but Jackson backed out of the deal and relinquished his claim, probably in early January of 1904, which was when the new claimant, Walter C. Buick, filed on the same claim just to the north of Conns. Jackson, who was not very well-off, was probably told by Conn to let the claim go because Conn's financial condition was quite bad by this time and he knew he would not be able to pay for both claims.

By the end of December, Creed Conn seemed to have given up hope of selling his claim, and had failed to appear to make final proof on December 26. Over the weekend Conn apparently had a change of heart, and a chat with friend Walter Buick, for on December 30 he met with Special Agent

Horace Jones, and made final proof. When Jones questioned Conn's witnesses he asked, "In case of a contest would you swear that he had taken this land for his own use, paid for it with his own money, and still holds possession and title thereto?" The question was an unusual one, and leaves the impression that Jones believed Conn had been out shopping for a buyer.

It seems that Conn had convinced Buick to take the adjoining claim, because Buick filed on it on January 7. Buick was a prosperous rancher, and would have been perfectly capable of coming up with the needed $410. Hope returned that the two claims could be sold together, and thus would be worth more money. Buick's witnesses were clerk Frank Payne, Creed Conn, T.J. LaBrie, and James R. Horning. Conn's witnesses were LaBrie and his most recent creditor, Al Geyer, Jackson, and George Emery.

Conn did manage to pay for his timber claim, on January 15, and it was patented after his death on October 22, 1904. Aside from his mounting debts, Conn's life got much more stressful, and his financial future much more bleak, when on February 12 all three of his freight wagons were destroyed by arson and on February 29 one of the brainy and practically irreplaceable leaders of his freight team was poisoned to death. These were unexpected losses that Conn was not prepared for. Without his team and wagons, his security, and a large part of his identity, were gone.

Conn's financial problems would probably have been common knowledge by March of 1904. The clerk that he had underpaid, the blacksmith and hay farmer he owed money to, the creditors on overdue loans, all probably told others about the sad state of affairs. Conn was so cash poor at the time of his death, that even his dues to the Baptist church and his newspaper subscription were past due. Shortly before he disappeared, on February 26, Conn had borrowed $200 from his brother, Lafe, so it is certain that the family knew something of his trouble. He was so broke that he could not afford to have his buggy repaired and had to charge the rental of a buggy from the Duncan livery stable in order to transport his witnesses in to the land office.

Just 10 days after Conn vanished from the streets of Silver Lake, his home town newspaper in far-off Roseburg knew something of his financial condition. "It seems that while Mr. Conn's business was in a most flourishing condition that he has had quite a number of reverses lately.... it is supposed that in a fit of despondency he went to the top of the bridge and there shot himself and the body falling into the swollen stream has been carried into Silver Lake about ten miles away."

All of the local talk about Conn's debt and financial ruin must be the reason for Lafe Conn's rush to settle his brother's debts, by declaring him dead when he was merely missing. All of the gossip about Conn's financial troubles probably made a lot of people rather edgy, and some began to speculate openly that he had 'gone on the lamb' to escape from his creditors. In mid-April, before the body was found, a citizen of Lake County was interviewed at Portland concerning what he knew about the strange disappearance. "There is one man who will be suspicioned as the cause of Conn's taking off if the body is not found," he said.

About one month before the disappearance, Creed Conn and Horning were at Lakeview together. On that same day, Horning paid for his claim at the land office. During the next four days, Conn realized, probably through a communication from his bank, that his account was overdrawn. When he inquired about the balance, he learned that most or all of the amount deposited with him by Martha Lane was gone. Conn, who was a careful bookkeeper, believed that some error had been made. He knew that he had not withdrawn the money, and could prove it with his daily transaction journal. Incredulous that so large a sum of money could have been misplaced by the bank, he worked by telephone to try to convince the men in far away San Francisco that they had made an error. Some of Conn's friends were sympathetic, but others that he already owed money to were less so. His lifelong friend, Tommy LaBrie, commiserated and agreed to provide the money to purchase the claims of the Duncans and Hornings, in addition to his own and his wife's. The lady he had married was a widow that inherited $5,000 in life insurance from her deceased husband, and had about $8,000 in the bank. The help of LaBrie came as a great relief to Horning, but he realized that he would have to do something to repay him as soon as possible.

Entryman Gus Schroder had become spooked fairly early on in the deal, and seems to have been pretty wary from the beginning because he insisted on paying the filing fees with his own money. When word of the loss of Lane's money reached him, Schroder stubbornly refused the offer of a loan from LaBrie. Schroder's interview one week before with Special Agent Horace T. Jones had left a lasting impression.

"What do you expect to do with your claim in order to realize from the investment?" asked Jones.

"I intend to hold it for a while until something develops," was Schroder's vague reply.

"Do you expect to sell it when you can obtain a good price for it?" Asked Jones, pressing him harder. At this question Schroder faltered, and answered both "yes" and "no." One answer is recorded over the top of the other in his testimony, making it impossible to know which answer came first from Schroder, who was obviously rattled by the directness of the Special Agent.

Schroder's insistence on waiting to pay for his two claims until he could raise the money more or less ruined the deal for Horning. Without the two patented claims of the Schroders, his nice block of two whole sections of timber was now broken apart in two places, making it far less desirable and more difficult to sell. Conn, who felt partly responsible for all of the trouble because the money had disappeared from his own account, attempted to help Horning by giving him $450 on February 26 so that he could pay the $75 that he had promised to each of the six entrymen.

Two nights after his return home, Conn's team was poisoned the night of February 29, and one of his leaders died the following morning. Clearly Conn was being maliciously targeted by someone with an axe to grind. But who? He had tried to assure his resentful creditors that he had every intention of paying them back in full, although he realized that his reputation in the community was suffering badly. His most recent debt of $1500 to Al Geyer was now 10 weeks past due. And, why was the team being targeted? First the wagons, and now the animals themselves? Stress, anxiety, and rage began to consume Creed Conn as he worked to discover the culprit in the face of a community that had begun to have serious doubts about his sanity and veracity.

It was in this condition that Creed Conn vanished into thin air on the morning of March 4, 1904. Early in April, Horning sold his large ranch on Buck Creek, that adjoined the Lanes, to Cliff C. Smith for $3,000, presumably so that he could repay LaBrie. Horning then moved his family to Klamath County. When clerk Frank Payne and his friend William Robinette learned the full particulars of Conn's loss of the money for Horning's timber deal, they quickly renewed their search for the body and turned their attention to Buck Creek, combing its banks and dragging it for several days during the first week of April. On April 16, Martha Lane appeared at the office of Virgil Conn and filed a claim against the estate to recover her $3,270. Lane trusted J.R. Horning, and in light of Conn's sudden and mysterious disappearance and all of the preceding events, she held the Conns responsible for the loss. Martha Lane was smart enough to bring an attorney with her, William J. Moore, who did most of the talking. When a 'timber deal gone wrong' was under discussion, it was best to play one's cards carefully. An examination of the probate records makes it clear that Creed Conn's bank account was empty, that he had very little cash on hand, and that Martha Lane was made to wait until October, after some of his assets had been sold, to receive her money.

Despite the very likely connection to a timber deal, the debt to Martha Lane was not the most suspicious one found amongst the probate records of John Creed Conn. On July 26, 1898, Conn had allegedly incurred a debt of $1,800 to George Winkleman for the purchase of grain. That debt was peculiar in several ways. In the year 1898, several types of grain could be had for about two cents per pound. If that debt was really for grain, then Conn would have purchased about 90,000 pounds of it, a tremendous amount for anyone to make use of. As of 1898 Conn did not own any animals at all, probably not even a riding horse, and did not purchase his team until sometime in 1900. But, even if he had purchased on credit the 90,000 pounds of grain, and paid Tommy LaBrie to deliver it out to the sheep camps on the desert through several winters, for what earthly reason had Winkleman allowed the debt to persist for almost six years? Most men would have sued for recovery of the money long before. And since such a massive amount of grain was involved, it was probably consumed over a number of years, which raises the question, why would anyone keep supplying grain to someone who was not paying?

Winkleman was paid the $1800 on September 3, 1904 by Virgil Conn, who was the administrator of the estate and had full charge of all of Creed's debts and worldly goods. Virgil also paid interest to Winkleman of $105.37, or eight percent. That too, was strange, because Creed Conn had only in the last two years begun to have financial problems, but with his other debts he had always at least paid the annual interest when it came due. Interest on this debt had not been paid since 1902.

At the time the Winkleman claim was recorded in probate, a three-year promissory note was presented, with a signature on it alleged to be that of Creed Conn, although the handwriting on the note was more similar to Virgil's. Even more interesting was the receipt written on September 3, alleged to have been signed by George Winkleman, even though the name Winkleman was misspelled as "Winkelman." After a careful and meticulous search of records of the General Land Office, the Oregon State Archives tax rolls for 1875 though 1900, and the censuses of 1900 and 1910, the author found that George Winkleman and his brother, Leonard F., consistently spelled their last name as "le," not "el." Why then, in the year 1904, after 54 years of spelling his last name as "Winkleman," did George suddenly and inexplicably misspell his own last name as "Winkelman" when he signed the receipt for $1,905.37 from the estate of John Creed Conn?

It is a fact that Virgil and Creed Conn were partners in business at least through 1895, and perhaps had still been partners in 1898. The bitter, bickering division of property between George and Virgil Conn that lasted from 1889 through at least 1901 also involved Creed. There was argument about

Creed's claim that he should earn interest, like his brothers, on the shares of the company that he owned. He was paid the interest on his shares, but in court Virgil asked to have the interest earned returned to him because the interest had not been guaranteed by a contract. At one point George did pay Creed $328 in back pay, but then Virgil demanded that the company reimburse him for half of it.

There were also counterclaims made by Virgil in which he asked to be reimbursed for two expenditures of a speculative nature in which the company had lost money. Those "speculative damages" were not allowed by the court because Virgil failed to file them on time. Whatever those two business ventures were, they were not described in any detail. It is possible though, that one or both of them involved the Conn's most enterprising younger brother, his new store at Silver Lake, and perhaps also his freight team.

Virgil himself did not own a freight team, but instead hired an independent teamster to do his freighting for him. His teamster was Len Winkleman. Perhaps he did not believe in the practice, and recognized that it was more economical to simply pay the team and driver per trip, rather than to keep and board them the year round. Was Virgil now, with his own unique brand of pettiness, attempting to recover the cost of feeding Creed's team after his death? A cost incurred before LaBrie took the animals to Silver Lake? If so, to what lengths was Virgil willing to go to get his money back?

Sources:

"A History of the Deschutes Country in Oregon," Deschutes County Historical Society, 1985, Redmond, Oregon, p 316-317, 425.

U.S. Census Bureau, Twelfth Census of the United States, 1900, Silver Lake, Lake County, Oregon.

In the Mater of the Estate of J.C. Conn, Deceased, Probate file of John Creed Conn, Probate Case Files, 1875-1927, Clerk's Basement South Storage Room, Lake County Courthouse, Lakeview, Oregon.

"Mysteriously Disappeared," *Roseburg Plaindealer*, March 17, 1904

Tax Assessments for John C., George, and Virgil Conn, Assessment and Tax Rolls for Lake County, Oregon, 1890, 1895, 1897, 1899, 1903, 1905, Oregon State Archives, Salem, Oregon

O.S. Root to J.C. Conn, November 25, 1895, Lot 4, Block "F," Silver Lake, OR, Deed and title records, vol 8, Lake County Courthouse, County Clerk's Office, Lakeview, Oregon. Recording of deed was witnessed by Virgil Conn. This is where Creed Conn built his store building sometime between 1897 and 1899.

Charles Hoskins to J.C. Conn, July 20, 1897, Lot 4, Block "E," Deed and title records, vol 8, Lake County Courthouse, County Clerk's Office, Lakeview, Oregon. Lot is across the street from the store building.

List of Taxable Property of J.C. Conn, Silver Lake pct., in the County of Lake, State of Oregon, for the year 1901, filed August 1, 1901, J.B. Blair Assessor. Schmink Museum basement storage room, Lakeview, Oregon.

"Homesteading the High Desert," by Barbara Allen, 1987, University of Utah Press, p 18-19.

"Local News," *Bend Bulletin,* December 11, 1903. Identifies Henderson as Chrisman's driver, having started that job around the first of December.

"An Illustrated History of Central Oregon," Western Historical Publishing, 1905, Spokane, WA, p 768, 915-916, 920, 1067.

U.S. Census Bureau, Thirteenth Census of the United States, 1910, Silver Lake, Lake County, Oregon.

"The County Convention," *Lake County Examiner*, April 7, 1904.

"Lone Pine Ranch,"by Maurice G. Emery, 2003, iUniverse, New York, NY, p 4-5.
Duncan Creek and reservoir in the vicinity of Lone Pine Ranch are named for the family of George C. Duncan.

"Voice of the People," (assorted tales from the Christmas eve fire of 1894) *Lake County Examiner*, November 27, 1969. In a telephone interview, Mark Partin said that George C. Duncan was a writer, and a relative, Eileen O'neil of Reno collected a scrapbook of his articles.

"Four Papers for Silver Lake," *Lake County Examiner*, March 5, 1903. Names Holder of the Review, and Bailey of the Journal.

"Local Items," *Deschutes Echo*, April 25, 1903. Identifies Percival as past foreman of the *Silver Lake Bulletin*.

"The Growth of Lake County, Oregon," by G.E.B. Stephenson, 1994, Book Partners, Inc, Wilsonville, OR, p 104.

"Local Items," *Deschutes Echo*, March 7, 1903. Names Bell as a partner of Holder.

"History of Oregon Newspapers," by George S. Turnbull, 1939, Binfords & Mort, Portland, OR, p 370-371.

Timber and Stone patent application file of Frank Elkins, serial #MV-0704-057, Bureau of Land Management, records of the General Land Office, National Archives and Records Administration, Washington, D.C. August through November, 1903 William Wagner was foreman of *Silver Lake Bulletin* and signed affidavit of publication for Elkins.

"They Came and Saw," *Bend Bulletin*, June 5, 1903.

Resolutions of Condolence in the death of James P. Combs, Prineville Lodge #76, AF&AM, obituary book #1, p 1, Bowman Museum, Prineville, Oregon. Notice names Baldwin as a member of the lodge. James P. Combs died April 1, 1900.

"Story of the Fire Again Told," *Lake County Examiner*, January 24, 1895.

"Impressions and Observations of a Journal Man," Fred Lockley, *Oregon Journal*, November 18, 1930. Interview with Ethel Lane.

"Portrait and Biographical Record of the Willamette Valley, Oregon," by Joseph Gaston, 1903, Chapman, Chicago, IL. Biography of Andrew V. Lane.

U.S. Census Bureau, ninth Census of the United States, 1870, Coast Fork pct., Lane County, Oregon.

U.S. Census Bureau, twelfth Census of the United States, 1900, North Harrisburg pct., Linn County, Oregon. Shows Frank W. Payne, age 19, living in the household of Martha Lane. Payne would probably have graduated from business college in 1901.

http://www.glorecords.blm.gov/PatentSearch/

"Marriage Records, vol. 2, 1895-1909, County of Lake, Lakeview, Oregon," 1995, Oregon Youth Conservation Corps, Lakeview, Oregon, p 29.

"Survived Tragic Christmas Eve Fire, pioneer reminsces about early-day Silver Lake life," *Bend Bulletin*, August 10, 1970.

"Local Items," *Deschutes Echo*, March 14, 1903 and March 21, 1903.

"Historic Douglas County, Oregon," by Douglas County Historical Society, 1982, Roseburg, Oregon, biography of Ferdinand LaBrie.

"Land of the Umpqua," by Stephen Dow Beckham, 1986, Douglas County Commissioners, Roseburg, OR, p 143

"Rails to the Ochoco Country," by John F. Due and Frances Juris, 1968, Golden West Books, San Marino, CA, p 71, 149

"Roads and Rails South from the Columbia," by John F. Due and Frances Juris, 1991, Maverick, Bend, OR, p 36, 108.

"No Appointments Now," *Lake County Examiner*, August 27, 1903.

"Holds up Knowles," *Oregonian*, July 7, 1903.

"Go Over His Head," *Oregonian*, December 23, 1903.

"History of the Oregon Country," by Harvey W. Scott, 1924, Riverside Press, Cambridge, vol. 1, p 346-348.

"Looters of the Public Domain," by S.A.D. Puter and Horace Stevens, 1908, The Portland Printing House, Portland, Oregon, p 446.

"Mr. Booth's Resignation," *Oregon Daily Journal*, February 27, 1904.

"Kribs in the Net," *Oregonian*, January 2, 1905.

U.S. Supreme Court, Booth-Kelly Lumber Co. v. U.S., 237 U.S. 481 (1915). Booth-Kelly Lumber Company, Stephen A. LaRaut, appts., v. United States No. 258. Decided May 17, 1915. Available online at: www.findlaw.com

Timber and Stone patent application file of Thomas J. LaBrie, serial #ORLAA 066402, Bureau of Land Management, records of the General Land Office, National Archives and Records Administration, Washington, D.C. Patented October 28, 1904.

Timber and Stone patent application file of Lulu C. LaBrie, serial #ORLAA 066403, Bureau of Land Management, records of the General Land Office, National Archives and Records Administration, Washington, D.C. Patented October 28, 1904. Lulu's first name was incorrectly entered as "Luke."

Timber and Stone patent application file of Augustus B. Schroder, serial #ORLAA 066408, Bureau of Land Management, records of the General Land Office, National Archives and Records Administration, Washington, D.C. Patented December 29, 1904.

Timber and Stone patent application file of Ida M. Schroder, serial #ORLAA 066409 , Bureau of Land Management, records of the General Land Office, National Archives and Records Administration, Washington, D.C. Patented December 29, 1904.

Timber and Stone patent application file of Warren M. Duncan, serial #ORLAA 066401, Bureau of Land Management, records of the General Land Office, National Archives and Records Administration, Washington, D.C. Patented October 28, 1904.

Timber and Stone patent application file of Ida A. Duncan, serial #ORLAA 066407 , Bureau of Land Management, records of the General Land Office, National Archives and Records Administration, Washington, D.C. Patented December 1, 1904.

Timber and Stone patent application file of John C. Conn, serial #ORLAA 058633 , Bureau of Land Management, records of the General Land Office, National Archives and Records Administration, Washington, D.C. Patented October 22, 1904.

Timber and Stone patent application file of Walter C. Buick, serial #ORLAA 058649 , Bureau of Land Management, records of the General Land Office, National Archives and Records Administration, Washington, D.C. Patented October 28, 1904.

"Local News," Lake County Examiner, June 18, 1903.

"1905 Klamath County Directory, Klamath County, Oregon, reference and business directory." This directory was transcribed by Todd Kepple, and is available online at: http:// ftp.rootsweb.ancestry.com/pub/usgenweb/or/ klamath/ history1905bizd.txt

U.S. Census Bureau, Thirteenth Census of the United States, 1910, 4th ward, Portland, Multnomah County, Oregon.

"The Growth of Lake County, Oregon," by G.E.B. Stephenson, 1994, Book Partners, Inc, Wilsonville, OR., p 55.

"The J.C. Conn Mystery," *Roseburg Plaindealer*, April 18, 1904.

"Has J.C. Conn Killed Himself," *Roseburg Plaindealer*, March 14, 1904.

"Local News," *Lake County Examiner*, February 11, 1904.

"Local News," *Lake County Examiner*, April 21, 1904. News item about the sale of the Horning ranch was picked up from the *Central Oregonian* at Silver Lake from the week before.

"Local Items," *Prineville Review*, April 7, 1904.

Photo of Ray Van Buren Jackson, inmate 3680, from the records of the Oregon State Penitentiary. Jackson was convicted of fraud and forgery in 1896 and sentenced to two years in prison. He was 26 years old when this photo was taken.

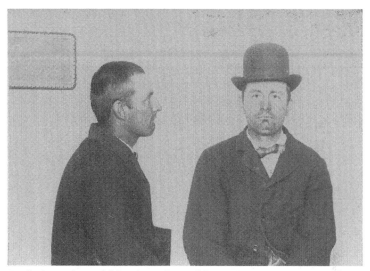

Back in prison, this time for robbery in 1899, Ray Jackson served one year for a crime he committed with an accomplice by the name of John Ryan in Baker County.

Chapter Eleven

A Life of Crime

Ray Jackson was born in Saline County, Missouri in December of 1869 in the town of Grand Pass. His first name came from Ray County in Tennessee, where his father had been born. His father, Martin, passed on his own middle name of "Van Buren," providing Ray with two middle initials. He was the youngest of three children, with an older brother and sister. His father was a civil war veteran, and resumed the life of a farmer after the war. In 1877 Ray's family arrived in Oregon, first settling at Highland in Clackamas County, but moved to Sodaville, near Lebanon in Linn County in 1879.

Very little is known about Ray's early life, except that the family continued to reside at Sodaville where he would have attended the local schools. Ray was different from his brother and sister and all of the other children. He was naturally left-handed, much to the embarrassment of his parents, and always had difficulty in school because of it. The teachers were determined to break him of the use of his left hand, and usually treated him like he was either mentally deficient or a problem and a rebel. He was frequently humiliated in school with various forms of punishment, and adopted a sense of shame at a very young age. He learned early that he could sometimes use his 'handicap' to appeal to the sympathy of others, to get his way, and to just get by.

Ray's parents were concerned about some of his other behaviors as well, such as the bed wetting that took way too long for him to outgrow and made him the target of a great deal of ridicule by his brother and sister. He was prone to out-of-control rages and was shockingly cruel to animals at times. All of those behaviors yielded the same outcome, a beating from his father and a continuing negative cycle. Ray was also fascinated with fire, and had deliberately lit several small blazes around the family home as a child. Despite the turmoil of his early life, through the force of his own will and to spite his teachers, Ray taught himself to write with his right hand. He became ambidextrous.

There are two accounts of a male teacher being assigned to the new Waterloo school near Sodaville in 1892, which would have been just about the time that Ray obtained his first teaching certificate, at the actual age of 23. There has been some confusion as to whether that teacher was Ray Jackson, or his brother William. But, since William was teaching at Brownsville at the time, and was married and living in Albany by 1893, the 1892 Waterloo teacher was probably Ray. Also, Ray had met the woman he would marry in 1893, Jessie A. Parrish, at Waterloo where her family lived, so Ray was probably living in the Waterloo area around 1892.

As a young man, Ray seems to have tried to emulate his older brother, William L. Jackson, who was a teacher and later a high school principal and school superintendent of Linn County. After the eighth grade the two boys attended Santiam Academy at Lebanon, a Methodist school, and Ray would have obtained his teacher's certificate there around 1891. His family, still residing in Linn County, hoped that Ray had finally settled down and would succeed in life, when in late 1893 he married Alda "Jessie" Parrish who was also a teacher. The couple had at least one child, born shortly after their marriage.

By 1895 Ray was teaching at Clackamas County in Beaver Creek District #33, and living at nearby Springwater south of Oregon City with the family of his uncle Marcus. B. Blackburn, his mother's twin brother.

Ray was about six feet tall, good looking, and had learned at a young age how to impress others with his speech and vocabulary. The mask of Ray was glib, cool, and confident. The real Ray on the inside was deeply angry, constantly resentful and envious of practically everyone, wanted respect, but was incapable of feeling respected. He resented the low pay that he was receiving from the school system, and believed he deserved more. People with money and things, with many possessions, fascinated Ray. If only he had money, lots more money, he knew that then people would respect him. On the 5th of April, 1895, Ray Jackson defrauded the school system by forging two pay vouchers to himself and then passing them on to others in payment for some debts.

The vexing problems that Ray had with handwriting as a boy had now morphed into what he considered his greatest asset. The ability to write with both hands allowed him to disguise his writing and to imitate the handwriting of almost anyone, and he practiced his "gift," as he called it, obsessively. He loved to demonstrate it to his students, especially to the older girls in his classes, and impressed upon them that the ambidexterity was a product of his superior intellect, even to the point where he began believing it himself. Forgotten were the torturous years of self-hatred in which he had struggled to force himself to learn to use his right hand.

When Ray arrived in Oregon City on July 18 of 1895 to attend the state teachers' convention, he had no idea that his 'creative writing' project was under investigation. He and his wife, Jessie, were driven by wagon to the train that morning by Ray's uncle Mark and cousin Elmer, who left them off at the Gladstone depot where they would catch the special train to deliver them to the convention at Gladstone Park.

Shortly after Marcus and Elmer Blackburn turned their wagon around and headed back toward Springwater, Marcus was killed in one of the goriest, bloodiest, and most shocking accidents that anyone in the area had ever seen. Ray, who bolted toward the sound of the commotion as soon as he heard it, could not believe his eyes. The young uncle who had always been the kindest to him of all of his family members, had been horribly mutilated, and the shock of that accident was so traumatic to Ray, that it became what is known in psychology as a "triggering event," from which point forward Ray, who was already deeply troubled, was terribly scarred.

The accident occurred, "just as they started across the railroad track to go up the Singer hill to Seventh street, when the Southern Pacific special came along and struck the horses killing one of them and dragging his mutilated remains along the track for a distance of seventy-five yards covering the ties and rails with gore." Reported the *Enterprise Courier*. Marcus Blackburn was dragged about 90 feet before he was run over, and his head was crushed by the wheels of the train. "His head was mashed and his brains were spattered on the ground for a distance of several feet." The one horse that was not killed instantly lost a leg and had to be shot. Elmer Blackburn was taken to the hospital at Gladstone and treated for injuries to his head and back, but survived.

The *Enterprise* article claimed that the passengers delivered to the depot were an older son of Mark, Thomas, and his girlfriend, but the author believes that because of the timing of the trip with the start of the teachers' convention, the passengers were actually Ray and his wife. Ray was close in age to Mark's older son Thomas, so the two could have been confused for one another. On the very morning of the accident, a large number of school teachers, superintendents, and college professors arrived at Gladstone Park, for the three-day convention. Notable among those gathered were Superintendent H.S. Gibson of Clackamas County, and F.G. Young, President of Albany College. The train depot where Ray was let off at Gladstone Park was less than a mile and a half from the scene of the accident.

The 10th street crossing was then and has always been a dangerous spot, located near the present site of the historic John McLoughlin House. Tenth Street joins the tracks at a 90 degree angle, but as it crosses the tracks it turns to the right so that wagons like Blackburn's were parallel with the tracks once they got across. The crossing was a deathtrap. The noise from streetcars and horses and carts clattering along made it impossible for Blackburn to hear the whistle of the approaching train. And once he got his wagon into the crossing, he was facing away from the train, which came up behind him at 15 miles per hour. Even if Blackburn had turned completely around in his seat to look for a train coming from behind him, he would not have been able to see it because his view along the tracks was obstructed by buildings and trees. The team was not only occupied with negotiating a turn while on the tracks, but also pulling uphill, and would not have backed away from the tracks under any circumstances. The train was not equipped with brakes.

On July 26, 1895 the *Enterprise Courier* reacted to the accident with a harsh attack on the conditions at the crossing. "It is high time that the road up that hill is either repaired or changed or that railroad trainmen should be governed more strictly while in the city limits," began the editorial. "The city council has been intending to improve the old road when it gets the road tax from the county court, which at this time seems quite doubtful as the court is not 'inclined' to give up any money unless forced to do so, but something should be done in this matter at once. Several teamsters report narrow escapes from accidents on this crossing.... It is almost impossible to tell when a train is coming if you are about to cross the track at these places..." As recently as 2007, the commissioners of Oregon City and the mayor were trying to improve the unsafe conditions at Singer Hill and 10th Street, the site of many accidents for over 100 years. No trestle was ever built, and the basic configuration of the crossing, with all of its inherent dangers, remains unchanged.

In 1896 the wife of Marcus Blackburn sued the Southern Pacific Railroad for damages, probably largely on behalf of her six fatherless children. The findings of the investigation by the Board of Railroad Commissioners of the State of Oregon admitted that the crossing was "very unsafe," and that "the view northward on the track is shut off by trees and buildings, so that it (the train) cannot be seen until within a few feet of the track at the Tenth-street crossing." Despite those problems, the board ruled that "the deceased and his son were careless in attempting to cross said track without seeing that no train was approaching before attempting to cross," and "nothing has been found from the evidence or other wise that would attach any blame to the Southern Pacific Company, nor to any of its employees in the matter."

Right on the heals of the horrid accident, during the first week of August, word reached Jackson that he was wanted by the sheriff for forgery, and he went into hiding. On August 29, as the law was closing in on him, he stole a horse from his cousin Henery "Lester" Blackburn at the home of his deceased uncle Mark, abandoned his wife and baby, and went to Linkville, now Klamath Falls, where he secured teaching positions for himself and his wife, who joined him. A warrant was issued at Linkville for his arrest as a horse thief on October 5, but Jackson was never arrested on the horse stealing charge.

At the end of August a reward for Jackson's arrest was published in the *Oregon City Enterprise*. "He is wanted for forgery," said the notice. "He is alleged to be guilty of forging the name of Mr. Harrington, a school clerk in that precinct, to an instrument to the amount of $35 and hypothecating the same."

R.V. Jackson taught school at Highland last year: later there turned up two school orders amounting to $70 bearing the forged signature of Clerk Harrington, and Jackson was charged with the forgeries. He promptly left the country when charged with the commission of the crime, and Sheriff Maddock has been looking for him ever since.

He was traced to Klamath county, thence away down into California, and there lost after officers had twice been at the point of nabbing him. Last Wednesday, he was reported to be in Jacksonville, Or., and Sheriff Maddock telegraphed Sheriff Patterson to arrest and hold him. Deputy Sheriff Hyatt returned with him Thursday. Jackson has been skillful in eluding pursuit, and it was only by the utmost perseverance that Mr. Maddock has been able to capture his man.

Last fall there was considerable commotion among some for the officers of Klamath county, who charged each other with having connived at the escape of Jackson, when he had been located and was about to be arrested. He was attending teacher's examination when caught, and had been teaching school in Antelope district in Jackson county.

The "commotion" referred to were accusations made against lady school superintendent, Mrs. Lenor I. Gordon, who had fallen victim to Ray Jackson's charms and then tipped him off when she was contacted by the deputy sheriff, who asked if anyone matching his description had lately applied for a teacher's certificate. Jackson was able to clear the state line into California about one half hour ahead of the Clackamas County Sheriff, who then had to petition the governor to continue the manhunt and have him extradited to Oregon when caught. Jackson managed to evade arrest for nine months. He spent the last half of 1895 in Shasta County, California where he was almost captured once when the sheriff thought he was cornered inside of a building, but Jackson was able to slip out the back door. He taught school in Antelope, Jackson County, from January through May of 1896 where he treated himself to a new horse and buggy.

After his arrest, Jackson boasted about his travels through California and showed no remorse for his actions, claiming that he was happy that he had finally been caught because he would now be able to collect the money owed him for teaching during the time he evaded arrest. Much to the embarrassment of his family, Jackson had made a name for himself during his crime spree. He was now notoriously known as "The Highland Forger."

On June 9, 1896, Jackson was sentenced to two years in the state penitentiary for fraud and forgery. Whatever problems Jackson carried forward from childhood, compounded by the mind-altering horror of the Blackburn accident, were magnified 100-fold during his days in prison, which in 1896 was very, very different than it is today. The state pen was a chamber of horrors, like hell on earth, that few if any young men of 27 could survive emotionally. Whatever Jackson's mental state was when he went in, by the time he got out in the summer of 1898, he was damaged far beyond the point of return. He went into the penitentiary angry, devious, and sociopathic, and emerged as a fiend and a monster. His dual middle name of "Van Buren" allowed him to change his name easily, and he thereafter used mostly the "B" as a middle initial instead of the "V" as he had before.

Upon his release from prison in 1898, Jackson went to work for Amos Riley and James Hardin's Double O Ranch, by all accounts a pretty rough outfit in those days before it was purchased by Bill Hanley in 1903. "The OO Ranch was considered one of the toughest operations in the state, measuring a notch or two above such rough outfits as those of Pete French, Pick Anderson, and the Prineville Land & Livestock Company," wrote David Braly. The Double O was headquartered near Harney Lake, and managed by superintendent Isaac Foster. While working at the Double O, Jackson probably became acquainted with Billy and Mike Mayfield, who started their own cattle ranching enterprise in north Klamath County. He may have done ranch work for the Mayfields for a short time, and Jackson probably knew the Mayfields from the Highland area in Clackamas County where both families had lived in the 1870's. The Mayfields moved to Riley in Harney County in 1880. One short biography on Jackson stated, "In 1898 he came to central Oregon and for a time was bookkeeper at the Double O Ranch." During this period of his life, Jackson acquired the nickname of "Tomcat," a name that stuck with him for the rest of his life because of his brazen womanizing.

One favorite phrase of Jackson's own making seems to have survived him, as recalled by Jess Gibson, whose father was good friend of Jackson's in his later life. Gibson was interviewed in 1991 by Edward Gray for the Harney County History Project. The quotation reveals some of Jackson's glibness and superficial charm, and shows that he considered himself quite the ladies' man. "I have an elegance sufficiency, any more would be supperflority. I have about all the (expletive) will take me."

Ray Van Buren Jackson was not able to stay on the 'straight and narrow' for long after his release from prison. On July 3, 1899 he was sentenced again to the state penitentiary as R. Jackson, age 29, for a term of one year after committing a robbery at Baker County. Jackson apparently had an accomplice, because a man named John Ryan was listed next to him in the prison register as having been sentenced on the same day, for the same crime, from the same county. Like Jackson, this was not Ryan's first time in the penitentiary. Ryan's inmate number was 4133, Jackson's was 4134, and the two men were released from prison on the same date, May 11, 1900. The prison photograph of "R. Jackson," when compared to the prison photo of "R.V. Jackson" shows the two men to be one in the same.

The remoteness of the town of Silver Lake around the turn of the last century made it a place where someone could conveniently 'disappear,' and a catchall for low-lifes, swindlers, and rustlers. It was "a natural hideout for fugitives from justice," according to Earl Small, who was born in Silver Lake in 1901. "Several such characters who drifted in stayed a while, and quietly moved on. Some worked as ranch hands, others were cardsharks, and still others were so bold as to indulge in a bit of horse and cattle rustling. When seen shirtless, some showed battle scars indicating a life of violence," said Small in a 1970 interview. Jackson was just such a man, and arrived in Silver Lake in June of 1902 where he was hired to be the local school teacher and moved into the old school house. Jackson taught his students to call him "Professor," although he had never taught anything above the eighth grade level.

Jackson was said to be living at Silver Lake in June of 1907 when his mother, Callie, passed away. Ranger Gilbert Brown, who was falsely credited with having found Wallende's body, worked with Jackson at Silver Lake before he went to Lakeview as Deputy Supervisor at the end of 1907. In a personal account printed in Melva Bach's "History of the Fremont National Forest" Brown referred to Jackson as "my assistant" during the time he was stationed at Silver Lake. Since Bach mistakenly credited Brown with having found Wallende's body "where it had been thrown into Silver Creek" after Brown had been promoted and left the area, it is likely that Wallende was found by another forest worker who was confused for Brown, and that Jackson was the man who at least participated in pulling the body from the stream. Both men were school teachers in Lake County in 1903, and began working for the Forest Service as seasonal 'guards' when they were not teaching, so were probably friends. A group photograph on page 41 of Bach's book shows a man in a ranger's hat who Bach identified as Gilbert Brown, but who bore an uncanny resemblance to Ray Jackson's prison photos.

It staggers the imagination to think that a man with Jackson's background could get a job teaching grade school, so there was apparently little effort made to learn what he had been up to since graduating from teacher's college about 1891. He had been held back a couple of years in school because of his left-handedness, as was routinely done in those days, and his family apparently lied about his age to help mask what they considered an embarrassing handicap. In 1880 when the census worker visited the family home at Sodaville, his mother Callie lied about his age, saying that he was only 9, instead of 11.

Shortly after prison, when Jackson drifted into Silver Lake, he developed a reputation among the school children as being a very mean teacher. A couple of accounts that have survived from the time, probably because they were so shocking, portrayed him as far more than mean, but actually malicious and sadistic.

The new teacher ruled with "an iron hand" according to writer Teressa Foster. "On the wall on either side of his desk were two black boxes containing buggy whips. They were kept locked until the older boys misbehaved. They usually received their punishment after school or during the noon hour after the other students were dismissed." Jackson's use of whips was confirmed by Russell Emery, whose brother Everett or "Slivers" was nine years old when the new teacher came to Silver Lake. One of Jackson's students around 1903 was Guy Foster, who was fortunate enough to have ducked in time to avoid a heavy glass inkwell that the teacher hurled at him. "Later Guy declared that had the inkwell hit him, he would have been killed or maimed." Ray Shaver, who had known Jackson later in life, said the former teacher had told him that he used to take a six-shooter and a baseball bat to school with him.

Writer Earl F. Moore, also a former student of Jackson's, dreaded going to school each day. "He saw no humor in youthful pranks and proved his displeasure in laying on the punishment for most any mischievous disobedience," wrote Moore. "He ruled by fear and the butt half of a rawhide buggy whip."

And now, for his prime method of punishment for boys; primitive and barbaric in every humane respect. This was what he called 'holding down knots.' The unfortunate one, or shall I say victim, was made to go up front before the entire student body, take off his shirt, bend over on one leg, the other stretched out behind and clear of floor. Now, with the point of one index finger touching the floor for balance and the other hand held forward you were ready to start the painful endurance.

Now if there was ever anything embarrassing to a young fellow, this was it. Well he bobbed around in this position till the back cramped and gave out and he sagged to the floor. This is where the rawhide whip came in. Lash after lash cut red welts over

the shoulders and back until the area looked
as though a red rope had been coiled up on it.
Then you were forced to try the torturous
procedure again or until the strength refused
entirely. The bigger the teenager, the more
Jackson seemed to enjoy the cruelty."

One such husky lad of about 19 was George Loucks, who one day while being "roughed up" decided that he had enough of Jackson's abuse and landed a right jab in the teacher's eye. "No mistake, the battle was on," wrote Moore. "Being pretty well matched, blow after blow sent one and then the other over desks, through library doors, down in the aisles and over more desks. The savage schoolhouse fight continued until both were pretty well winded and slowing considerably, when some girl screamed, 'Sock him a couple for me, George!'"

"The fight ended by virtue of exhaustion on the parts of both combatants, and school was dismissed for the day." George Loucks came away with a broken hand. Moore recalled that all of the children the next day were chilled to the bone with fear when the teacher "walked in nonchalant like and placed a sixshooter on his desk with a challenge to anyone or all who wished to continue the scrap."

From the context of Moore's story, the altercation with George Loucks occurred at the Paisley school, probably between 1906 and 1908. In June of 1908 Jackson was elected as Lake County Superintendent of Schools and moved to Lakeview. It was around that time that began one of the saddest and most tragic chapters of his sordid life, and his involvement in certain events proved that prison had not reformed him. He exercised the same insensate charm over women, and was still capable of great treachery in financial matters.

About the same time that he was elected, Jackson became involved in the Ana River Irrigation Company, formed in 1908. He was president of the company; Jesse W. Nelson was a director; M.W. O'Brien was vice-president; Curtis Duvall, another Lake County teacher and an engineer, was secretary and treasurer; and J. "Frank" Barnes was a director. The basic idea was to force water up to ground level to create an irrigation system. The project, in which Jackson must have been an investor, ultimately failed and broke the Nelson and Barnes families financially.

"The reckless grandiosity of psychopaths usually causes them to fail at any enterprise, often spectacularly," wrote Robert I. Simon in his book, "Bad Men Do What Good Men Dream." In 1910 a 14-foot dam had been constructed and the board voted to install a pumping plant at a cost of $3,000.

Anyone with a passing knowledge of teachers' salaries for the period has to wonder where Jackson got the money to invest in the irrigation company. In 1910 he was only making $58 per month as school superintendent.

In February of 1910, Ray Jackson came up with another big wad of cash when he laid plans to launch a new mercantile store at Paisley in partnership with William M. Dobkins, who had previously operated a store there. "The Chewaucan Mercantile Company" filed articles of incorporation in the county clerk's office during the first week of June. Jackson would again fill the chair of president in this second new company. Other officers named were William Y. Miller, and Stephen P. Moss. Frank Dobkins, son of William, was a stockholder. Jackson had known the Dobkins family since about 1906 when he began teaching at Paisley, although he was not the Dobkins children's teacher because they were beyond school age.

Emma was the oldest of the three children of William and Jane Dobkins, and was in her early 20's when she met Jackson. Emma began teaching school herself between 1904 and 1909, and may even have been influenced to become a teacher by Jackson around 1906. In July of 1909, Emma was assigned a privileged position on the eighth grade examination board, for which she earned twelve dollars, and the summer job put her in close contact with the school superintendent. Emma Dobkins died on March 2, 1910, and there are several oral history accounts that blame her tragic death on what was considered a "tainted" relationship with Ray Jackson. In one of those accounts, Vera Addington Wagner described how Emma's father absolutely hated Jackson after Emma's death, and was never able to get over the loss. It was Wagner who described Jackson as a "no good womanizer," and said that, "He got one of the Dobkins girls pregnant.... the girl committed suicide."

"Many people who knew the family thought Emma Dobkins committed suicide because of a tainted relationship with Ray B. Jackson," wrote Edward Gray, who interviewed several people who had been neighbors of Jackson later in life. Gray took an interest in the premature death of Emma Dobkins, and obtained a copy of her death certificate from the Oregon State Center for Health Statistics that gave the cause of death as "angina pectoris" and stated that Emma died in Lane County. Angina is not usually a fatal condition in and of itself, but describes a stabbing chest pain that is sometimes a symptom of a heart attack. Angina could be caused by extreme fatigue or by the action of some toxin that cut off the supply of oxygen to the heart.

In early June of 1909 superintendent Jackson took a tour of all of the schools in the county, and filed a claim of

$122 for his travel expense, a large sum of money in 1909, about two months pay for a skilled laborer. The timing of his 'tour' was exactly nine months before Emma Dobkins died of mysterious causes.

"Dobkins had a sister, the way I understand it, and she committed suicide over Ray or something," said Shelby Petersen in a 1991 interview. The Petersens had also known Jackson later in life, and Edward Gray, who interviewed Petersen, speculated that Emma Dobkins had been raped. Emma's brief obituary left many questions unanswered, and her family was probably reticent to talk about the tragedy. Those factors combined to open the door for speculation and innuendo amongst members of the next generation.

Died

Emma, daughter of Wm. and Jane Dobkins, honored pioneers of Lake County, died suddenly Wednesday, March 2d, at 8 p.m.

Emma was born in Siskiyou County California, 29 years of age, coming to Oregon with her parents when 13 months of age, where she has since resided at the family home near Paisley.

She was a young woman of sweet and lovable disposition, beloved by all who knew her. Her loss will be keenly felt by the community. And her going leaves the family heart broken.

The funeral services were conducted Friday March 4th, by Rev. T.L. Young, pastor of the Methodist Church. A large congregation of friends from Paisley and surrounding country were present. Tender hands laid in the grave the body, to await the reunion which is to come.

The Methodist pastor named was probably Reverend Frank L. Young, who arrived in the Paisley area around 1909 and was a friend and ally of Jackson's in irrigation matters. The two men were also active in the first town government of Paisley in 1911, where Jackson and Virgil Conn were both city councilmen, and Young was justice of the peace.

Neva Schroder Warner, who was born in 1899 and lived in Silver Lake her whole life, stated that the version of the story she remembered was that Emma Dobkins had been raped by Jackson, but that she had never heard anything about

Emma dying by suicide. Her brothers Burtt and Hawley Schroder had been friends of Emma's brother, Frank, around 1939 and leased a large portion of Frank's land at Wagontire for cattle ranching.

Because Jackson and Emma Dobkins were connected in several ways, through teaching, through Jackson's friendship with the men in her family, and through the Chewaucan Mercantile Company in the town where Emma lived, it is very possible that the two had some sort of relationship. Due to the facts that Emma suffered some kind of heart trouble at the time of her death, and that she died in Lane County, it seems likely that she died in childbirth in a far off hospital where Jackson and her family had hoped that the arrival of the illegitimate child could be kept quiet. Many women died in childbirth in the early 1900's, and a preexisting heart condition could have made it impossible for Emma to survive labor.

Regardless of the exact fate of Emma Dobkins, many who knew the family were unanimous in the belief that Jackson had a hand in her death. She was buried next to her grandmother Margaret at the Paisley IOOF Cemetery, where a large marble pillar, with the words "Gone, but not forgotten," marks her grave. Her parents William and Eliza "Jane," and brother Frank are all buried in the same plot, number 41. In an adjoining plot, number 40, which is near Emma's headstone, there is buried an unknown infant that could have been her child.

Emma Dobkins died about the time of the democratic primaries in Lake County, and despite whatever scandalous talk was afoot, Jackson again captured the nomination for Superintendent of Schools and managed to get himself reelected. But, his days of being a big shot, an elected official, president of an irrigation company, and president of a mercantile company, were short lived. By the fall of the year 1910 he was under investigation for having embezzled a large sum of money from the Lake County school system.

> *R.B. Jackson, county school superintendent, was indicted for refusing to pay over public money at the time provided by statute. He paid the money into the county treasury after the time provided by law had expired, but such act apparently does not clear him in the eyes of the law.*

He was indicted for embezzlement in October of 1910, and later resigned his position as superintendent. His resignation was officially accepted by the county on September 1, 1911. In 2009 the author attempted to get a copy of circuit court case file #40, which would have described in more detail exactly how, and how much, money was embezzled by Jackson, but circuit court personnel were unable to locate the file. Jackson's appropriation of county school funds for his personal ventures would have made fascinating reading.

The embezzlement did not escape the notice of the Conn family. Lafe Conn was still practicing law at Lakeview, and would for many years to come. And Bernard Daly was still county judge, and signed an order for the exhumation of the body of John Creed Conn only about two months after the investigation into the school fund had begun. The timing of those events suggests that Lafe Conn had long suspected Jackson as having a hand in his brother's financial ruin and subsequent death. The following article appeared in the *Roseburg Evening News* of November 23, 1910.

The remains of the late J. Creed Conn, who was murdered about five years ago by unknown parties at Silver Lake, Oregon, arrived here today and were taken in charge by the brother of the deceased, Henry Conn, of near Melrose, and interred at the Masonic cemetery this afternoon. The deceased was well known here being a native of Douglas County, and the circumstances leading up to his death is still fresh in the minds of many persons. Prior to his demise he was a prosperous merchant at Silver Lake. When the body was discovered, two bullet wounds gave unmistakable evidence of the cause of death, but the party or parties responsible were never apprehended. The body was brought from Silver Lake to Klamath Falls, a distance of 200 miles, by private conveyance and then expressed by rail from the latter place to Henry Conn, who was in the city today to take charge of the remains and give them proper burial in the local cemetery.

On November 19, 1910 Creed Conn's coffin was removed from the Silver Lake Cemetery and put on a wagon. When it arrived at Klamath Falls on November 23, a Lake County mortician by the name of Alva E. Kenworthy performed an autopsy at the county morgue, applied the necessary chemicals to the remains, and placed them in a new coffin which departed for Roseburg on the train, arriving there on the 24th. Henry Conn saw to it that Creed received the proper Masonic service and burial that he deserved, and he was reinterred in the family plot at Roseburg, next to his parents and sisters, Annie and Mary, on land that had been a part of the farm where Creed grew up.

Another article about the exhumation in the *Roseburg Review* described the circumstances of Conn's death. "One day he mysteriously disappeared and it was about two months afterward his body was found a short distance from the town, a bullet wound in the breast, another in the head, and a revolver lying nearby." That article offered the second of only two references ever published about the strange hole found in Conn's right temple that had originally been mistaken for a bullet wound, and added, "The relatives emphatically assert that it was a case of murder."

From Silver Lake, William Holder recalled, "The belief was so strong at the time that Conn knew who the sheep killers were and was murdered by some of the gang, that the Governor offered a reward of $2,000 for the apprehension and conviction of the murderers."

Little is known about Jackson's activities from 1912 through 1916, although the obituary of his father, Martin, who died in January of 1917, stated that he was still living in Lake County. Ray B. Jackson staked out a homestead claim of 640 acres on the east side of Wagontire Mountain in 1921, but had been involved in ranching there since at least 1916. He was partners in the ranching business with Frank Dobkins, probably from about 1912. Dobkins had some land south of Sycan Marsh in Lake County, and his wife had a homestead claim down near Ana Reservoir. Their partnership seems strange in light of the tragic death of Emma Dobkins, although Frank's willingness to accept Ray as a partner could support the theory that Emma died in childbirth, something that not everyone would say was completely Jackson's fault.

Frank Dobkins and Jackson seemed to have had a classic toadie-bully relationship. Jackson was a large man, and had been toughened by his stints in prison and his days with the Double O outfit, and was just the kind of man that Frank Dobkins would have admired. "He was a little bit of a guy, and like lots of little guys, he tried to act big," said Vera Addington Wagner about Dobkins. "He could cuss faster than anybody I ever heard.... couldn't imagine any man using such foul words. The only way I can explain Frank Dobkins is, he was a little piss ant. He was all bark and no bite."

Amongst the files of the Harney County Oral History Project, one finds numerous other snide comments from people who had been neighbors of Ray Jackson, veritable gems of insight into his character.

"He was a school teacher for a while. But he was a deadbeat, he was kind of a crook," said Russell Emery, who recalled that Ray had admitted to him having spent time in the penitentiary and knew that Jackson had the habit of stealing tools from his neighbors.

"Old Ray was pretty smart too, but he didn't seem to get too far," said Shelby Petersen.

Jess Gibson said that Jackson had moved out to Wagontire "on account of his health," another way of saying that he moved because he was unwelcome elsewhere and knew what was good for him.

Vera Addington Wagner told about the day that she and her father had made a discovery at Jackson's house that haunted them for years. "Out in that country when you was out riding on the range, if you got hungry you just went into somebody's house and fixed yourself a meal. And Papa and I was riding for some reason or other over, clear over at Harry Arnold's place to gather up the cattle one year. And we came by and stopped at Jackson's and he wasn't home.... Papa and I went in and fixed ourselves something to eat. And he had a well kept pantry, his pantry was just stocked with good stuff. So I reached up to get... a can of peaches... and doggone if it wasn't empty. And we found out something that we shouldn't have found out.... He would take a can of peaches or a can of pears and be careful with the label, and he'd open them on the bottom and use the fruit out of them, and wash them and put his roll of money in there, and put it back on, and set it back up in the shelf. And about every three or four can you pulled down off the shelf had a roll of money in it."

In a 1934 interview for the *Lake County Examiner*, neighbor Link Hutton told about one encounter he had with Jackson. "Dobkins and Jackson drove a herd past my place one day and I saw some of my brand. My cattle were supposed to be 30 miles away, down at Alkali Lake for the winter. I got on my pony and intercepted them. Dobkins answered my question as to what they were doing with my stock away up there by cussing me. Jackson threw back his coat and showed me a revolver. I said, 'Jackson, are you carrying that for me? If you are, I'll go get mine.' He denied that he was carrying it for me, but I did not understand why he should unbutton his coat on a winter day to show me he was armed."

The years that Jackson lived at Wagontire Mountain also revealed quite another 'side' to his character. To describe Ray Jackson as duplicitous would be putting it mildly for, like many sociopathic characters, Ray lead a double life and operated under two separate identities. Around Bend and Klamath County, he was known as Roy Jackson. Around Wagontire and Burns he was most often referred to as "Tomcat Jackson," although his neighbors also knew him as Ray B. Jackson. He alternately lived in two different places, spending six months of the year at each, which allowed him to maintain relationships with different women, and to illegally file upon and claim two separate homesteads.

Ray B. Jackson filed on a 640 acre stock raising homestead on the east side of Wagontire Mountain in sections 8, 9 and 17 in township 26 south, range 24 east in December of 1921, and began immediately renting the land to Frank Dobkins for grazing at a cost of $320 per year. In January of 1927 he filed on the same piece of land again, because he had failed, just barely, to meet the residency requirement of spending six full months on the land each year. Jackson made final proof on his claim on October 10, 1931. He spent the winters away from Wagontire, and told his neighbors and witnesses to his claim there that he was away working. According to his testimony, Jackson was gone from the mountain each year from some time in October through about mid-April. Witnesses to this claim were Frank Dobkins, John W. Kirk, and P.L. and Bertha Forbes.

When Jackson relinquished his original claim and refiled on the same piece of land in January of 1927 he testified, "That the reason I relinquished is that I was unable to comply with the requirements of the homestead law--by reason of climatic conditions. I could not keep my stock in that section of the country--that I could not procure sufficient feed for my stock to keep them through the winter season. I could not procure feed in that section of the country." He stated that he was a native born citizen of the United States, over twenty one years old, and "a single man." He also claimed that "It was through no fault of my own that I was unable to live upon the land as required by law." His claim was suspended for a time, when he failed to pay related fees amounting to about $26, Jackson finally did furnish the money, after first accusing the notary at the Burns land office of having pocketed the money he had already paid.

On November 15, 1926, Roy B. Jackson of Crescent, as he was known thereabouts, appeared before H.C. Ellis, U.S. Commissioner at Bend, and filed on a homestead in township 23 south, range 9 east, sections 25 and 26. George Snodgrass, who was a witness on this claim, testified that Ray, or "Roy" had established residence in February 1927, and was a married man. The claim had recently been relinquished by Martin J. Thomas.

This second claim was dissected by Highway 97, and Jackson had a business selling cans of gasoline and renting small cabins on the property to travelers. On July 18, 1929 Jackson inquired as to whether the size of the claim could be doubled by designating it as a stock raising homestead, but since the land was not located in a major stock raising area like Wagontire, the request was denied. From the beginning Jackson had stated that the claim in north Klamath was primarily valuable for grazing purposes, although he operated a small resort there, and was probably influenced to take the claim by his old friends the Mayfields, whose ranch adjoined the homestead.

On April 15, 1929 "Roy" asked to make commutation proof on the Klamath claim, meaning that instead of fulfilling the residency requirement for three more years, he would pay a lump sum for the land and acquire title to it earlier, as was allowed by law.

In July and August of 1929 he communicated with the land office by mail from Klamath Falls, and stated that he was spending weekends at the homestead on highway 97. That was during the time (May 1 to November 1, 1929) that he also claimed to have been living continuously at Wagontire in order to fulfill the residency requirement there. In fact, from 1927 through 1929 he claimed to have been living year-round in north Klamath County, when in reality he was spending the spring, summer, and early fall of each of those years at Wagontire. His witnesses for the land on Highway 97, Roy T. Moore and George C. Snodgrass, backed him up by denying any knowledge of extended absences by Jackson.

On November 15, 1926 when "Roy" filed on the Klamath County homestead, he signed an application falsely stating that, "Since August 30, 1890, I have not entered and acquired title to, nor am I now claiming, under an entry made under any of the non mineral public-land laws, an amount of land which, together with the land now applied for, will exceed in the aggregate 320 acres; and that I have not heretofore made any entry under the homestead laws." And, "I do solemnly swear that I am not the proprietor of more than 160 acres of land in any State or Territory."

In a letter dated August 4, 1929 from La Pine, writing as "Roy," he referred twice to having a wife. "My reason for commuting was so that I could take the wife to Oakland who Aunt is in the hospital and has been for the last two years, who depend upon us entirely." And, "The altude is to high here for the wife and her health demands and climate change," wrote Jackson, signing the letter "Roy B. Jackson." It is interesting to note that a self-proclaimed professor of higher learning such as Jackson should have so poor a grasp of the English language.

The wife was also mentioned at the time "Roy" testified to make final proof on the claim, when he was asked, "Are you married or single?

"Married."

"If married, of whom does your family consist?"

"Self, wife and two dependents."

Although, in October of 1931 when Jackson made final proof at Wagontire, he would state that he was single and had no family.

Taking a look back at the time when Roy Jackson and his family established residence on Highway 97, he stated that, "We lived in a log house while building." That would mean that they moved into an existing log structure, and the only known log house in that area in 1927 was on the homestead of Etta Cane, that was patented in 1919 and adjoined Jackson's claim on the north. The Cane log cabin would have been no more than a quarter mile from the site where Jackson built his house.

In 1920 Rosetta "Etta" Cane Glazier and her sister Veronica Cane lived in Bend at the corner of Louisiana Avenue and Sisemore Street. Etta's husband Eugene Glazier and an elderly aunt of the girls', Mrs. Mary Daub, lived in the same household. Veronica was a school teacher, and would have been 38 in 1927. In one of his letters to the land office, "Roy" mentioned that he and his wife cared for an elderly aunt of his wife, and Veronica's occupation could be more than a coincidence. Etta and Veronica were sisters of Mary Cane, who in 1924 owned and operated the Cane Variety Store on Bond Street in Bend, and of Benitta Cane who was Deschutes County Clerk that same year. A directory for 1924 showed Benitta and Mary living together in a house on Newport Avenue. The sisters had come from Ontonagon, Michigan where Veronica had begun teaching by 1910. Although there is no record of a marriage between any of the Cane girls and Jackson, it is possible that theirs was a union of the common-law type.

Could there have been another man living in central Oregon at the same time with the name of Roy B. Jackson? The 1920 census for the State of Oregon shows only one person by the name of Roy Jackson living in the state, a 15 year-old boy in Baker County. That boy would have been only 24 by the time the Klamath homestead was proved up. But the Roy who proved up on the homestead stated that he was 50 years old and born in Missouri, the same age and birthplace as Ray B. Jackson. The Oregon State Archives has no public records for a Roy B. Jackson, such as taxes, marriage, or divorce. Genealogy and tombstone transcription records show that no person by the name of Roy Jackson, born in the year 1869, was ever buried in Oregon. And finally, there is the uncanny resemblance in the handwriting of the two men, especially evident in their signatures.

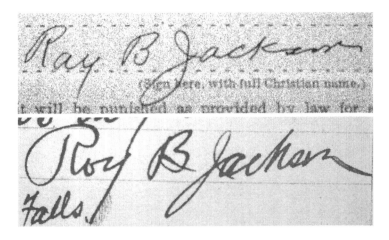

Compare the signatures of Roy and Ray.

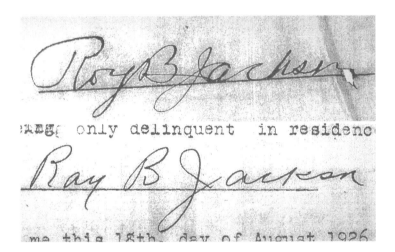

Ray had a tendency to drop the "o" in Jackson, even when he was masquerading as Roy.

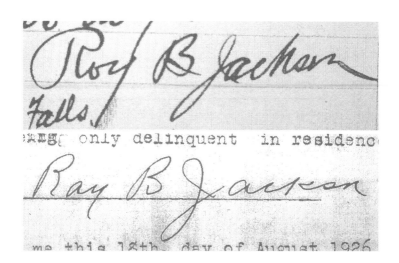

Note the similarity in the "B"s

Roy Jackson of near Crescent in 1929 formed his "R"s almost identically to Ray. This signature of R.B. Jackson was taken from the timber claim file of John Creed Conn, where Jackson served as a witness in 1903.

Ray Van Buren Jackson, masquerading as Roy B. Jackson, patented a homestead in north Klamath County in November of 1929. Shortly afterward, in December, he purchased the 2,240 acre ranch of Louisa Egli that adjoined his Wagontire claim.

There was one man who seemed to have caught on to Jackson's game, or at least had some knowledge of his criminal past. A government examiner for the General Land Office by the name of Clyde B. Walker wrote to Warden H.W. Meyers at the Oregon State Penitentiary on January 2, 1930. "Will you please inform me as to the record of the Penitentiary with regard to one Ray B. Jackson who was convicted and sentenced for a term in the penitentiary many years ago on a charge said to be forgery," wrote Walker. "The offense was committed in some town in the Willamette Valley. I wish the information for official use in the Department."

Walker was apparently investigating Jackson in connection with his and Frank Dobkins' homesteads at Wagontire, and his letter and the response of Warden Meyers became a permanent part of his inmate record, now on file at the Oregon State Archives. "Our records show that one R. V. (underlining his) Jackson was received at this institution June 9, 1896 from Clackamas County for forgery to serve 2 years," replied Meyers. "His description at time of receipt was as follows:"

AGE	24 years
NATIVITY	Missouri
HEIGHT	5 11 1/4
WEIGHT	160
COMPLEXION	Medium
HAIR	Dark Brown
EYES	Brown
OCCUPATION	School Teacher

In a July 1933 letter that Jackson wrote to the government in which he complained about his Wagontire patent having been held up for investigation, he stated that he wanted it patented so that he could put all of his property up as collateral to receive a large loan from the government. Despite all of his double dealing and deception, Jackson did, contrary to the law, acquire patent to the homestead of 360 acres at Wagontire in October of 1933. Dobkins' Wagontire homestead was canceled because it included a water hole that was needed by other stockmen in the area.

The end of Ray Jackson's life fit a typical pattern, as described in Martha Stout's insightful book, "The Sociopath Next Door." He was found dead from a gunshot wound in the upstairs bedroom of his house at Wagontire. "Global sociopaths most typically come to no good end, and this sharply downward tendency is displayed by the more local ones as well," wrote Stout. "In the final analysis, sociopathy appears to be a losing game, regardless of its scale.... For the extraordinarily patient observer, one technique to determine whether or not a questionable person is a genuine sociopath is to wait until the end of her life and witness whether or not she has ruined herself, partially or maybe even completely."

The coroner's jury who held the inquest over Jackson's body determined that "R.B. Jackson took his life by shooting himself thru the body with a 30-30 rifle," a verdict that was very much in keeping with Stout's conclusions. "A person without conscience, even a smart one, tends to be a shortsighted and surprisingly naive individual who eventually expires of boredom, financial ruin, or a bullet," she wrote. And, "There are additional reasons, less obvious, for the long-term failure of living without a conscience, reasons that are endemic to the psychology of sociopathy rather than the rage of other people. And the first of these is boredom, plain and simple."

Jackson's death certificate, signed by Dr. B.F. Smith and Deputy Coroner Holt Grimes gave the cause of death as: "Suicide by shooting himself thru left chest with a 30-30 rifle. Death by suicide determined by a coroner's jury." The bullet was a steel-jacket hollow point.

The tendency toward suicide was also described by Simon when he wrote that sociopaths "have 'stimulus hunger,' a need for constant stimulation, perhaps to dispel their diffuse sense of the meaninglessness of life. Some find this state unbearable and kill themselves."

"R.L. Hutton arrived here from Wagontire about 1 o'clock this afternoon, bringing information that R.B. Jackson, well known rancher and livestock operator of that section had ended his own life about 9 o'clock this morning with a rifle," reported the *Burns Times-Herald* on the day of the incident. "Henry Welcher, who had been staying with Mr. Jackson this winter heard a shot shortly after 9 o'clock Tuesday morning and upon investigation found Mr. Jackson's body," stated the *American* on the 4th. Welcher "found Jackson's body lying with the gun along side. He at once went to the James Sutherland home and took Frank Foster back to the Jackson ranch and Mr. Foster said he noted the rifle and a stove poker, indicating that had been used to fire the gun."

Next to arrive at the Jackson ranch were Sheriff C. W. Frazier, District Attorney J.S. Cook, and Acting Coroner Holt Grimes. Members of the coroner's jury were William Butler, Frank Welcome, Eldon Johnson, Charley Bedell, Claud Gray, and W.G. Bardwell. The bullet entered the body over the heart on the left side and emerged at the point of the right shoulder.

Aside from the evidence of the stove poker, there was another indication that Jackson had made some provision for the disposition of his property on the day before his death. Carley Parker had talked with Jackson at the Wagontire post office late in the day. "It was found that Mr. Jackson had some legal papers notaried by the post mistress at Wagontire the previous day, but no papers could be found about the ranch house and it is thought Mr. Jackson had mailed the papers while at the post office," reported the *Times-Herald*. Sheriff Frazier, who returned to the ranch to make further investigation the day after Jackson's death stated that the evidence was quite conclusive that Jackson had taken his own life. He was buried on February 4, 1938 at Burns.

Two-faced thief and coward, sadist and bully, abuser of women, perpetual liar, fraud and forger, a man filled with self-loathing, Ray Jackson was all of those things. He was also the man who had breakfast with John Creed Conn immediately before he disappeared on the morning of March 4, 1904.

SOURCES:

"Veteran Oregon Publisher Dies at Albany at Age 81," *Oregonian*, February 15, 1949. Obituary of William L. Jackson.

"Portrait and Biographical Record of the Willamette Valley, Oregon," by Joseph Gaston, 1903, Chapman, Chicago, IL, p 816-817. Biography of William L. Jackson.

Certificate of death, Linn County, Oregon #3931, Callie G. Jackson, June 25, 1907.

R.B. Jackson to H.H. Heeney, December 3, 1907, Deed and title records, vol-- p 299, Lake County Courthouse, County Clerk's Office, Lakeview, Oregon.

"Impressions and Observations of the Journal Man," by Fred Lockley, *Oregon Journal*, March 18, 1933. Sketch of William L. Jackson.

"Death of Mrs. M. Jackson," *Lebanon Express*, June 28, 1907.

"History of the First Methodist Church of Lebanon, and of its Associate, Santiam Academy," by Anna D.S. Pratt, from "Yesterday and Today in the First Methodist Church, 1850-1950." Available online at: http://

www.linncountyroots .com/Churches/
history_of_the_first_methodist_c.htm

"Martin Jackson," *Lebanon Express*, January 24, 1917. Obituary.

Oregon State Board of Health, Certificate of Death, Martin Van Buren Jackson, January 22, 1917. State index #19. Local Registered #6.

Ninth Census of the United States, Saline County, Missouri, Grand Pass township. Shows Ray at 8 months of age.

Tenth Census of the United States, Linn County, Oregon, Lebanon township. The adult interviewed is obviously Ray's mother Callie, who mistakenly gives the state of her husband's birth as Virginia, when it was actually Tennessee.

Thirteenth Census of the United States, Lake County, Oregon, Paisley precinct.

Tenth Census of the United States, Linn County, Oregon, Waterloo precinct. Jessie is 4 years old, daughter of William W. and May E. Parrish.

Marriage records of Linn County, Oregon, book H, #01748, December 3, 1893. Marriage of R.V. Jackson and Alda J. Parrish.

"Coroner's Verdict," *Enterprise Courier*, July 26, 1895.

"Bad Railroad Accident," *Enterprise Courier*, July 19, 1895.

"Horrible Accident," *Enterprise Courier*, July 19, 1895.

"The Teachers' Inning," *Oregonian*, July 19, 1895.

"Teaching Teachers," *Oregonian*, July 20, 1895.

Web site of the McLoughlin Memorial Association, http:// www.mcloughlinhouse. org

"Commission Report: City of Oregon City, to the Honorable Mayor and Commissioners," Agenda item 9a, local agency agreement No. 23,904, rail-highway crossings program project, Singer Hill/10th Street RR crossing safety improvements, April 4, 2007.

"The Singer Hill," *Enterprise Courier*, July 26, 1895

"Biennial Report of the Board of Railroad Commissioners of the State of Oregon to the Legislative Assembly, regular session, by Oregon Board of Railroad Commissioners, 1897. Available online at: http://books.google.com

Record of the Justice Court of Linkville Precinct, Klamath County, Book no. 28, 1890-1899, p 241, R.V. Jackson (1895). Available online at www.co.klamath.or.us/museum / justicecourt

"Oregon Geographic Names," by Lewis A. McArthur and Lewis L. McArthur, sixth edition, 1992, Oregon Historical Society Press, Portland, Oregon, p 65.

Circuit Court, (proceedings of the), *Enterprise Courier*, June 12, 1896.

"Sheriff Maddock Offers a Reward," *Oregon City Enterprise*, August 30, 1895.

"Gave Him the Word," *Oregon City Courier*, September 6, 1895.

"Jackson Caught," *Oregon City Courier*, May 22, 1896.

"Slick Forger Arrested," *Oregon City Enterprise*, May 22, 1896.

Thirteenth Census of the United States, Siskiyou County, California, Yreka township. Lenor was the wife of Charles N. Gordon.

Inmate record (and photo) of R.V. Jackson, inmate #3680, sentenced from Clackamas County, June 9, 1896, Oregon State Archives, Salem, Oregon.

The State of Oregon vs. R.V. Jackson, Oregon Circuit Court at Clackamas County, indictment, November 16, 1895, Circuit Court Case Files, Oregon State Archives, Salem, Oregon.

"Pioneer Rancher Takes Own Life," *Harney County American*, February 4, 1938.

"An Illustrated History of Early Northern Klamath County, Oregon," by Edward Gray, 1989, Maverick, Bend, Oregon, p 76-87. A map on page 87 shows the claim of Etta Cane with a log cabin on it in section 25 where it would have adjoined the claim of Roy Jackson, also in section 25.

"History of Cottonwood, Now and Then," by Dottie Smith. Excerpts available online at: http://www.ohs.org/education/ oregonhistory/narratives/subtopic. cfm?subtopic_ID=460

"Cattle Barons of Early Oregon," by David Braly, 1878, American Media Co., Prineville, Oregon, p 21-22, 44.

"William 'Bill' W. Brown 1855-1941, Legend of Oregon's High Desert," by Edward Gray, 1993, Your Town Press, Salem, Oregon, p 40, 166, 170-173, 193-194.

Inmate Record of R. Jackson, #4134. Oregon State Archives, Salem, Oregon. Record contains only a photograph of Jackson, but he and Ryan are also listed in the penitentiary's Convict Record on page 102.

Correspondence between author and Mary L. Solomon, Information Specialist of Oregon Department of Corrections, February 2, 2004.

"Survived Tragic Christmas Eve Fire, pioneer reminisces about early-day Silver Lake life," *Bend Bulletin*, August 10, 1970.

"A History of the Fremont National Forest," by Melva Bach, 1990, Forest Service, USDA, Pacific Northwest Region, Fremont National Forest, p 19, 35, 41.

"Lake County Teachers," *Lake County Examiner*, October 22, 1903.

"Register of Teachers," *Lake County Examiner*, July 23, 1903. Ray gives his name as Ray V. Jackson, also listed is Gilbert Brown.

Timberlines, Thirty-year Club, Region Six, U.S. forest Service, vol XIV, June 1960, p 49-53. A short sketch of the career of Gilbert Brown.

"Settlers in Summer Lake Valley," by Teresa Foster, 1989, Maverick, Bend, Oregon, p 19-20, 94, 124, 157-161, 178.

"Bad Men Do What Good Men Dream," by Robert I. Simon, M.D., American Psychiatric Press, Inc, Washington, D.C., p 28-30.

"WPA Interviews," Linnie Hutton Harbin, and Nettie Gibbard Bruce Glass, transcribed by Patricia Dunn of the Lebanon

Genealogical Society. Available online at: http://www.lgsoregon.org/ resources/wpa

"Western Echoes," by Earl F. Moore, 1981, Tremaine Publishing, Klamath Falls, Oregon, p 72-73.

"Supt. Jackson Talks of Schools," *Lake County Examiner*, May 6, 1909. Jackson comments editorially about his disdain for the Portland Irrigation Co.

"Supt. Jackson Thinks Improvements are Necessary," *Lake County Examiner*, June 10, 1909.

"The Teacher's Examination," *Lake County Examiner*, July 8, 1909.

"News Notes from Paisley," *Lake County Examiner*, February 10, 1910.

"The County Court," *Lake County Examiner,* July 15, 1909.

Creditor's claim of A.E. Kenworthy, November 30, 1910, in the Mater of the Estate of J.C. Conn, Deceased, Probate file of John Creed Conn, Probate Case Files, 1875-1927, Clerk's Basement South Storage Room, Lake County Courthouse, Lakeview, Oregon. Itemized bill of Kenworthy shows that chemicals were applied to the body, and a fee for the use of the morgue at Klamath Falls.

"Grim Reminder of 1904 Range War," *Lake County Examiner*, November 24, 1910. Story was originally published in the *Silver Lake Leader*.

Stock raising homestead patent application file of Ray B. Jackson, serial #1066515, Bureau of Land Management, records of the General Land Office, National Archives and Records Administration, Washington, D.C.

Homestead patent application file of Roy B. Jackson, serial #1032174, Bureau of Land Management, records of the General Land Office, National Archives and Records Administration, Washington, D.C.

Bureau of Land Management, records of the General Land Office, land patent of Frank Dobkins, serial #ORLAA 063342, http://www.glorecords.blm.gov/PatentSearch

Harney County History Project, oral history interview #377, Vera Addington Wagner, July 10, 1991, p 38-43.

Harney County History Project, oral history interview #380, Jess Gibson and Leora Houston Eggers, June 19, 1991, p 27. The word "supperflority" incorrectly recalled by Gibson is not an actual word. The word "superfluity" would better fit the context of the sentence, as in, the state of being superfluous. So Jackson began by claiming that he had a sufficient amount of elegance, and any more would be superfluous.

Harney County History Project, oral history interview #66, Ray Shaver and Russell Emery, August 16, 1991, p 6.

Harney County History Project, oral history interview #382, Russell and Mary Emery, August 16, 1991, p 4, 9- 11.

Harney County History Project, oral history interview #381, Shelby Petersen, August 4, 1991, p 5-6.

Harney County History Project, oral history interview #53-B, Neva Schroder Warner, June 22, 1992, p 8-11.

"Died," *Lake County Examiner*, March 10, 1910. Obituary of Emma Dobkins.

"County News, Paisley and Summer Lake," *Lake County Examiner*, December 30, 1909. Frank L. Young is named as an opponent of the Portland Irrigation Co.

"County Court, claims against Lake County," *Lake County Examiner*, September 22, 1910. Jackson earned $116.66 for two months salary.

"County News," *Lake County Examiner*, February 10, 1910. Names William Dobkins as the partner of Jackson in the new mercantile store.

Research by author at Paisley IOOF Cemetery, December 20, 2009.

USGenWeb tombstone transcription project, for Paisley IOOF Cemetery, Paisley, Lake County, Oregon. Available online at: http://files.usgwarchives.net/or/lake/ cemeteries/ paisleycem.txt

"In the matter of the resignation of R.B. Jackson," *Lake County Examiner*, September 28, 1911.

"In the Circuit Court," *Lake County Examiner*, October 20, 1910.

Interview with R. L. "Link" Hutton, title unknown, *Lake County Examiner*, December 6, 1934.

Twelfth Census of the United States, Ontonagon Village, Ontonagon County, Michigan

Thirteenth Census of the United States, Ontonagon Village, Ontonagon County, Michigan

Fourteenth Census of the United States, Bend, Deschutes County, Oregon

Polk's Deschutes, Crook and Jefferson Counties Directory, 1924-25, by R.L. Polk & Co., Inc., 1924, Portland, Oregon, p 71, 98.

http://www.findagrave.com shows that Rosetta "Etta" Cane Glazier, wife of Eugene Richard Glazier was born in Ontonagon, Michigan in 1894.

"Dobkins Homestead Cancelled by U.S.," *Burns Times-Herald*, May 30, 1930.

"Georgie Boydstun Stephenson Collection," Lake County Museum, Lakeview, Oregon, p 4. Names Jackson and Virgil Conn as both being on the first city council of Paisley in November of 1911.

"The Sociopath Next Door," by Martha Stout, PhD, 2005, Broadway Books, New York, p 184-185, 191.

Oregon State Board of Health, Certificate of Death for Ray B. Jackson. Date of death February 1, 1938.

"Suicide is Verdict of Coroner's Jury in Jackson Death," *Burns Times-Herald*, February 2, 1938.

Funeral announcement for R.B. Jackson, *Burns Times-Herald*, February 3, 1938.

"R.B. Jackson Ends Life With a Rifle," *Burns-Times Herald*, February 1, 1938.

"Pioneer Rancher Takes Own Life," *Harney County American*, February 4, 1938.

Photo of the Hutton Ranch taken by Rufus W. Heck in early 1926. The corral is visible through the gate at the far side of the yard. Garage is at far right of photo.

Front view of Hutton garage, taken by Rufus W. Heck shortly after the murder. Note the large doors that swing outward. Harold Bradley fell in front of the building, near the post that divides the two empty bays.

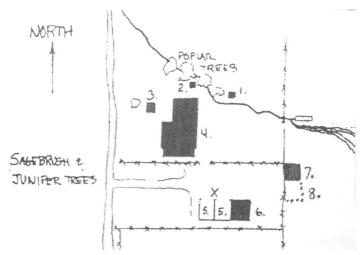

Map of the Hutton Ranch. (1) Outhouse (2) Spring House (3) Cold Cellar (4) Main House (5) Empty carport bays (6) Garage bay where Hutton kept his car (7) Barn (8) Corral

Chapter Twelve

Harold

"Harold is the eldest son of Mr. and Mrs. Ira Bradley. He was born at Lakeview, Oregon, April 13, 1902, aged 23 years. He was quiet and unassuming with a sunny disposition and everyone who knew him was his friend.... In the untimely death of Harold Bradley the community loses one of its best young men, while the family loses a faithful son and brother whose loss words are inadequate to describe. The sympathy of the community goes out to the bereaved ones."

-Silver Lake Leader, January 7, 1926

"Harold Bradley was a very, very close friend of ours. He and my brother, oldest brother, were the same age, and herded sheep together for Bill Brown. Harold was a very nice guy, very nice young man.... Harold was our mail carrier... he carried the mail from ... Stauffer to Wagontire for years. He was not murdered." *

Harold Bradley was ambitious, fun loving, and a very responsible person. He was like a father to his siblings, teaching them to be self-reliant and independent. He took over the fatherly chores when the kids were attending school. During the summer he helped with the daily tasks involved with living at Wagontire. Give him a job to do and Harold Bradley could handle it.

-Bradley Family History

Harold was a very mild, even tempered guy. Never did see him lose his temper. He took care of us kids mostly. He just took the lead and took care of us kids. He never got mad at us.... He had red hair, but he wasn't very big.

- Grace Bradley Gowdy

Between 6 and 7 o'clock on the morning of December 29, 1925, before daylight, Harold Bradley, age 23, was shot to death in the shadows of a a shed-like carport on the ranch of Robert Lincoln 'Link' Hutton at Wagontire Mountain. Vera Addington Wagner was only about 7 years old at the time, and her parents kept the post office at Wagontire and knew Bradley very well. Bradley was also friendly with Link Hutton, and in addition to his two-day mail route had worked for Hutton for several years on his ranch. Bradley was liked and trusted by Hutton and his wife, Leona, so the whole countryside was thrown into a state of shock when Hutton was charged with Bradley's murder.

Harold had built two small cabins at his homestead claim on Bradley Meadows, which was just over the Lake County line near Wagontire Mountain. He was a small man, like his father, about 150 pounds and five foot, seven inches tall.

Hutton had been away at a cattlemen's association meeting at Grants Pass, and returned home on Christmas eve and put his car in a shed that had spaces for three cars. The shed more or less faced the house, and was located about 75 feet to the southeast of the front porch. Hutton kept his car in the stall furthest from the house, at the east end of the shed.

"Hutton had been away, he and his wife having been separated for several weeks," reported the *Silver Lake Leader*.

Leona Hutton filed suit for divorce after the shooting, alleging cruel and inhuman treatment. "In her complaint she charges that in November, 1925, Hutton declared his intention of leaving her and that he did leave and remained away until the night of December 24 when he returned and threatened to kill her." The same article in the *Leader* claimed that Harold Bradley, a mutual friend of the Huttons, had twice intervened when Link Hutton had threatened Leona.

"On the evening prior to the tragedy Mr. and Mrs. Hutton had been at the Jackson place where they went to have some legal papers drawn. Harold, who was employed as a farm hand by Mrs. Hutton, was taken along as a witness," said the *Leader* of January 7. Bradley spent the night at Hutton's, and early the next morning went outside to do some minor repairs to his car, probably in order to complete his mail route. The only persons known to have been at the ranch at the time of the shooting were the Huttons and Harold Bradley.

What happened next has been the subject of considerable debate for all of the years since, and no eye witness ever came forward to describe the shooting death of young Bradley. He was shot with a 30-30 rifle by an assailant that no one saw. One bullet entered his chest just below the left nipple. Another shot entered the left lower jaw and ranged upward, cutting his tongue and damaging his jaw so badly that he was unable to speak, then lodged in his right temple. It is not known which shot was fired first, although the following statement by Leona Hutton for the inquest leaves the impression that the shot to the chest was first:

> "My name is Leona Hutton, that I reside at Wagontire, Harney County, OR, on what is known as Hutton's ranch. Am 46 years old and wife of Link Hutton. On morning of 29 Dec. 1925, Link left house between 6 and 7 o'clock to fix his car. Harold Bradley was outside. I heard shot, then immediately I heard Harold scream and said, 'Link, you shot me. Oh, please don't shoot me again.' Immediately after this heard second shot. I immediately went for help. No quarrel or cross words either night before or next morning between them. Not light enough to see them."

> *-Sworn testimony of Leona Hutton in the shooting death of Harold Bradley*

When Leona Hutton fled the scene she went to the home of John Kirk, who lived about two miles to the north.

The next person on the scene was none other than Ray B. Jackson, who was staying at the old Egli ranch about 3 miles north of Huttons. The two men carried Bradley to the house, placed him on a bed and removed his boots. Hutton left to get help, and went to the ranches of the Kirks and Donovans. They were not at home, but he found another neighbor, Ole Soderberg, and returned home with him. In his statement to the coroner's jury made the next day, Jackson would claim that Hutton had come to his ranch looking for help at about 7 o'clock, bypassing several other occupied ranches along the way.

While Bradley was left alone in the care of Jackson, the young man died, approximately one hour after he had been shot. Jackson and Hutton left Soderberg with the body, and drove to the nearest phone, at the home of Wood Best and waited for the authorities to arrive. The Best home was located about 20 miles northeast of the Hutton ranch, and the two men waited there for about six hours, or until around 2 P.M. Hutton was put under arrest. Deputy Sheriff Locker and District Attorney Cozad returned to the Hutton ranch, then a short time later, Coroner Clevenger and a professional nurse arrived.

The next day, the coroner's jury, of which Ray B. Jackson was a member, returned a verdict that "Harold Bradley came to his death... from two gun shot wounds in the body and head of the deceased, and that said shots were fired by R.L. Hutton." Other members of the jury were J. C. Cecil, Ony Thompson, Luther J. Addington, Ole Soderberg, and Harry Z. Smith.

"My name is R.B. Jackson, 56 years old. That I reside at my ranch, near Wagontire.

Mr. Hutton came to my place about 7 o'clock yesterday (29). He said, 'I guess I killed a man this morning.' I asked if accident, and he said 'No. I shot him.' I asked if he was dead. He said, 'I don't know. I shot twice. Don't know whether I hit him second shot.' He said he came after me and asked me to go over and see what could be done for him.

When we got to the body, I shook it and he did not move. I then touched his eye and he moved and attempted to speak. We put him on a canvas which Hutton procured and we carried him a short way, and he motioned to stop. We put him down a moment and then he nodded (and asked if we) should go ahead and he nodded assent. We brought him on to house. I removed boots, and prepared water and fire in stove preparatory to rendering aid, and in probably 25 or 30 minutes he died.

Hutton went to Kirk's and on to Donovan's for help. They were not at home, but he found Ole Soderberg at Kirk's and brought him back. As soon as we got this help, Hutton and I left and went to Wood Best's and had Mr. Best phone in to officers at Burns. We stayed there until officers came from Burns. Should I say about 2 o'clock.

Hutton, Mrs. Hutton and Bradley all came to my house the night before about 8 o'clock, and Mrs. Hutton asked me to prepare some agreements or contracts between her and Link, and I did this. She dictated terms and they both agreed and both signed. No quarrel or dispute of any kind, nor any harsh words between any of them and all appeared in good humor and jovial. Link told me 'goodbye,' and said he was leaving for the south next morning and would probably go to Peru. Mrs. Hutton took the two agreements. Link said he did not want them, and would leave settlement and sales of property all with Mrs. Hutton. She asked to have clause in agreement to effect she should have full control and custody of property.

-Sworn testimony of Ray B. Jackson in the shooting death of Harold Bradley

Jackson's account of what happened raises almost as many questions as it answers. Why would Hutton, as he went for help, bypass several occupied ranches in order to get to Jackson's place? Why did Hutton go for help a second time, this time going to the homes of his nearest neighbors? Did Hutton fetch Jackson, or did he arrive on his own?

According to Ray Shaver, Jackson never did own an automobile, or learn how to drive one. "Old Jackson rode in there one day," said Shaver. "He didn't drive, he didn't have a car or nothing. When he went any place, unless somebody took him, he just rode this old horse."

Bradley's wounds, from how they were described at the inquest, may have been survivable, so long as the bleeding could have been stopped and a doctor could have been located. The shot through the chest did not strike the heart, and the bullet that damaged his face and jaw seemed to have missed the brain. Just what happened at the Hutton ranch during the time when Jackson was left alone with the dying boy? From Jackson's account, it sounds as though Bradley was dead by the time Hutton and Soderberg returned.

Why is it that Hutton does not, in Jackson's version of the story, name Harold Bradley? Hutton knew Bradley well, knew he was out in the yard at the time of the shooting, and like any person with a normal degree of empathy, would have ran to the injured man and attempted to help him. Was Jackson trying to make it sound like Hutton shot a man in the yard, not knowing that the man was Bradley?

What Hutton allegedly said to Jackson about the shooting contradicts the account of Leona Hutton. Bradley was obviously shot at fairly close range, so the shooter, if it was Hutton, would have known that he had hit his target, especially when the second shot took off part of the lad's face and stopped his outcry.

The events of the evening before, according to Jackson, were also highly questionable in light of the complaint that Leona would soon file against Link Hutton, accusing him of cruel and inhuman treatment and suing him for divorce. Obviously there were serious problems in their marriage, yet when they allegedly got together to write what was probably a power of attorney, there was an unusual lack of bitterness. Also, events of the years to come would show that Link Hutton had no intention of disposing of his property, and maintained ownership of it until 1946. At any rate, if such a deal had been struck, Hutton was certainly smart enough to have kept a copy of the agreement for himself. Was this Jackson's attempt to explain why Leona had two suspicious documents in her possession? That power of attorney document must have later been found to be fraudulent, because Link Hutton maintained a continuous residence and ownership of the ranch. As for going to Peru, Jackson was probably referring to the historic mining camp near Lake Tahoe in California.

The statement allegedly made by Hutton that he was taking off to travel south with no plan of returning was strange, too. Was that a suggestion of a plot to get rid of the well-heeled rancher? Indeed, neighbors like Vera Addington Wagner spoke of a plot involving Leona to get rid of Link Hutton and take control of his large cattle ranch. "Not knowing to Link, why Woodard and Leona Hutton decided that they were in love, and that they were going to take the Hutton property away from Link.... Unbeknownst to Link, this was all planned out," said Wagner.

"She had been stepping out with the neighbor for quite a little while," said Grace Bradley in a 1991 interview. "And she was out that night with that neighbor... with the neighbor man. I don't know how far he really lived.... She'd been stepping out with him for quite a while. Everybody kind of knew that."

On Wednesday, December 31, Hutton was charged with murder in the first degree, waived preliminary examination, and was released on $10,000 bail. Several newspaper accounts printed during the week after the killing placed the blame on Hutton and claimed that he had shot in self-defense when Bradley threatened him with a hammer. No source was ever named for the story about the hammer, which could have been an invention of Jackson's.

Witnesses that were called to testify when Hutton was indicted were Ray Jackson, Ole Soderberg, John and Pauline Kirk, Harry Smith, Coroner G.W. Clevenger, Harold Bradley's father Ira, John Simpson, and Deputy Sheriff Leonard Locher.

Hutton hired photographer Rufus Heck to take photos of the scene of the crime, *"showing the buildings, their relation to each other* and showing, so far as possible, the condition at the time that said alleged crime was committed." Hutton wanted Heck to testify at the trial so that the photos could be introduced as evidence, but was not allowed to use Heck or his photos. Leona Hutton could not be found by the sheriff of Lake County, E.A. Priday, who attempted to serve her with a summons, and so the trial lost one of its most important witnesses. Hutton requested 12 witnesses for his defense, and about half of those men appeared as character witnesses.

"Ole Soderberg and J.C. Cecil were members of the Coroner's jury and among the first people that were upon the ground after the said alleged crime was committed and that they will testify as to the conditions that they found at that time, *particularly with reference to my position and the position of the deceased*, together with other circumstances that were indicated by the conditions at the time," wrote Hutton in his request for witnesses. It is interesting to note that Hutton did not request Ray Jackson as a witness. Cecil did appear as a witness for the defense, but Soderberg did not.

Ira Bradley and Soderberg appeared against Hutton as a witnesses for the state. Hutton's choice of words about his position at the time the shots were fired and the relative locations of the ranch buildings indicate that the defense was trying to show that Hutton could not have fired the shots.

Hutton was probably deep inside of the east bay, the 'garage' portion of the carport with a lantern at the time the shots were fired. Leona stated that he had gone out to fix his car, and that was where his car was kept. He may have been planning to leave early to visit his brother, Tom, who was in the hospital at Burns as the result of a car accident that occurred two days prior. One news story about the incident said that Hutton "was getting ready to remove and repair some 'flat' tires." Another said that Hutton stood and talked to Bradley for a moment, then went into the garage nearby. The front of the west bay was fitted with two doors, each about six feet wide, that swung out to open. That was probably what Hutton meant when he wrote, "with reference to my position and the position of the deceased." What he was trying to say was that he could not see Bradley from his position. That in order to have seen Bradley, or to have shot him for that matter, he would have had to walk six feet beyond the opening of the garage bay, past the door, and turned to his left. Incidentally, if Hutton had been standing in that spot at the end of the garage door and facing Bradley, he would have been in the direct line of fire between Bradley and the corral, which was the direction from which the shots came.

Was the killer waiting for Hutton to come out of the garage to shoot him? With the two men, both of the same height and weight, moving around in the darkness, with deep shadows and the high contrast of a lantern or two, coming together to talk, then parting, then moving again, the killer could easily have become confused and shot the wrong man.

"That I further state that several of the same witnesses will testify as to the reputation of John Kirk and Pauline Kirk as to their bad reputation for truth and veracity in case they should appear as witnesses against me and testify to statements that are not true," wrote Hutton, much in the tone of a man who felt he was being framed. It is interesting to note here that the Kirks were friends of Jackson and had appeared as witnesses to his homestead claim at Wagontire. It is also interesting that the Kirks were not at home at the time of the killing or when Hutton stopped at their ranch when he was looking for help. They were probably included as witnesses because Leona ran to their house after the shooting and hid there, possibly until they arrived home.

When the case went to trial in April of 1926, Hutton was acquitted after the jury deliberated for only one hour. Leona could not be located, making Ray B. Jackson, the first man on the scene, fraud and forger, womanizer and ex-convict, the prosecution's star witness.

The author believes that Jackson, an enterprising sociopath, decided that he wanted all that Link Hutton had, and so set out to destroy him by charming his way into Leona's lonely life while Link was away. In the stock raising community around Wagontire, Link Hutton, although only slightly built, was the 'king of the mountain.' "Link was approximately five foot eight inches tall and weighed around one hundred forty pounds," wrote Edward Gray. "That guy could throw a fifty or sixty foot loop at the end of a rawhide rope. He was a roper and a good one, Link had an awful good personality. Just to meet him anybody would like him," said Jess Gibson in an interview with Gray. Jackson wanted control of the Hutton ranch, and wanted to have everything that Hutton had, his status, his home, his cattle, his money, and his wife.

Jackson must have had some special reason for hanging around the mountain during the holidays. As he stated in his homestead application, between the years 1921 and and 1931 he was normally gone from his claim from about November until May. He would not buy the Egli place until late in 1929, but he was apparently staying there at the time of the murder.

Shelby Petersen told Gray about an incident that occurred in January of 1926:

> *"Shelby was on the Wagontire Road returning to Burns from Paisley when the lights went out on his Model T Ford. Nearing Ray B. Jackson's house (the old Egli place), he saw lights on. He knew Ray and decided to pull his car into the front yard where he drained the radiator before entering the house. As he turned towards the house the lights had been turned off. He went ahead and opened the door and lit the coal lamp and began gathering wood for the cook stove. The stove was still warm, but no one was in the house. Shelby fixed a pot of beans and went to bed. Underneath one of the pillows he found Jackson's pearl handled Colt 45. Just as he was about to fall asleep, Jackson hollered from the porch asking who it was. Shelby said he came in and talked most of the night. Jackson told him that Leona had walked from Kirk's house the day after the shooting (of Bradley) and wanted protection from Link. Shelby said, 'When he heard the car coming with no lights he just turned the lights off and beat it. He was so scared he had forgotten his gun.'"*

Leona spent the morning of the 30th, the hours before the inquest, at Jackson's house, which would have given Jackson ample time to coach her on what to use in her statement, particularly the words she heard Harold cry out between the first and second shots, *"Link, you shot me. Oh, please don't shoot me again!"* When what she really heard was probably more on the order of, *"Link! He shot me!"* During their morning planning session, Jackson and Leona probably also brewed up the fake power of attorney papers, with Jackson forging the signatures of both Link Hutton and Harold Bradley. With Hutton still alive and kicking, Jackson needed a fresh plan for getting control of the ranch. Once Leona had power of attorney, he could negotiate the purchase from her. And, as far as Jackson was concerned, the best witness to the fraud was a dead witness.

On the morning of the murder, Jackson laid in wait for Hutton outside. He had arranged with Leona to send Hutton out on some pretext, like the flat tire that was mentioned in an article on January 2. The plan was to shoot Hutton, then to frame Bradley for the murder, putting both the rancher and his ranch hand and friend out of the way. But Jackson mistakenly shot the wrong man in the darkness, as both men were of similar height and weight. As the young man cried out, Jackson shot him again, then quickly disappeared to get rid of the rifle. There was no mention of the murder weapon having ever been found, another fact that probably helped to clear Hutton. If Bradley had been Jackson's intended victim, he might have shot the boy with Hutton's rifle so that he could frame Hutton, but he did not use Hutton's rifle.

Bradley was shot as he walked toward the garage to put away the tools he had been using, possibly a hammer and fell a few feet in front of it. That was an interesting fact that was brought out in a news article that appeared in the *Leader* on January 7. That single item is of great interest because it seems to have come from Ray B. Jackson. Link Hutton was not quoted in the article, and was probably told by his attorneys not to talk about the case because he might say something incriminating. Leona was not the source for that individual fact, for in her testimony she stated that it was too dark to see what had happened, and she fled for the neighbors immediately after hearing the second shot. Also, the source of that information misquoted her statement of Bradley's last words. *"Link, you shot me. Oh, please don't shoot me again,"* was changed to, *"Don't shoot me any more Link, you've shot me once."* One person saw the direction Bradley was walking, one person saw Harold Bradley fall, and that person was the killer.

Vera Addington Wagner provided a hand-drawn map of the Hutton property for Gray's book, "William 'Bill' W. Brown" that showed the location where Bradley fell and died. A photograph of the carport shortly after the crime is contained in the same book, and shows the front of the carport and a dark stain on the ground in the place where Bradley fell.

Both of those sources show that Bradley fell a few feet in front of the carport building, near the post that divided the west bay from the center bay. The "garage" referred to was actually the the third bay on the east end of the carport that was the larger of the three, that had doors on it, and that contained Hutton's car, some tools, and some other items he had stored there. Bradley must have put his own car in the west bay of the carport, and was shot just after he came out of the bay and turned to walk east toward the east bay. The shot seems to have come from the corral, which was located in the southeast corner of the yard and is plainly visible in one photo through the Hutton's gate. Bradley's left side would have been most exposed to gunfire from the corral, and the bullets struck him in the left chest and left jaw.

Jackson, although he was not quoted directly in the January 7 article, does seem to have been that writer's primary source because he cast Jackson in so favorable of a light:

Harney Rancher Kills Harold Bradley
Silver Lake Leader, January 7, 1926

On Tuesday morning, Dec. 29, R.L. Hutton, aged 54, shot Harold Bradley, a Silver Lake boy, near Wagontire, who died an hour later from the wounds.

Previous to the killing Hutton had been away, he and his wife having been separated for several weeks. Hutton had returned the day before and on the evening prior to the tragedy Mr. and Mrs. Hutton had been at the Jackson place where they went to have some legal papers drawn. Harold, who was employed as a farm hand by Mrs. Hutton, was taken along as a witness. At this time both seemed to have been on the best of terms.

The following morning, Mr. Bradley, who has the mail contract between Wagontire and Stauffer, left the house to start with the mail for Stauffer. He was detained a few minutes fixing a part to the car, when Hutton came and stood and talked with him, then going into the garage nearby. Soon after, Harold having made the repairs to his car, started for the garage to put away the tools he had been using, when Hutton opened fire on him, shooting him in the abdomen. Mrs. Hutton hearing the shot, opened the door in time to hear Harold say: 'Don't shoot me any more Link, you've shot me once,' when another shot was fired which entered the left lower jaw, ranging upward, cutting off the tongue at the roots, the bullet lodging in the right temple. As the mail leaves early and it was not yet daylight Mrs. Hutton was unable to see the shots fired.

Hutton, after the shooting, went to the Jackson place, when he told Mr. Jackson what he had done, Mr. Jackson started with him to Burns but was met at Silver Creek by a deputy sheriff who took him in charge. He is now in the county jail at Burns and it is understood he will plead insanity.

After hearing the second shot Mrs. Hutton went to the nearest neighbors, and it is well she did as it is claimed Hutton went to the house in search of her, and it is believed that if he had found her, her life would have been taken.

Harold is the eldest son of Mr. and Mrs. Ira Bradley. He was born at Lakeview, Oregon, April 13, 1902, aged 23 years. He was quiet and unassuming with a sunny disposition and everyone who knew him was his friend. The body was brought to Silver Lake Thursday where funeral services were held in the afternoon, conducted by Elder G.W. Reynolds, interment being made in the local cemetery.

In the untimely death of Harold Bradley the community loses one of its best young men, while the family loses a faithful son and brother whose loss words are inadequate to describe. The sympathy of the community goes out to the bereaved ones.

Nursemaid to the injured; paralegal and expert on contracts; law man who brought an insane killer to justice; news reporter; confessor; liar; forger; killer. How could Jackson have been all of those things? Because he was a psychopath, and a psychopath will portray himself as a hero even as he takes another man's life.

The behavior of Leona Hutton during the whole ordeal was also very strange. When she gave her statement to the coroner's jury, she said that she was standing in the doorway with a view of the whole yard when the second shot was fired, yet she saw nothing. On a dark morning, the flash of the gun would have been visible as the second shot was fired, but Leona said she didn't see it. Then, knowing that her husband, Link, and her friend, Harold, were outside in the yard where she heard two shots fired, she did nothing immediately to help them. She didn't go outside to see if they had been shot, but instead skedaddled off to the neighbor's house.

Suppose that Leona was so frightened by the shooting that she ran away to the neighbors. Wouldn't it be natural for a woman who was badly shaken up to later go back to the comfort and security of her own home? Wouldn't she want to find out if her husband had been hurt? Instead she spent the next day, and possibly even the night after the killing, at the home of Ray Jackson, indicating some loyalty or attachment to him.

By the time of the trial, Leona could not be found. What was she hiding? Didn't she have any sympathy for the Bradley family? Didn't she want to help bring Bradley's killer to justice? Maybe it was shame that kept Leona away. Shame over her affair with Jackson and a fear of the mudslinging that would surely come during the trial. Shame that she had not stayed to help Harold. Shame that she conspired in a plot that ended in the tragic death of a nice young man like Harold Bradley.

Jackson was certainly the first person on the scene. But, despite that fact, Hutton rejected him as a witness for the defense. It seems that Hutton distrusted Jackson from the outset, or even suspected him. Although at the time of the shooting, Hutton trusted him enough to leave him alone with Harold Bradley as he lay dying, in later years Hutton developed a distinct animosity toward the man. Shelby Petersen's account of Jackson's fear of Hutton will be remembered here, along with the Hutton's account of Jackson throwing back his coat to display his gun. The animosity between the two men after the death of Harold Bradley was common knowledge around Wagontire.

There was some gossip that circulated around Wagontire during the years after the murder about another man who was a hired hand for the Huttons, Clarence 'Link' Woodard, who Leona later married. According to those tales, Woodard was a bootlegger and had a still at nearby Bunyard Springs and was allegedly responsible for turning Harold Bradley into an alcoholic. Prior to the time when Bradley was shot, those stories say that it was Woodard who developed a relationship with Hutton's wife, Leona. But, since Woodard was not named as a witness for the inquest or trial of the Bradley murder, and was not mentioned in the articles that described it, it does not appear that he was in the area or on the ranch at the time.

In 1991 Edward Gray interviewed a man by the name of Ray Shaver, who had been a friend of Jackson's in the mid-1930's. He told the following story about an incident that happened around 1936:

> *"He (Jackson) told me he met Link Hutton coming down that road that runs off the mountain.... That lane that runs by Highway 395. He said he met old Link and Link got out of his car and said, 'Jackson, get off your horse, I'm going to kill you.' Jackson said to him, 'If you're going to kill me, shoot me off my horse.' About that time they seen dust and another car coming so old Link jumped in his car and took off."*

According to writer Edward Gray, in 1926 Jackson felt so fearful of Hutton that he had him placed under a peace bond. Hutton had to put up a sum of money that would be lost if he threatened or harassed Jackson in any way. In light of certain events, Hutton's hatred of Jackson now seems understandable.

SOURCES:

Harney County History Project, oral history interview #377, Vera Addington Wagner, July 10, 1991, p 1-11. Wagner's statement that Bradley "was not murdered" seems to stem from her belief that Hutton's intention was to shoot another man who he believed was having an affair with his wife.

"Fatal Shooting at Wagontire Ranch," *Harney County News*, December 31, 1925.

"Harold Bradley Shot Tuesday by L. Hutton," *Burns Times-Herald,* January 2, 1926.

"Details Meagre in Harney Tragedy," *Lake County Examiner*, January 7, 1926.

"Harney Rancher Kills Harold Bradley," *Silver Lake Leader*, January 7, 1926.

"R.L. Hutton is Found Not Guilty of Murder," *Burns Times-Herald*, April 17, 1926.

Coroner's inquest records in the death of Harold Bradley, December 30, 1925,
Harney County Courthouse, Clerk's Office, Burns, Oregon.

Stock raising homestead patent application file of Ray B. Jackson, serial #1066515, Bureau of Land Management, records of the General Land Office, National Archives and Records Administration, Washington, D.C.

"William 'Bill' W. Brown 1855-1941, Legend of Oregon's High Desert," by Edward Gray, 1993, Your Town Press, Salem, Oregon, p 160, 164-165, 169-171, 176, 184, 191,

Harney County History Project, oral history interview #381, Shelby Petersen, August 4, 1991, p 8-9.

Harney County History Project, oral history interview #66-A, Ray Shaver & Russell Emery, August 16, 1991, p 5.

Harney County History Project, oral history interview #192-A, Ray and Grace Bradley Gowdy, June 18, 1991, p 28-32.

The homestead cabin of Ira Bradley was about one and a half miles west of the county line between Harney and Lake counties, within the jurisdiction of Lake County authorities.

The Bradley family in 1912. Harold, the oldest, stands in back behind his parents, Ira and Ada. Other children from left are Hosmer, Leah, Lena, Lora, and Ruth.

Chapter Thirteen

Ira

The body of Ira Bradley, well known Silver Lake man, was found Saturday afternoon at his homestead cabin near Wagontire mountain, apparently the victim of cold blooded murder.

- Lake County Examiner, May 8, 1930

Ira stood only five foot seven and weighed 145 to 165 pounds, but he was one heck of a cowboy. In his youth he went to work for the ZX Ranch at Paisley where he gradually worked through the ranks to become one of the ranch's foremen. Ira also worked for Bill Kittredge and helped in driving a herd of horses from Oregon to Missouri having to work his way back.

- "William 'Bill' W. Brown," by Edward Gray

Bradley is said to have been a very mild mannered, inoffensive man who took no part in neighborhood differences. He had raised a

*family of eight children and worked hard to
give them an education.*

- Burns Times-Herald, May 9, 1930

Ira Bradley's body was discovered in the same cabin
on Lost Creek in township 25 south, range 23 east, section 23,
where his son, Harold, had been living when he was murdered
only about four years and four months prior. He was found by
another son, Hosmer, who was about 19 years old, and his
friend, Jesse Pennington, who went to the cabin for a visit on
the evening of Saturday, May 3. "He had been brutally clubbed
over the head, the entire upper part of his skull beaten to a
pulp," reported the *Burns Times-Herald.* The horrifying
nature of the discovery was compounded by the state of
decomposition the body was in, and authorities estimated that
Bradley had been killed about three days prior, on or around
May 1.

Bradley, age 62, lived alone and was described by
those who knew him as having a similar temperament to his
deceased son, Harold. At the time of Ira's murder, his wife Ada
and their seven children were in Silver Lake, where they lived
part of the year so that the children could attend school. Mild
mannered and inoffensive, kind and gentle, Ira Bradley was
very fond of animals, especially horses. "He told the children
never to abuse an animal, especially the horses. He was not a
hunter of wild game and is known to never have killed a deer
even though he was surrounded by them. He hated to cut
down a living tree."

"A watch, pocket knife, and $2.50 in change were
found on the body. No signs of a struggle were to be seen about
the cabin, where the tragedy took place, the killer apparently
striking without warning." The murder weapon was some
unknown heavy instrument.

News of the killing reached Burns shortly after 7 P.M.
on Saturday, May 3. The first officials on the scene Saturday
night were Deputy Sheriff Gould, District Attorney Sizemore,
and Coroner Clevenger of Harney County. They completed an
investigation and search of the area around the Bradley cabin
where they reported that they had found no trace of the killer,
then conducted an inquest early Sunday morning and
departed for Burns with with the body where it was embalmed
and the clothing that had been on the body was incinerated.

Unfortunately, all of those official acts were highly
negligent to the point of a miscarriage of justice. Bradley had
been murdered in Lake County, not Harney County. His cabin
was about a mile and a half inside the county line. So, the
investigation and inquest should have been carried out by the
Lake County authorities, who were not informed of the

homicide until 10:30 A.M. on Sunday, well after the men from Burns had departed with the body. Sheriff Priday, District Attorney Charles Combs, and Deputy Coroner W.N. Robinson learned of the snafu, drove to Riley late Sunday evening and went on to Burns, expressing dismay that so much evidence had been destroyed by the embalming of Bradley and the burning of his clothes.

On Monday, the Lake County men went to the Bradley cabin and found "that activities of the Harney officers had served to disturb the scene of the crime to such an extent that little creditable evidence could be found." Hosmer Bradley and Jesse Pennington helped search the vicinity of the cabin, and found the tracks of a man "off some distance from the corral and ranch house," and the tracks were measured.

When the Lake County men broadened their search to the ranch of Bradley's neighbor, Harry H. Thompson, they found "a pair of shoes that fit the tracks, also a hardwood club and a pair of overalls covered with blood."

Harry Thompson had left Wagontire on Sunday after the body was taken away to Burns, and drove to Paisley, then returned to his ranch on Monday where he was arrested as a suspect in the crime because of the bloody items found on his property. The Harney County authorities apparently had not considered Thompson a suspect on Sunday, because they made no attempt to detain him. But, Thompson had an alibi. He had been away from home in Burns buying a new Ford car at the time the killing was believed to have taken place.

While Thompson was away at Paisley Sunday night and Monday morning, someone had been working to turn the tables on him. Someone who lived on the highway and saw him drive off toward Paisley on Sunday afternoon, and reported seeing him leave; someone who planted the evidence at Thompson's ranch; who participated in the first inquest and investigation, such as it was, but who neglected to tell the Burns men that they were in the wrong county; someone who came around to help the Lake County investigators on Monday and knew where to look for the footprints; who enjoyed cavorting under the noses of both sets of officials as he played the role of a concerned and helpful neighbor. That someone was Ray B. Jackson.

Just like in the murder of the younger Bradley, a Lake County paper reported that Jackson became involved immediately in the incident, allegedly because those who found the body had sought him out, asking for help.

> *"Due to a delay in wire services, word of the tragedy did not reach local officers until 10:30 Monday morning, though the message was filed at Burns shortly after 7 o'clock*

Saturday evening, by R. Jackson to whom young Bradley and Pennington had imparted the news. Jackson, who was formerly county school superintendent of Lake county, endeavored to notify officials at once and in so doing Harney county officers gained knowledge of the affair and rushed to the scene.... The Harney county officers held an inquest and departed for Burns with the body. This action was taken after they had been told by Jackson that the cabin at which the crime took place was located in Lake county."

As in the earlier Bradley murder, Jackson's name was featured so prominently and favorably for the part he played in the investigation, that there can be little doubt that he himself communicated directly with the newspaper. As for the claim, which must have come from Jackson, that the Harney County men had ignored his warning and deliberately acted outside of their jurisdiction without so much as a phone call to Lakeview, it can only be said that no district attorney or coroner who sought reelection would be so careless when handling a capital crime.

Jackson realized that for an ordinary rancher like Harry Thompson to have killed his friend and neighbor, an all-around good guy like Ira Bradley, there had to have been a motive. And so the story was invented. "As a motive for the murder it is reported Thompson accused Bradley of having stolen some liquor from his ranch home," reported the Burns paper of May 9.

The Bradley and Thompson families went way back. The Thompson homestead of 320 acres adjoined the Bradley claim at Bradley Meadows to the north, and the two houses were about a mile apart. Ira Bradley started spending a lot of time around Wagontire in 1915 when both he and Thompson were buckaroos for Bill Brown. Bradley's wife Ada and their children would come up to the mountain during the summers, and their daughter Grace was born there in the Thompson house in 1917. Apparently, the Bradley family lived with the Thompsons at least part-time from 1917 through 1919. The cabin where Ira's body was found was a small wood frame structure with a wood floor that had been built by Harold near Bradley Spring. The Thompson's received the patent on their homestead in 1923. Their ranch was located just off of the main road between Stauffer and Wagontire, and Harold Bradley would have passed the Thompson house coming and going from his mail route in 1925.

Harry Thompson was known around the community as a maker of bootleg whiskey and beer, and the Bradleys' acquaintance with him roughly coincided with the years of prohibition, from 1919 to 1933, when the sale, manufacture, and transportation of alcohol for consumption was illegal. "Ray Houston, who knew the Thompsons well, told me that when he was buckarooing for Brown in 1926, Brown's horses had broken away and he set out to find them," wrote Gray about a 1992 interview. "Between Bill's Lost Creek corrals and Bradley meadows he came upon an open area where his horse dug in. There was a still going with a hot fire." Another man who knew the Bradley's believed that Ira had been involved in the bootlegging operation, and that his son Hosmer and a young friend had raided the whiskey stash.

> *"Old man Thompson and Bigfoot (Thompson's son Orrin) was making whiskey with Ira Bradley, and they had made a 50-gallon barrel for each one of them.... And they made it over against the hill from the Bradley place. Up on the mountain there was a spring come out and that's where they made it. And they took their 50-gallon barrel, each one of them, and buried them in the hillside there, and put brush all over them, and was going to just, go and get them as they needed them. And it was well understood that each one of them owned a 50-gallon barrel of whiskey. Well, Hom (Hosmer) Bradley and... I did know who was with him.... they saw them hide the whiskey, so they went and stole the whiskey, the whole thing.... Anyway they stole the whiskey and took it way off someplace else and buried it, and when Thompson went up there to get his whiskey and it was gone, he thought Ira Bradley had done it, so he went down there and killed him."*
>
> *- Jess Gibson*

It should be noted here that when Jess Gibson told the above story, he said that Ray B. Jackson "and my dad was pretty good friends." Gibson's father, William S. Gibson, lived near Wagontire Mountain from at least 1910, the same year that Jess was born, through 1927 when he patented his homestead there. Jess Gibson was about 20 years old when Ira Bradley was killed, and the story that he told about the two boys stealing whiskey and Thompson killing Bradley could have come from Ray B. Jackson himself. Harry Thompson must have been able to prove his alibi, because he was never tried for the murder of Ira Bradley. Jackson seemed to continue to blame Thompson for the crime long after Thompson's name had been cleared.

Despite his long and friendly association with bootleggers, Bradley's daughters, as they recorded the family history, swore that Ira Bradley had never drank whiskey in his life. None of the inquest records from either the Lake County or Harney County investigations into the death of Ira Bradley have survived. Paul Wilson, who was 35 years old when Bradley was killed, and had also been a buckaroo for Bill Brown, said in a 1991 interview, "I... they tried, burned his feet and everything trying to make him tell where he had his money buried. He was a moonshiner."

Vera Addington Wagner, whose parents operated the Wagontire post office, stated that she believed their mail carrier, Harold Bradley, had been involved in the alcohol trade. Although her oral history recollection of the Bradleys is full of factual errors, there may have been a kernel of truth in the way she associated Harold Bradley with illegal alcohol. "He never drank until he started drinking Woodard's rot gut whiskey, and that's what drove him crazy," said Wagner, who thought that another neighbor, Link Woodard had kept a still at Bunyard Spring. The name of the spring may have been a typographical error, because there is a "Boneyard Spring" about one half mile north of the Hutton ranch house where Harold Bradley was killed. "He was a moonshiner, and they got Harold started in drinking that rot gut stuff," said Wagner. During prohibition, mail carriers were often enlisted to deliver illegal whiskey along their routes, and thus could claim a share of the profits. Perhaps Harold Bradley was trying to make a little money on the side to buy his homestead from the government?

To what extent the Bradley's were involved in the moonshine trade is not known, but they were, at the very least, closely connected to a maker of bootleg whiskey. And that association with Harry Thompson and his stolen stash of liquor, as reported in the Burns paper at the time of Ira's murder, could have been the very thing that caused the black cat to cross Bradley's path. Whoever the killer was, he had to be a local person who was familiar with the Thompsons and Bradley, too. Jackson had already been imprisoned at least once for theft by physical force. In Jackson's homestead application, he stated that he returned to Wagontire for the season on May 1. He went to Bradley's little cabin that night, where he was let in as a trusted neighbor, proceeded to torture Bradley until he told what he knew about Thompson's operation, and then clubbed Bradley to death.

Like most sociopathic killers, Jackson's disordered personality gave him a distorted sense of self and poor impulse control. He would probably have been prone to abuse alcohol himself, and when he started clubbing Bradley, he didn't know when to stop. He probably wanted the whiskey partly for his own consumption, but primarily was after the money. The money that he could make by selling it, and any bootleg money that Thompson had hidden.

Sunday, around 10 A.M., when Jackson realized that Thompson was out of the way, he planted the bloody club, overalls, and shoes at the Thompson ranch, and called the Lake County authorities to the scene of the crime. He participated in the first inquest and both investigations, and communicated with the newspapers. That compulsive need to come back to the murder site and remember those moments has been referred to by experts as "rolling in it." It allowed Jackson to relive the torture and murder, that seemingly sacred time when Ira Bradley was so pathetically helpless, and he, Ray B. Jackson, was all-powerful, and blissfully, temporarily, relieved of his own relentless self-contempt.

A second inquest was held over the body of Ira Bradley at Silver Lake before he was buried next to his son, Harold, at the Silver Lake cemetery. Both were neighbors of Ray B. Jackson and considered him a friend; both were from Silver Lake; both were small men and considered very kind and mild-mannered; both lived in the same cabin; both had injuries to the head; Jackson attempted to frame someone else in both murders; Jackson involved himself in both investigations, and 'played cop' as it were; Jackson painted himself as a hero who said he came to the rescue when he was summoned to the scene of both crimes; and bootleg whiskey was referred to in connection with both of the Bradley murders.

SOURCES:

"H.H. Thompson Suspected in Ranch Murder," Burns Times-Herald, May 9, 1930.

"Well Known Man Apparently Victim of Cold Blooded Murder," *Lake County Examiner*, May 8, 1930

"William 'Bill' W. Brown 1855-1941, Legend of Oregon's High Desert," by Edward Gray, 1993, Your Town Press, Salem, Oregon, p 160-162, 168-171, 175-177, 180-184, 189, 190-194, 197-201, 217. One of Gray's sources was the Bradley Family History, a genealogical document available at the Burns Public Library's Claire McGill Luce Western History Room.

Harney County History Project, oral history interview #53-A, Jack and Doris Kittredge, June 22, 1992, p 16.

Harney County History Project, oral history interview #58-A, Paul Wilson, April 20, 1991, p 13.

Harney County History Project, oral history interview #380, Jess Gibson and Leora Eggers, June 19, 1991, p 1-27. Gibson speculated that the friend of Hosmer Bradley was either Jesse Pennington or Spike Pointer.

"The Psychopathology of Serial Murder," by Stephen J. Giannangelo, 1996, Praeger, Westport, Connecticut, p 27, 308, 302.

Stock raising homestead patent application file of Ray B. Jackson, serial #1066515, Bureau of Land Management, records of the General Land Office, National Archives and Records Administration, Washington, D.C. In one of his sworn statements, Jackson said that he returned to his Wagontire homestead on May 1, 1930 in order to meet the residency requirement. The date may be approximate.

This pearl handled .45 caliber single action Colt revolver was manufactured in 1893. Colt sold over 50,000 of these guns in the .38 caliber version. Ray Van Buren Jackson's gun was either a .38 or a .45.

Advertising artwork for Davis' Pain Killer, the brand of Laudanum that Conn carried in his store. An intact bottle of this patent medicine was found on the body.

Chapter Fourteen

Deduction

Throughout the course of this book it has been shown that many of the facts of the Conn murder case have survived in printed sources for over a hundred years. This chapter will review the pertinent facts of the case, and describe conclusions arrived at through deduction, with Ray Van Buren Jackson as the prime suspect, and his motivations for having chosen Conn as his victim.

Beginning from a time several weeks prior to Conn's disappearance, we learn that he became ill and went to see a doctor who prescribed laudanum, a widely used and addictive medicine made of opiates and ethyl alcohol. "In the vest pocket was found a bottle of laudanum which had never been opened. The merchant carried this in stock in his store, and a physician said he had prescribed it for Mr. Conn's use in the treatment of some bodily ailment."

> *"The bottle had never been opened. It was this laudanum that influenced the jury most strongly for a verdict of suicide. But it is believed that Conn himself had taken this*

laudanum with him, for a physician had prescribed its use to allay hemorrhages with which he was troubled."

When the contents of Creed Conn's store were inventoried for probate, there were 10 bottles of Davis' Pain Killer on his shelves, a type of laudanum and nationally advertised patent medicine. The jury was interested in that little 4-ounce bottle because of a strong social stigma existing at the time against people who used laudanum. It had been the drug of choice in many suicides, and because of its addictive properties, person's who used it habitually were often viewed as crazy, suicidal, or both. But laudanum was effective for suppressing excessive bleeding, and was widely prescribed for tuberculosis. It also relieved pain and helped the sufferer to sleep. To this day, it is still sometimes used to control diarrhea.

On April 21, Conn's body was found frozen, yet remarkably well-preserved and clean, with the hands positioned up over the head, as if Conn was "in repose" or asleep. Those facts, combined with the care taken by the killer not to reveal the hiding place, indicate that the body had been stored somewhere cold and dry, with a temperature just above the freezing point, where it was kept clean, probably wrapped in something such as a tarp. Most of the houses in the town, especially those built before 1900 in the days before electric refrigeration, were equipped with root cellars. The cellar was ordinarily built on the north side of the house, away from the sun, in an area where snow would accumulate and create a 'cold battery,' generating cold that would penetrate the ground and keep food items near the freezing point for several months. Just such an early style house was the former dwelling of Frank West, who was the brother of Henry F. West, the man responsible for platting the town of Silver Lake, in township 28 south range 14 east, in 1888.

Frank West's sturdy home was located in the southeast quarter of section 22 at the same spot shown on early maps as the location of the Silver Lake school house. A large gray stone school was later built just to the west of the original school. West received a homestead patent for the whole west half of the southeast quarter of section 22 in 1889.

The distances traveled by those who appeared at the coroner's inquest point strongly to the school house as the location for those proceedings, and it was probably the only public building that was vacant and available for such use on a Sunday in the month of April. It was also revealed by dates on the coroner's documents that the body was held at the location of the inquest overnight, and then hauled to the cemetery on Monday by Warren Duncan and buried. This, too, points strongly to the existence of a root cellar at the school house, and the building had probably been used for inquests and the storage of bodies on prior occasions. From these facts it could be inferred that the body had been stored in the root cellar of the former West home, and that any tracks leading to its location would naturally point to one man, the school teacher.

It will be remembered that one of Creed Conn's horses died of poisoning only four days prior to his disappearance. But there was another, now long-forgotten, poisoning death that occurred in the small town of Silver Lake during the time that Conn was missing. A young girl who was a student at the Silver Lake school at the time of Conn's disappearance can be seen through the haze of time as she stands pointing to that very school building. Her name was Ethel Martin. Her father, James M. Martin, was a friend of Creed Conn's and both men were very active in the town's branch of the Republican Party. She was also the niece of Martha Lane, and the sister of the wife of Frank Payne, who it has been shown both had close relationships of trust with Conn. The 1900 census reveals that Ethel Martin and her family lived only two doors away from the school house. Her real name was Zelma Ethel Martin, and she died on April 1, 1904 at the age of 11, although the county paper reported her age incorrectly.

Death of Ethel Martin

Word reached here last Saturday morning of the death, at Silver Lake, of Miss Ethel Martin, daughter of ex-commissioner J.M. Martin. Miss Martin was 14 years old. She was attending school, and had returned home from school on Friday evening. There was no one at the house at the time, and shortly afterward her father heard her scream, and went to the house, where he found her in convulsions, apparently from poison. Mr. Martin asked her some questions but could get no satisfactory answer from the sufferer, but found strychnine near by. She had taken the poison, but nothing could be learned here to justify an intent to commit suicide. The above is as near a true statement of the case could be learned. It is the belief that her death was the result of accidental poisoning.

The tragic death of little Ethel Martin reveals some important things. She arrived home from school in the *evening*, later than usual, so she probably remained at the school for some time after all of the other children had gone home for the day, and was also probably alone with the teacher. Suicide is unlikely and uncommon in little girls, and the article tells us that "nothing could be learned here to justify an intent to commit suicide," and that the death was ruled an accident, revealing that the people present did not believe it was a suicide either. Moreover, it shows the feelings of incredulity felt by the friends and family over the tragedy. They concluded that the girl's death had to have been an accident. Surely, no one would murder such a sweet and delightful child. No one but a sadist. A man with a predilection for imposing his cruel will on the children left in his charge. Who whipped them viscously, hurled heavy objects at them, beat them, and threatened them with a loaded pistol. No one but Professor Jackson.

It was concluded that Ethel Martin had accidentally ingested strychnine, but did that conclusion hold water? Strychnine is one of the most bitter substances known, and its taste is detectable in concentrations as low as one part per million. Any normally adjusted little girl, finding a horrendously bitter substance in her mouth, would have automatically gagged or spit it out. And, although the symptoms of convulsions and an inability to speak do match strychnine poisoning, the timing of Martin's death does not. Those who ingest strychnine do not die for two to three hours, yet Ethel Martin, or so we are told, arrived home, took the poison, and died shortly afterward. It was more likely that the girl died from another type of poison, one that was tasteless, yet produced similar symptoms and killed more quickly, like arsenic.

Arsenic was readily available as arsenious oxide in 1904, commonly sold as rat poison and insecticide, and well known for its effectiveness. Because of her sudden death, Ethel consumed a relatively large amount of arsenic by eating or drinking it, and died approximately 30 minutes later. Thirty minutes prior to her death, Ethel Martin had been at the school house. Since her death was ruled an accident, there was no autopsy or test performed to determine the exact type of poison she was exposed to.

When we ask ourselves if the poisoning of Ethel Martin could have been connected to the disappearance of Creed Conn, we must consider the dates of both events. Since the poisoning occurred almost a month after the disappearance, it seems unlikely that the girl witnessed anything on March 4 that was of concern to the killer. Moreover, she was not named as a witness for the coroner's inquest. Ethel Martin was probably poisoned at the school house, which was also probably the hiding place for the body, therefore she was probably deliberately poisoned, and her poisoning had something to do with the body itself. It could be postulated that in her extracurricular activities at the school house, Ethel happened upon the body, and Jackson moved swiftly to silence her with something that he had on hand.

Arsenious oxide, or white arsenic, was considered an almost perfect homicidal poison. Not only was it tasteless and colorless, it was fatal in a small quantity. Its symptoms, when administered in non-lethal doses, would mimic common gastroenteritis. If the killer was cunning and exerted enough control and influence over circumstances, the death could be made to seem like an accident or the result of natural causes. So long as foul play was not suspected, the authorities would not order an autopsy or test for arsenic. Around 1900 the symptoms of persons who had survived a non-lethal dose of arsenic were often misdiagnosed as cholera, a bacterial infection that caused the same abdominal pains, vomiting, and bloody diarrhea as arsenic.

Ray Jackson probably lived at the school house because teachers in 1904 Oregon were notoriously undercompensated, and because his predecessor had lived there. But, being a bachelor, he probably took his meals at one of the hotels, and had breakfast with Creed Conn at the Silver Lake Hotel on at least one occasion, that being the morning of the disappearance. It would have been relatively easy for Jackson to have slipped some of the white powder into Conn's breakfast several weeks before, about the first week in February when Conn concluded that his bank account had been tampered with. Conn had probably seen doctor Witham at Paisley for his gastroenteritis on his trip south in the first weekend in February. But Jackson miscalculated the amount of arsenic needed to kill someone like Conn, and his intended victim survived. If anyone suspected that Conn had been poisoned, they would have realized that the poisoning occurred at approximately the same time as the sheep kill at Reid Rock.

Jackson knew Creed Conn pretty well, and developed a typical 'parasitic' attachment to the merchant when he arrived in Silver Lake in June of 1902. Jackson had a real love of firearms and took a keen interest in the antiquated six-shooter that Conn kept in his desk drawer. He also knew Conn's morning routine, and that he liked to pick up his mail after breakfast and before going to his store.

In both of the Bradley murder cases, it was shown that Jackson could not resist the opportunity to involve himself in the investigation of his crimes and to communicate with the newspapers. In the case of the murder of John Creed Conn, Jackson exhibited the same signature behavior. He was listed among the prime witnesses who gave testimony to the coroner's jury, along with clerk Frank Payne; the almost-eye witness Mrs. Mosby; doctors Hall and Witham; and the two 'ear witnesses,' George Parker and Royal E. Ward. His statements as the last person who had an extended conversation with Conn before the disappearance, and his reptilian coolness, gave Jackson the ability to sway the jury toward any conclusion that he desired.

Not a one to miss the chance to see his own name in print, Jackson apparently offered his services as the primary source for the very first article written about the disappearance, which came off the presses of the *Central Oregonian* at Silver Lake. Judging from the actual writing style, the author has surmised that Jackson was interviewed by Samuel M. 'Mart' Bailey.

There were several lines of that article that point very strongly to Jackson's influence. *"No one noticed anything strange in Mr. Conn's manner as he seemed to be in his right mind up to the time he disappeared,"* was eerily similar to the phrase given by Jackson in the Harold Bradley murder when he described the chummy behavior of the recently estranged Huttons as, *"No quarrel or dispute of any kind, nor any harsh words between any of them and all appeared in good humor and jovial."* Both observations were offered up with the same profound inability to relate to human emotion, to understand human nature, that is so typical in sociopaths. Would a man, recently poisoned, made the target of terrorism, and hovering at the point of insolvency, actually show no signs of anxiety whatsoever? Or, how about a man alleged to be on his way to committing suicide? Surely, this was the reasoning of a maladjusted mind.

"Mr. Conn, in company with Prof. R.B. Jackson and one or two others ate breakfast at the Silver Lake Hotel about 7 o'clock. Mr. Conn and the Prof. left the hotel together. Mr. Conn made his way direct to his place of business." Ray Jackson never had been, nor ever would be, a professor of any institution of higher learning. He was a grade school teacher. But, with the characteristic grandiosity of most sociopaths, he managed to work his imaginary title into the article twice. As for the other persons who were present at breakfast, they were apparently not worth naming in the mind of the school teacher, who was so profoundly self-centered and prone to giving himself airs that he placed himself in a category entirely by himself.

"Being natural actors, conscienceless people can make full use of social and professional roles, which constitute excellent ready-made masks that other people are loath to look behind."

Other information apparently provided by Jackson was the statement, *"Mr. Conn was recognized as one of the leading merchants of Lake county and was always found upright and honest in all his dealings."* It was taken from Ray Jackson's own personal 'garden of words' and found elsewhere, in a letter that he wrote in 1929 to the General Land Office about his homestead in Klamath County. *"I had far more building than was required and had shown good faith in all my dealings,"* he wrote using the alias "Roy B. Jackson."

The Silver Lake article, titled "Mysteriously Disappeared," should weigh very heavily in the mind of anyone interested in the solution to the Conn murder, not only because it was strongly influenced by the prime suspect, but also because it was the first article written on the subject to come out of Silver Lake. For those reasons, it has been transcribed exactly and in its entirety.

Mysteriously Disappeared

Prominent Silver Lake Merchant Not Seen Since Friday Morning

J.C. Conn, a prominent merchant and business man of this place, mysteriously disappeared last Friday morning between 7 and 8 o'clock, and up to this time nothing has been heard or seen of the missing man. Searching parties composed of every able bodied man in the valley were organized, horsemen scoured the entire country to the snow line and a thorough search was made in which Silver creek was dredged for over a mile, but in vain.

Some think it was suicide while others talked of foul play. Generally speaking the entire community is thunder struck and a black cloud hangs over the mysterious event. The people of Silver Lake and surrounding country will not give up until something is brought to light of the lost one.

No one had noticed anything strange in Mr. Conn's manner as he seemed to be in his right mind up to the time he disappeared. Mr. Conn in company with Prof. R.B. Jackson and one or two others ate breakfast at the

Silver Lake Hotel about 7 o'clock. Mr. Conn and the Prof. left the hotel together, Mr. Jackson went to the school house while Mr. Conn made his way direct to his place of business. Frank Payne, who is clerking for Mr. Conn was sweeping, when Conn walked in and asked the clerk if he had been to breakfast. Frank informed him that he had, he then asked if the Prineville mail had arrived being told that it had he turned and walked out.

T.J. Roberts who is clerking for F.M. Chrisman, was in the postoffice at this time and says he is confident that Mr. Conn called for his mail. He was seen a short time after he left the post office by Mrs. R.H. Mosby and her two small boys as he was walking up the Prineville road about one-half mile west of town. Mrs. Mosby says after he passed the house a short distance he stopped and looked back toward town then went on up the road. A very short time after he had vanished from Mrs. Mosby's sight, R.E. Ward who resides about three-quarters of a mile west of town heard a pistol shot somewhere near the Silver Lake bridge, thinking it was some of the boys that were hunting, he thought nothing strange and gave it no further attention until Saturday noon, when Mr. Payne began to grow uneasy as to the whereabouts of his employer as he had left early Friday morning without leaving any word with him and had gone without his overcoat or overshoes. After investigating it was found that he had not occupied his room or had not been seen by any one since Friday. Mr. Payne suspecting something was wrong went to the drawer where Mr. Conn kept two revolvers. He discovered that one was gone and the one missing had not been in use for a year or more. Payne immediately informed the citizens of the full details of the strange affair, and a searching party was organized at once composing of at least 50 men. Mrs. Mosby and R.E. Ward were interviewed, in which it was found that the lady had seen Mr. Conn pass up the road about 8:15 o'clock. A short time after Mr. Ward hearing the report of a shot near the Silver creek bridge and upon inquiry in the matter it was found that no one in the vicinity had fired a shot of any kind in that vicinity at any time during that day. This is strong evidence of either suicide or foul play, which leads the citizens of the valley to believe that the body of the missing man lies in the bottom of Silver creek and the distance will not exceed one mile from this place.

On account of high water it is impossible to make any further search in the creek at present, but just as soon as the creek falls it will be dredged thoroughly for the body and no doubt it will bring about some development in the case.

John C. Conn was born in Douglas county, Oregon in 1860, being 44 years of age. He came to Lake county in 1886 and clerked for his brother Virgil in a general merchandise at Paisley until 1892 when he came to Silver Lake and started in the merchantile business, of which he conducted until late Friday morning. Mr. Conn was recognized as one of the leading merchants of Lake county and was always found upright and honest in all his dealings.

He was a man that was very conservative, although he had many warm friends. He took very little interest in anything outside his own business.

Mr. Conn was a member of the Paisley Lodge A.F.&A.M. He has three brothers in Lake county who survive him. Virgil and George who are prominent merchants of Paisley, and L.F. of Lakeview, present prosecuting attorney for this district.

--Silver Lake Oregonian.

Notice that Conn was considerate enough to offer young Frank Payne the chance to go eat breakfast, and that would seem to indicate that Conn was just 'popping in,' and only planned to be gone for a very short time to the post office. When Conn left the store, his only intention was to go get the mail. If he was on his way to meet someone, he would not have offered to let the clerk off for a breakfast break, but would have said something very different to Payne, such as, "Can you mind the store? I'm going to be out for a while."

That short exchange between Conn and Payne indicates that Conn received word to meet someone with his mail. Furthermore, if Conn was already planning to be out for a while, he probably would have grabbed his overcoat and overshoes instead of leaving them at the hotel. Lafe Conn himself seemed to believe that there had been something of interest in Creed's mail, because after the disappearance he and brothers George and Virgil spent several days inside the store studying all of Creed's private letters and business correspondence looking for "evidence of why he so strangely left."

Conn's stopping to look back toward town shows that the person whom he was to meet was expected to come from that direction, and the statement that Ray Jackson next went to the school house was obviously made by Jackson himself. The accuracy of Mary Mosby's eyesight, at age 37, was previously called into question, but the eyesight of her sons was not. David E. Mosby, age 13, who was with her at the time, probably had excellent vision.

Very little was ever written about Creed Conn during his lifetime and during the days following his disappearance, but from what was written about him, we can surmise what sort of person he was. By all accounts, Creed Conn was a good man. He extended credit to his customers, beyond the amount that made sound business sense. He was considerate of others, even to the young clerk Frank Payne. He loved animals, particularly horses and mules, and was obviously despondent over the loss of one to poisoning. He loved the outdoors and hunting. He had a social conscience, and worked within his political party to make a difference in his community. He was a reserved man, rather reticent and conservative. The photograph that was taken of him shortly before he died leaves the impression of someone who was self-conscious, with just the faintest suggestion of a smile, and an intelligent and quality about the eyes. "His friends are legion," and "he had many warm friends" said the newspapers. At Christmas time he stocked his store with items for children. He was a member of the Baptist church, and supported the church financially, so probably had Christian values.

Early in 1904, the Baptist minister living at Silver Lake was James H. "Jimmy" Howard. On February 11 he performed a marriage ceremony for Lenora Easterly and Morgan L. Troth, who was one of the men who would later stand guard over Conn's body at the Sandy Knoll before the coroner and others arrived at Silver Lake. Conn's clerk, Frank Payne, was one of the witnesses for the happy couple, and given those relationships it seems likely that Conn himself had been present at the wedding.

Reverend Jimmy Howard and family moved to a house in Silver Lake from the Dillard area of Douglas County in 1901, and remained in Silver Lake until the summer of 1905. A family history later recorded some excerpts from letters the reverend wrote to his daughters during his years at Silver Lake, and he described one sermon that he gave on a Sunday evening in April of 1904. The topic was the life of Paul, taken from Acts 20, verses 16 through 38, and he called it, "Three Glimpses at the Life of Paul." He wrote that the congregation filled the house on that night. Creed Conn was missing all through the month of April, his inquest was held on the last Sunday of the month, and the sermon seems to have been written with Creed Conn in mind. The verses selected by Howard (see appendix B) offer some important insights into the hearts and minds of the Silver Lake congregation as well, with reflection upon the type of man that Conn was; their feelings of loss; and what seems to be a reference to the sheep kill at Reid Rock:

> *"Therefore take heed to yourselves and to all the flock, among which the Holy Spirit has made you overseers, to shepherd the church of God which He purchased with His own blood. For I know this, that after my departure savage wolves will come in among you, not sparing the flock."*

The verses encompassed Paul's emotional departure to attend Pentecost at Jerusalem from Miletus, with no intention of returning, and with the belief that he might be killed. "Chains and tribulations await me. But none of these things move me; nor do I count my life dear to myself," said Paul. After saying goodbye and kneeling down to pray. "Then they all wept freely, and fell on Paul's neck and kissed him, sorrowing most of all for the words which he spoke, that they would see his face no more. And they accompanied him to the ship." The comparison to Silver Lake's loss of a good friend can easily be drawn here, along with the general belief among the people of that town that Conn did not commit suicide, but was murdered.

Perhaps that particular chapter of Acts was also selected because it told something of Paul and his character, comparing him to Creed Conn. Paul who served the Lord with all humility, who kept back nothing that was helpful, and coveted no one's silver or gold or apparel. "Yes, you yourselves know that these hands have provided for my necessities, and for those who were with me. I have shown you in every way, by laboring like this, that you must support the weak," said Paul. "And remember the words of the Lord Jesus, that He said, 'It is more blessed to give than to receive.'"

In the chapters describing the murders of Harold and Ira Bradley, it was learned that they both were considered exceptionally kind men, both caring and helpful. And, although very little is known about the character of the other Silver Lake victim, Julius Wallende, he was really only just a boy when he died. An innocent. Creed Conn's goodness was probably his final undoing. It was used by the killer to lure him to a secondary location in a fringe area where he would become easy prey. Conn's kindness and consideration for others overruled any suspicions that he many have had. When Creed Conn got the letter, he took off from town without even stopping to grab his coat. His sense of obligation rooted in his attachment to other people, his conscience, carried him along, just as Ray Jackson knew it would.

"We have an extremely hard time seeing that a person has no conscience, but a person who has no conscience can instantly recognize someone who is decent and trusting," wrote Stout. "When a sociopath identifies someone as a good game piece, she studies that person. She makes it her business to know how that person can be manipulated and used, and, to this end, just how her chosen pawn can be flattered and charmed."

The letter that Conn received that morning probably contained an appeal of some kind. It appealed to Conn's sympathy. Jackson, who disguised his handwriting, had no regard for the social contract, but he knew how to use the social contract to his own advantage. He knew that he would be granted special dispensation by Conn by presenting a pathetic image in that letter. "Good people will let pathetic individuals get by with murder, so to speak, and therefore any sociopath wishing to continue with his game, whatever it happens to be, should play repeatedly for none other than pity," wrote Stout, describing the sociopath's typical fondness for sympathy. It was the most reliable trick to get Conn to the bridge quickly, alone and unarmed. Any other approach, such as a challenge, would have put him on guard and made him wary.

The book, "Profilers," by John H. Campbell and Don DeNevi, described the effectiveness of the sympathy method used by serial killers. "The organized offender often uses a ruse or con to gain control over his victim. This is a man who has good verbal skills and a high degree of intelligence, enough to lure the victim into a vulnerable area. Control is of the essence for the organized offender, and law enforcement personnel learn to look for control as an element in every facet of the crime." The book also described how Ted Bundy commonly "feigned injuries or the need for help to disarm his victims."

The information that Conn was seen going toward the bridge, but had no intention of doing so when he 'popped in' on clerk Payne at the store, was corroborated by Conn's district attorney brother when he applied to the county for permission to administer the estate. "Without giving any notice of his purpose or intention of absenting himself, and was seen shortly thereafter walking along the County road leading westerly from said town of Silver Lake to where the same crosses Silver Creek; that shortly after he was seen traveling along said road, affiant is informed, and therefore alleges it to be a fact."

A bit more detail about the final moments before the disappearance came from an article in the *Plaindealer* on March 14. "As he neared the approach of the bridge he was seen to stoop down as though he was tying a shoe string or rolling up the bottom of his pants and was seen to turn around as if to return but a few minutes afterwards he was seen on the top of the bridge and that was the last seen of him."

The letter Conn received in his mail, the pitiful letter that made him respond with sympathy, led him to the bridge to meet someone. And, as he approached the bridge he did not see anyone standing on top of it, so he looked back toward town to see if the person was coming behind him. Then he crouched down to try to make out the person who he thought he saw standing *underneath* the bridge in the shadows. Also, if Conn was really spotted on top of the bridge, that would have to mean that he crossed it, and probably went down the opposite bank to meet the person that he had seen in the shadows.

The creek had to be the place where Conn was killed, and that was one thing that the searchers did get right. The stream had been the primary focus of the search. The bridge was a fringe area, and the ideal place for a homicide because it was out of sight of everyone. The shooting could have only been seen by someone who was standing in the stream bed, and Jackson knew that when he selected that meeting spot in advance. When Conn left the restaurant on the first floor of the hotel, Jackson went out right behind him, but abruptly turned left and walked, undetected, up the stream bed, a distance of about three quarters of a mile, to the meeting spot and arriving there well before Creed Conn did.

Mrs. Mosby claimed to have seen Conn approaching the bridge around 8:15, but Lafe Conn noted that Creed "disappeared from his place of business between the said hours of 7 and 8 o'clock." The merchant had breakfast at 7 o'clock, or probably started his meal at that time, and could have easily finished eating, checked-in with Payne, picked up his mail, and made it to the bridge by 7:45. That kind of timing would have made it possible for Jackson to shoot Conn, stash the body, return to the hotel via the stream bed, and get to the school around 8 A.M. to start the day.

Traces of Jackson's cunning were found in Bennett's May 10 "Reign of Terror" article, like fingerprints that he left in the ink of that issue of the *Oregonian*. From the context of that article, it appears that Bennett had visited Lakeview and read the inquest testimony. The following excerpt from "Reign of Terror" seems have been drawn from the testimony of Ray Jackson:

> *"It was said the horse was poisoned and Conn was afraid the others might suffer the same fate. He had the horses in a pasture three miles from town and it was his practice each morning to walk out to look after them.*

> *Friday morning, March 4, about 8 o'clock after getting his mail and eating breakfast in company with Prof. Jackson, who noticed nothing unusual in his demeanor, he left Silver Lake to go to the horses as was his custom."*

> *Right after him went the stage and if Conn had taken the road where his body was found seven weeks later the driver would have observed him. Another team at that same time passed over the road and the ill-fated man was not seen."*

Here Jackson again exhibited interpersonal ineptitude. He claimed that Conn had taken off on a walk of several miles with no coat or overshoes in 25 degree weather to do something completely unnecessary, and at a time when he was needed at his store. It was unnecessary because his team was now boarding at the ranch of his friend, James R. Horning, where they were looked after and cared for. None of the local accounts describing the day of the disappearance mentioned anything about Conn going to check on his team, and none said that he did so on a daily basis. Conn owned a fine saddle horse, and a team and buggy, so it seems unlikely that he would have set off on foot.

Note that Jackson was mentioned in the same sentence describing Conn's activities that morning, and that the trip to the post office and breakfast were transposed in time. Jackson said that Conn went to the post office first, next ate breakfast, and then walked out of town, and did not even mention that he stopped in at the store to check on Frank Payne. Jackson was trying to hide the fact that Conn left town suddenly after getting his mail, and also lied about the team to make it look like Conn had some reason other than the meeting at the bridge for walking off the way he had.

Those lies during the inquest show that Jackson was suspected, as naturally anyone would be who was around the victim immediately before he disappeared. Because it was brought out during the inquest that no one saw Conn on the road beyond the bridge, we know that at least one of Jackson's lies was uncovered. And, during the week after the disappearance, when Mart Bailey wrote that first detailed account of the events of that morning, he revealed that Conn had not dressed for the weather, casting further doubt on the idea that he had gone to check on his team.

Since Bailey's article was published at Silver Lake less than a week after the disappearance, it seems likely that Jackson lied about where Conn was going from the very beginning. He wanted to create the impression that Conn was killed far beyond the edge of town to throw off the investigators. That intention can also be seen in the way that the search was turned to Buck Creek, two miles northwest of town, in early April.

Jackson's resentment of Conn had been growing since he was forced to relinquish his timber claim in January. It sprang from his jealousy of the man who seemed to have everything. And when his attempts to ruin Conn by poisoning his team and burning his wagons, and to kill the merchant with arsenic failed, Jackson's hatred grew. When Conn hinted that he suspected Jackson was behind all of those acts, and had also tampered with his bank account, Jackson resolved to end Conn's life.

One of the signature aspects of the Conn murder was the severe damage done to his face. That was something that was done to the victim beyond what was needed to end his life. His features were described as "obliterated" and also "maimed and mangled" to such a degree that Conn's pocket watch had to be used to identify the body. The trauma to the face was not believed by the doctors to have contributed to Conn's death, so it was probably done well after he was dead. Conn had a peculiar hole in his right temple (see appendix B) that was not a gunshot wound, so a different weapon was used on the face.

The trauma to Conn's face was not done to hide his identity because Jackson left personal items in his pockets such as papers with his name on them and the pocket watch, but destruction of the man's face divested him of his identity, of who he was. According to the book, "Profilers," at times "the depersonalization of the victim by the attacker manifests itself in an attempt to obliterate the victim's face or in mutilation after death." How those facial injuries were explained by the jury is not known, although they could have blamed them on animals, as they worked under the assumption that the body had been out in the open for seven weeks.

Jackson, using the keys that he found on the body, had stolen Conn's gun from the store on the night of March 4 before the search for the body had been initiated. He had been planning the murder carefully for weeks, obsessively going over every little detail time and time again. He wanted to incriminate the ZX cowboys and make it appear that the murder had happened on their property. And his tactic did succeed in throwing the investigators off the track for a time, because physical evidence weighed very heavily in such matters.

Conn's body was placed on the Sandy Knoll on a snowy night. And, that snowfall is as significant to the reader now as it was to the killer then, because there had been only traces of precipitation in the little town of Silver Lake since Creed Conn had disappeared seven weeks prior. The killer clearly waited for and counted upon a weather system to arrive in order to hide his tracks, and from that it can be deduced that the killer lived very near or in town, and realized that his tracks would give away the location where he had stored the body, and thus his identity as well. He waited for the right opportunity, and delivered the body to the Sandy Knoll later in the night, after the temperature had dropped and the snow had stopped falling, for Conn's clothing and the contents of his pockets were not dampened.

> *"Evidence of symbolism within the spatial or temporal organization of the crime scene could provide clues regarding the identity of the killer."*

> *-Dirk C. Gibson in "Clues From Killers"*

That behavior was highly controlled, and revealed a great deal about the nature and thinking of Jackson. He had a strong desire, a compulsion to control every aspect of the crime scene, was very organized, and willing to take a tremendous risk in selecting someone like Creed Conn. Forget that he was in possession of pure dynamite, the dead body of the biggest man in town; the brother of a district attorney; the man everyone was looking for. It was more important to him to remain in control of the situation. The knoll itself was selected because it was a good place to make a graphic display of the body and because it was on ZX land. Throughout his crimes against Conn, the arson, poisoning of his team, and murder, and after the murders of both of the Bradleys and

Julius Wallende too, Jackson had always tried to pin the crimes on someone else. And, since March 4 he had been working to place the blame for Conn's disappearance on the cowboys of the ZX Ranch.

More can be gleaned from what was found at the Sandy Knoll than the fact that the body was kept in a cool, dry place, which allowed for some flexibility after the period of rigor mortis had passed. Jackson made an effort to make Conn appear to be asleep, probably as a mocking reference to Conn's 1899 comments about the death of James O'Farrell. Since Jackson did not live in Lake County in 1899, he must have read what Conn told the newspaper, that he had seen O'Farrell alive. That was when the wide-awake merchant unwittingly trespassed into the killer's private life.

O'Farrell was alleged by Creed Conn to have been *seen walking the streets of Silver Lake after he was declared dead by suicide.* Conn was declared dead by suicide in an article strongly influenced by Ray Jackson *after he had been seen alive on the streets of Silver Lake.* The murder versus suicide debate was a strong theme in the death of James O'Farrell, and that same theme was recreated in the murder of John Creed Conn by the confusing combination of murder and suicide clues that were deliberately left. It seems likely then, given all that was communicated by Jackson at the Sandy Knoll, in the media, and during the inquest, that he was also the killer of James O'Farrell.

The murder weapon is considered an important key to most investigations, but in the Conn murder case, questions about the gun that was used seem to have been left unanswered or swept under the saddle blanket. The facts of the case are that Conn's own antique 38-caliber six-shooter was found by his left side, although Conn was right-handed. Two rounds had been fired from the gun, and the empty shells were still in it. One shell was underneath the hammer. There were two entrance wounds in the chest, and one exit wound in the back. A .38 caliber bullet had penetrated the ground underneath the body, and seems to have lined up perfectly with the exit wound. The doctors who examined the body said that the body had not moved since that second shot was fired.

Ballistic fingerprinting was in its infancy in 1904, and had only been used for the first time in court in 1902 to prove that a specific gun was a murder weapon. The science of ballistics matching would not hit its stride until 1925 when Calvin Goddard published his groundbreaking article, "Forensic Ballistics" describing the use of the comparison microscope invented by Charles Waite. If a comparison was ever made between the slug found in the ground, the one found inside Conn's body when it was exhumed in 1910, and Creed Conn's antique six-shooter, it was never written about.

There are several references to Ray Jackson having owned and carried a pearl-handled "six-shooter." His gun was not referred to as a "revolver" or a "pistol" by the people who knew Jackson, but as a "six-shooter," which was the name most commonly attached to older sidearms. All of the articles that mention Conn's gun found on the Sandy Knoll referred to it also as a "six-shooter."

The fatal first shot probably came from Ray Jackson's own gun. There was no mention of a break-in or a robbery at Conn's store before the disappearance. It seems likely that the newspapers would have reported such a crime if it had occurred because they reported the arson on Conn's wagons and the poisoning of his freight team. Therefore, Jackson would not have had access to Conn's antique gun until after the murder, when he took the keys to the store in the merchant's pocket. Also, working from the premise that Jackson had already tried to kill Conn once, by poisoning, and failed, it seems more likely that he would have wanted to use a weapon that he was familiar with, to take no chance that Conn would survive again.

"When he took charge of that school or something, he had boots on and a big hat. He had a pearl-handled six-shooter that was under his pillow one night when I come by there after--Link had killed that boy, he had them all scared," said Shelby Petersen about Ray Jackson. "Anyway, why he had this six-shooter and he called the roll and had them all stand up. Called the roll, he stood up, and he'd hammer on the desk with his six-shooter."

Ray Shaver recalled a conversation he had with Jackson about his teaching days at Paisley and Silver Lake. "He said he used to take a six-shooter and a baseball bat to school with him," said Shaver.

In his book, "Western Echoes," Earl F. Moore wrote of Jackson, "He walked in nonchalant like and placed a sixshooter on his desk with a challenge to anyone or all who wished to continue the scrap." The book contains a work of poetry by Moore titled, "A Knot-hole Peek at Paisley" with the following verse:

Paisley had a day of diversion
Professor and student fought to a draw
Next morning down the barrel of a Colt Six
We read the warning of a graveyard excursion

Then there was the encounter that occurred between Link Hutton and Ray Jackson during the 1920's when, "Jackson threw back his coat and showed me a revolver," according to Hutton. "I said, 'Jackson, are you carrying that for me? If you are, I'll go get mine.'"

Those accounts about Jackson make it clear that he was in the habit of carrying his six-shooter with him during his teaching days, whereas Creed Conn did not habitually carry a gun. "It is further believed that Conn did not have his revolver with him when he was killed. It was not his practice to carry a gun. He always kept a weapon in his store, but it was not his custom to lug it around with him," wrote Bennett in the *Oregonian*.

Jackson's gun, according to details provided by Moore, Shaver, Peterson, and Hutton, was a Colt pearl-handled six-shooter, and Petersen thought it was a .45. Colt did manufacture Winchester Center fire 38-caliber pistols, beginning at least as early as 1893, and made 50,520 of them. That particular model was available with a pearl handle.

The doctors who examined Conn's body said that they believed both entrance wounds were made by 38-caliber bullets, although some questioned that assumption. "It is to be regretted that at the Coroner's inquest a complete autopsy was not made and the first bullet fired into Conn's body through the heart, located. If it had been found to be a 38-caliber bullet it would simply have indicated that some other 38-caliber gun was used by the assassin. If it had been found to be any other sized bullet it would have settled the matter beyond controversy, but the jury thought such an examination was not necessary," wrote Bennett.

The first and fatal bullet was left inside the body when it was buried at the Silver Lake cemetery the day after the inquest, so there was no physical evidence tying any weapon directly to the murder. In later years, an attempt could have been made to match that slug to either the slug that was found underneath the body to Conn's own gun, or to the gun of a suspect. That bullet may have been what Lafe Conn had in mind when he had the body exhumed and autopsied in late 1910.

Forensics in 1904 was a lot more dodgey, a lot more speculative, and a lot less scientific than it is today. Mistakes were made, and people were wrongfully convicted. It was also a lot more spooky to people who, due to circumstances beyond their control, found human remains on their property. Creed Conn's body had been found on the Sandy Knoll, inside of a fenced pasture belonging to the ZX Ranch, and the alleged arson of his wagons while they were parked inside of a ZX barn was still fresh in the minds of everyone in town. The injuries to the body, the two bullet holes, and the trauma to the head made it appear to be a case of murder to a lot of people, and the lack of visible powder burns around the first fatal shot through the heart should have launched a full-blown murder investigation.

Fred Austin, a ZX employee, had found Conn's body on the Sandy Knoll, and quickly returned to the spot with the foreman of the ZX at Silver Lake, James M. Welch. Both men testified as witnesses at the inquest. William D. West, who seems to have been the foreman of the coroner's jury, had been a vaquero for J.D. Coughlin at his Paisley ranch up until he sold it to the Chewaucan Land and Cattle Company in 1900 and it became the foundation of the ZX Ranch there. George Lovegrove was the secretary of the ZX Ranch, and was also a member of the coroner's jury.

At some point during the inquest the proceedings seem to have broken down, and the inquest stopped being about determining the means and manner of death, and started being about protecting the image of the ZX Ranch and protecting the cowboys who worked there. It was the duty of the jurymen to offer two opinions. The means of death was a statement of what specific injury caused death, and they concluded, "That he came to his death by two wounds inflicted with a 38-calibre revolver." The second opinion was the manner of death, whether from natural causes, suicide, accident, or homicide, and that finding decided whether or not there would be an investigation.

It is the firm belief of the author that officials of the ZX Ranch took a protective stance in the Conn homicide. After all, they were friendly with the Conn brothers, and knew that their own men were innocent. But, the ZX managers were very troubled by what seemed like deliberate attempts to pin the crime on their men. The body had obviously been transported and placed on their property and shot there a second time, yet no guilt for either the previous arson or the murder could be proven against any of their cowboys. Since the victim was the brother of the district attorney, the officials of the ZX Ranch knew that a verdict of murder could mean that one of their men would be convicted and have his neck broken in the penitentiary. Since they were not able to produce a good and convincing suspect who was not a ZX employee, it was in their best interest to avoid a verdict of murder.

Bennett even referred to the jury's approach when he wrote, "The charitable view that the public took of the Coroner's jury that rendered the verdict of suicide in the death of J.C. Conn in Lake County was that the men on the jury had not fully weighed the evidence, that *they were honestly deceived by the efforts to make it appear a case of self-destruction*." And, "From the evidence developed at the inquest the jury could not point to any one man and say, 'You did the deed.' It was just as wrong for them to malign the dead as it would have been to arraign the living.... The only verdict the jury could have rendered consistently was that the deceased came to his death by unknown hands."

The jury first went off track when they stated that "two wounds" were the cause of death, despite the fact that the second shot struck no vital organ. And, if it alone had been fired, Creed Conn would probably have survived. They ignored the fact that the second wound seemed to produce no blood, therefore it was fired some time after Conn was already dead. They ignored the fact that Conn was already dead when the shot that came from his own gun, the shot that went into the ground, produced no blood. Or, did they? It will be remembered here that the bottle of laudanum in Conn's pocket *"influenced the jury most strongly for a verdict of suicide."* Aside from being a common sleep aid and pain reliever, laudanum was commonly prescribed to staunch excessive bleeding of any kind. Even in Creed Conn's case, it had been prescribed for "hemorrhages."

When it was proven that Conn had been prescribed laudanum several weeks before, and so may have been taking it habitually for some time, the laudanum explained the lack of blood from the second bullet hole, at least to the satisfaction of those concerned. There had been a few cases on record where suicide victims had actually shot themselves twice, and in Conn's case, the second bullet hole had powder burns. That was the bullet hole that seemed 'suicidal.' "The testimony of the physicians at the inquest was that the shot through the heart was fired first, but they said they did not know when asked what was the manner of death." In other words, the doctors would not commit to either a verdict of homicide, or suicide.

So, just how did that bottle of laudanum come to be in Creed Conn's vest pocket? It is possible that he could have picked it up at the store when he 'popped in' on Frank Payne, although it was never stated that he had done so. Conn had not been to the store before breakfast, so did not take the bottle with him then. He could not have put the bottle in his pocket in order to deliver it to someone at the stream, because he only decided to go to the stream after he left the store for the last time and picked up his mail.

If Creed Conn himself put that bottle in his pocket, he probably did so at least one day prior to his disappearance, and the jury apparently made the assumption that Conn was still using the laudanum to treat his gastroenteritis symptoms and the associated bleeding. It seems strange that the bottle had never been opened, because when a person carries medicine with them, it is usually because they really need it. Because they are using it. If Conn needed the medicine and put it in his pocket the day before, it would have been opened by Friday. Also, he had taken ill several weeks prior, so by March 4 he was probably far along enough in his recovery to not need the medicine any longer. And, how often do people with full-blown gastroenteritis and bloody diarrhea report for work at 8 o'clock in the morning?

This process of reasoning and the elimination of several possibilities leads us to the conclusion that the bottle was probably planted on the body by the killer after the murder. As the star witness for the inquest, just what did Ray Jackson have to say about Conn's use of laudanum? Apparently, quite a bit was said about it because, "It was this laudanum that influenced the jury most strongly for a verdict of suicide."

The bottle made it possible for the jury to say that Conn killed himself, because some of the jurymen noted that the second bullet wound did not seem to have bled much, or at all. Conn could not have shot himself if he was already dead, unless he habitually used laudanum, and his injured heart was not beating strongly. Then it would have been possible for a second suicidal bullet to bleed very little, or so was their reasoning.

The noncommittal behavior of doctors Hall and Witham helped shape the outcome of the inquest, and allowed the jury to say that two bullets caused Conn's death. And, as long as the shot from Conn's own gun, which caused powder burns, was included in the cause of death, the jury could justify a verdict of suicide. The doctors could have told them to ignore the second shot, but they apparently did not.

The jury was obviously on the defensive. Take, for example, the obviously defensive tone of juror Ervin K. Henderson as he tried to justify the suicide verdict. *"There was not a particle of evidence to show that he was murdered. On the contrary, every circumstance showed that J.C. Conn took his own life,"* wrote Henderson. *"The evidence clearly and beyond any reasonable doubt showed suicide."* And, while refuting another criticism of the jury, Henderson even suggested that men were being shielded. *"I presume he means to insinuated that the cattlemen would try to shield the guilty parties if possible,"* wrote Henderson.

Bennett also noted Henderson's defensiveness when he wrote, "Does he show the spirit of the impartial investigator, the Judge who is anxious to see that justice is meted out? Is he not rather an attorney who tries to present but one side of the case? Why is Mr. Henderson taking such an interest in the matter of suppressing an investigation?"

Contradictory testimony is often a 'dead giveaway' in a lie, and in the matter of the powder burns there is a very clear cut contradiction. Henderson wrote that, *"The entire jury who viewed the remains will also attest the fact that the clothing above both wounds was badly powder burned."* He also claimed that the written testimony of doctors Hall and

Witham, contained in the inquest records, described powder burns around both entrance wounds.

Opposite of Henderson's claims were statements made by Alfred S. Bennett in one of his Series of Four articles about the Conn murder. From the context of Bennett's articles, it is obvious that he visited Lake County, read the inquest records, and interviewed important witnesses in the case. *"It is a certain fact that the jurors, the examining physicians and the Coroner have stated in private conversation that there was no powder burn around that first shot through the heart."*

Why was there so much confusion over the presence of powder burns? Both doctors and all of the jurors had viewed the body and the bullet wounds. Why should there be any disagreement? The answer to that question, which played such a key role in deciding the verdict, could come from certain other conditions that were present. Creed Conn was wearing a vest. We know that he was because the laudanum bottle had been found in his vest pocket. The style of men's vest worn around 1900 had a rather small neck opening, so that the vest itself would have covered the heart area. An example of that style appears in the photograph of Creed Conn which was taken shortly before his death. The first shot struck the upper part of the heart, so would have entered through the dark cloth of Conn's vest, making it more difficult to see any powder burns that existed.

After Conn was shot the first time, Jackson must have rolled him over onto his back. In that position, blood flowing from the entrance wound in the heart would have pooled on the chest. If powder burns had been present on Conn's dark vest, underneath that pool of dried blood, the jury and the doctors would not have been able to see them. Or, so was their reasoning. The jury could have assumed that the powder burns were there, but just not visible.

Even until recently, forensic scientists have struggled to see and record powder burn patterns in cases where the clothing is dark in color, or blood stained. A variety of exposures with infrared film, or a video spectral comparator are used now to create images of burn patterns. But, neither of those methods was available in 1904.

The second shot was probably fired through Conn's white shirt long after he was dead, and probably also in a bloody area because blood would have flowed up toward Conn's collar as he lay on his back. However, any powder burns in that area would have been more visible because they did not have the background of dark cloth, and because they were *on top of* the dried blood.

Since the presence of powder burns around the first bullet hole could not be confirmed or denied, that point became null for the sake of argument. But, since powder burns were definitely visible around the second wound, and the doctors included that wound in the cause of death, it was possible to make a case for suicide as the verdict.

George Lovegrove, secretary of the ZX Ranch, was the person who acted as stenographer at the inquest. And it was he who later took the compressed shorthand version and extended it to 5,800 words of testimony. Was something lost or manipulated in the translation? That could explain how, after the inquest, everyone who saw the bullet wounds said only the second shot was powder burned, but that the written record of the proceedings described powder burns around both shots, supporting the verdict of suicide.

Bennett wrote that the jury "had not fully weighed the evidence, that they were honestly deceived by the efforts to make it appear a case of self destruction." Certainly, the doctors would have examined the whole body on all sides during the postmortem. But, how had the body been presented to the jurymen? Was the body lying face up? Did they have a chance to examine the exit wound in the back? To see that it had produced no blood, and so was fired well after Conn was dead so could not have contributed to his death? "The entire jury who viewed the remains will also attest the fact that the clothing above *both* wounds was badly powder burned," wrote Henderson. Both. As in two. Not three, but two bullet wounds. From that statement, and no other statement about the exit wound, it would seem that the jury did not examine Conn's back.

Whether or not powder burns were present around the first bullet hole does not tell us anything about the identity of the killer, but the argument over that question and the diametrically opposed statements that were made on the subject do tell us that some men did not want there to be a murder investigation. Some men did. And one of those who did was Lafe Conn.

Suppose, for a moment, that what was testified regarding the powder burns was not conclusive. That could explain why the verdict of the jury was later summarily overturned and thrown out by a higher authority. The governor of the State of Oregon himself declared Conn's death a murder when he offered a reward for the killer or killers on May 19th, 1904. And that action by Governor Chamberlain was probably done at the behest of Lafayette Conn. His ongoing interest in solving his brother's murder was proven in 1910 when he had the body exhumed and autopsied. It is possible that Chamberlain could also have been influenced to overturn the verdict by Bennett's first article, "Reign of Terror," although its attempts to connect the Conn murder to the sheep kills was obviously very flimsy and circumstantial. By the time that Chamberlain offered his reward, he knew about the trouble that Williamson, Gesner, and Biggs were in, and knew that they were behind the sheep kills. He probably also knew that those same men were behind the "Reign of Terror" propaganda. In their article describing Chamberlain's reward, the *Burns Times-Herald* reported, "The Governor was induced to take this action by letters received of prominent citizens of Lake County."

Chamberlain offered a reward for the sheepshooters at the same time that he offered the reward for Creed Conn's killer or killers. Just one week prior he told the press that there was nothing he could do about the problem, and wanted local people to handle it. Perhaps it was during that week that Chamberlain received the letters from a Crook County rancher, possibly Roscoe Knox, informing him of who was behind the sheep kills. Marion R. Biggs had been appointed as judge of Crook County in May of 1903 by none other than Chamberlain himself, and given all of the trouble that Biggs had gotten into, it would be natural for Chamberlain, being the pure politician that he was, to distance himself from Biggs by offering some sort of condemnation.

Lafe and Creed Conn were apparently very close as brothers. They were close together in age, with Creed being only two years older. When Creed found himself short on cash, he went to Lafe for a loan of $200 on February 26. Lafe Conn had been at Silver Lake investigating the poisoning of the team, but left on the morning before Creed disappeared. Under those circumstances, it is easy to see how the younger brother might have felt somewhat responsible for Creed's death. Lafe had known that Creed was having financial trouble, that he was being harassed by someone, and yet he went back to Lakeview. Then, when Creed disappeared, he was unable to find him, for the killer was very organized and had planned everything out. He left no footprints, no blood evidence, and made sure there were no witnesses. When Creed's body appeared on the Sandy Knoll, it was almost more than Lafe Conn could deal with, and he was confounded by the strange assortment of clues and injuries to the body. He appointed another attorney, John D. Venator, to act in his place at the inquest, although he and brothers George and Virgil were also present. Lafe Conn did not pursue the nomination for District Attorney that year. The primary election took place during the time that Creed Conn was missing.

The author had a short interview with Larry Conn of Lakeview in 2003, who is the grandson of Lafe Conn, and the son of Ted Conn, who also had a lifelong career as an attorney of Lakeview. According to Larry, the murder of Creed Conn was something that his family just never talked about, perhaps because the subject was just too painful.

In terms of brother Virgil's grudge against Creed for the debt involving a large amount of grain, it does not seem likely that Jackson was hired to kill Creed Conn by Virgil. It is unlikely that Virgil would have tolerated the mess that Jackson made of things. Most contract killings are done as cleanly and simply as possible--just one shot, and the killer walks away. Most contract killers will not mutilate the head, hold onto the body for seven weeks, involve themselves in the investigation, then shoot the body a second time.

The use of a contract killer also does not track with the harassment that Conn suffered during the months prior to his death. Creed Conn would have had a much more difficult time repaying his old debt to Virgil after his team was poisoned and his wagons were destroyed. The use of a contract killer also does nothing to explain all of the missing cash that belonged to Martha Lane, and there is no evidence of Creed Conn having spent over $3,000 shortly before his death. The things that were done by the killer beyond what was necessary to kill, his signature behavior and communication, left clues about his identity. A professional killer would never go to all of that bother, but would take a short and simple approach to "the job."

Take, for example, the similar signature behavior found in the Whitechapel murders of 1888. Jack the Ripper also liked to use the bodies of his victims as a communication medium, a means of expression. Jack would place his victims in degrading positions, and leave them in places where they would be easily discovered. Creed Conn was placed in an embarrassing position for a "wide awake" Republican, a position that made him look asleep. A bottle of laudanum, a common sleep remedy, was placed in his vest pocket. His formerly very handsome and strong facial features were horribly mangled to the point of being obliterated. And, the body was displayed like a billboard on the Sandy Knoll where it could be seen from the main road.

Lafe Conn was correct in looking toward the stream when the search began, but was confounded by what was found, and what was not found, at the Sandy Knoll. He may have assumed that the signature aspects of the crime, the unnecessary things that were done to the body, were done out of hatred or revenge against Creed or the Conn family. He probably went looking for the killer's motive, one clear reason from Creed's life that caused the killer to strike. But, what was done at the Sandy Knoll was more an outgrowth of who the killer was and the killer's own life. His hyperactive fantasy world; what the killer felt about himself; what he wanted to express; what he needed and what he enjoyed. The signature aspects did not reveal the motive of the killer, as they would in an ordinary crime of passion, but rather the *motivations* of a deranged and utterly self-centered man.

"Sociopaths, people with no intervening sense of obligation based in attachments to others, typically devote their lives to interpersonal games, to 'winning,' to domination for the sake of domination," wrote Stout. "The rest of us, who do possess conscience, may be able to understand this motivational scheme conceptually, but when we see it in real life, its contours are so alien that we often fail to 'see' it at all."

In 1904 there were very few people on earth who understood anything about serial killers, and those who did were mostly psychologists. It would be many years before that understanding would find its way into rural law enforcement, and everyone with a television would posses at least a rudimentary understanding of how serial killers operated. The phrase "serial killer" would not come into usage in the U.S. until the mid-1970's when it was coined by Robert K. Ressler of the FBI.

Jackson presented a contradictory set of circumstances at the Sandy Knoll. The trauma to the face, the second gun shot wound, the positioning of the body and arrangement of the clothes, the placement of the gun on Conn's left side rather than the right, all seemed to point to murder. Yet, the addition of the laudanum bottle, the deliberate powder burns, and using Conn's own gun as 'a throw down' all pointed to suicide. Most murderers would have tried to fake a suicide, and they certainly would not have held onto the body for seven weeks.

Jackson did those things because it made him feel powerful to see half the people in town combing the sagebrush looking for the body, to see the stream dragged and dynamited, to witness all of the panic and anxiety of the people of Silver Lake. It was all so exciting, and he and he alone knew the real truth of what had happened to Conn. Holding onto the body was a huge risk and a liability, but that excited him too. As long as he held onto the body, he held control over the whole town. It made him feel so superior, so much smarter than everyone else. And taking part in the inquest and participating in the search kept him right where the action was.

In describing the driving force in the life of another sociopath, Stout wrote, "He had been to court and jail countless times, and this was the way he lived his life--robbing, watching, going to jail, getting out of jail, and robbing again. But he was unconcerned, because the eventual outcome of his scheming was irrelevant to him. From his perspective, all that mattered was playing the game and seeing, at least for an hour or so each time, the irrefutable evidence that he... *could make people jump....* Controlling others--winning--is more compelling than anything (or anyone) else."

The evidence left at the Sandy Knoll was put there to cause confusion, to prolong the investigation. He hoped the shock of it would cause a huge outrage and a sensation that would be carried in all of the newspapers. For Jackson it was about doing whatever he wanted to do with the body and 'winning.' He delighted in the confusion of the jurors and doctors, and probably objected loudly when the murder investigation began to slide into the obscurity of other known suicides.

> *"What sociopaths envy, and may seek to destroy as a part of the game, is usually some-thing in the character structure of a person with conscience, and strong characters are often specially targeted by sociopaths."*

> *- Martha Stout in the Sociopath Next Door*

Ray Jackson, with his deeply entrenched self-loathing and intense envy of Creed Conn, could not resist the opportunity to make the local celebrity appear foolish, to mock him as a wide-awake Republican who made a comment on the O'Farrell case. He hated Creed Conn's handsome face, but moreover, he hated his intelligence and how highly regarded he was. Jackson at an early age had had the notion ground into his head that he was mentally inferior, even stupid, and so the head trauma he consistently inflicted on his victims was a reflection of that particular brand of self-loathing. It was the core of his signature aspect.

Creed Conn had many of the outward symbols of status and power, including nice clothes and a flashy team for his buggy, and that galled Jackson no end. In his book, "Bad Men Do What Good Men Dream," Robert I. Simon described the sociopath's admiration of outward things like "beauty, wealth, power, adoration by others--and what they discount (and despise) are hard-won abilities, achievements, acceptance of responsibility, and loyalty to ideals." Simon believed that a sociopath's antisocial acts are driven by the need to exploit and depreciate others in order to maintain a grandiose and powerful view of himself. "All serial killers are power mad in the extreme," he wrote. "In their relationships they devalue the other person, they are greedy, they appropriate others' property or ideas and feel entitled to do so."

When all of Creed Conn's worldly goods were being sold off a few months after his death, Jackson purchased Conn's buggy team for $125, which could have been an outward expression of his envy of Conn, and his desire to imitate him. And, it should be remembered here that a few years after the murder, Jackson himself opened a mercantile store at Paisley.

In his insightful book, "Clues from Killers, Serial Murder and Crime Scene Messages," Dirk C. Gibson studied over two hundred serial killings and came away convinced that most serial killers communicate during and after the killings, and many communicate more than once. Some like Jackson use the victim's body to communicate. Others leave notes at the scene, or talk to the media. The primary reason for the communication seems to be the same reason that serial killers enjoy involving themselves in the investigation. It allows them to relive the episode, to keep it fresh in their own mind and in the minds of everyone close to the subject. Serial killers are exceptionally cruel people who also derive some satisfaction from tormenting the friends and families of victims.

"Each of these repeat murderers felt the necessity to share parts of their homicidal experience with someone, in some fashion, during and/or after the fact," wrote Gibson. "This consistent compulsion to communicate characterizes these serial killers."

If there was any real motive at all in Jackson's behavior, it was probably revealed, in what was *not* found at the Sandy Knoll. "There seems no doubt that the body of Conn was searched after his death. A daily journal, or diary that he always carried with him is missing. In this he made memoranda of all his daily transactions," wrote Bennett.

In chapter ten it was stated that a large sum of money, deposited by Martha Lane, seemed to have disappeared from Creed Conn's bank account around the first week of February. Conn was no doubt making every attempt to track down the missing cash, which at first he believed to be a banking error, and all of his cash flow notes would have been contained in that journal. He may even have had other evidence in it, such as the original forged promissory note returned to him from the bank.

Also not found were tracks, blood spatters, other trace evidence, and eye witnesses. Jackson had committed his crime in a secluded place early in the morning when the temperature was around 25 degrees. The ground was frozen so hard that he probably left no trace at all. Late that same night, when he went to retrieve the body from where he had hidden it underneath the bridge abutment, the ground was also very frozen. The next day he got a lucky break. It began to rain. The search in the area of the stream, which did not begin until Sunday, had to be called off on account of the downpour.

"All through March the weather was very severe and stormed almost every day. The precipitation was unprecedented in that part of the country for that month. It rained or snowed almost continuously until the last day of March," wrote Bennett. "Never in the history of the county has there been so much rain and snowfall as there has been this month," wrote editor Beach of the *Examiner*. On the Friday that Conn disappeared, Lake County got .22 inches of rain, Saturday brought only a "trifle" or a sprinkle, and Sunday, the day that the search of the stream began, there was a quarter of an inch of rain. On Monday about one third of an inch fell, and Tuesday got a whopping eight tenths of an inch of rain. All of that rain, particularly the rain that fell on the day of the disappearance and murder, probably washed away any trace evidence that was left behind.

The thing that gave Jackson his reptilian coolness, his strength, and the ability to pull these murders off, was that he had no conscience at all. He could carry the knowledge of a murder with him and exhibit no outward sign of it. He could lie about it constantly and consistently without the slightest glimmering of guilt. Jackson exhibited all of the traits of a true psychopath. He was known for his glibness, his superficial charm, and his grandiosity. He enjoyed the thrill of a risky situation and was a pathological liar. He often lived off of others like a parasite. He had been a juvenile delinquent, and drank too much. He was irresponsible and exhibited a shallowness of emotion.

In "The Sociopath Next Door," Dr. Martha Stout wrote a description of one type of sociopath that should chill to the bone anyone familiar with the life of Mr. Ray Van Buren Jackson.

Shelby Petersen, who knew Ray Jackson when he lived at Wagontire, described his fast talking ways and glibness, and so did Jess Gibson when he recalled Jackson saying, "I have an elegance sufficiency, any more would be superfluity."

Although Jackson seems not to have been the sort of killer who required a motive to kill, the missing cash could have been what caused him to turn on Conn after a period of parasitic friendship. Between Christmas and New Years at the end of 1903, the two men had been friendly enough for Jackson to appear as a witness for Conn's timber claim. But during the first week of February, Conn took ill, possibly from poisoning. On the 12th his wagons were destroyed by arson, and on the 29th his team was poisoned. On March 4 he was shot.

We know that Jackson embezzled money from the school system at Clackamas County, via forgery, in 1895. We also know that he committed robbery in Baker County in 1898. That he embezzled money from the Lake County school system in 1910. And, that he seems to have been involved in a plot to separate Link Hutton from his valuable ranch in 1925 by killing him and buying the property from his widow. That he used an alias and swore falsely in order to obtain title to two separate homesteads at the same time. From these facts it seems evident that Jackson loved money, and was willing to do almost anything for material gain, identifying him as a "serial enterprise killer." The Highland Forger probably struck the bank account that Conn kept in San Francisco. He learned about Martha Lane's deposit into that account through his involvement in Conn's life and timber dealings.

It is apparent that the money was missing, and that Conn himself did not spend it. After Creed Conn disappeared, seemingly having taken the money with him, J.R. Horning was forced to sell his ranch on Buck Creek for $3,000. He had to raise the money he needed to pay for the timber claims on Dead Indian since the money he had borrowed from Martha Lane was gone. During the first week of April, Frank Payne and William Robinette suddenly shifted their search for the body to Buck Creek where the Horning Ranch was because, by that time, there was considerable talk that Conn's disappearance had something to do with the missing money.

Some of Conn's friends apparently objected to the mud slinging, and chose to believe that he had killed himself out of remorse for having failed financially and lost Martha Lane's money. The *Crook County Journal* of April 28, in an article about the discovery of the body, stated, "A love affair is supposed to have been a partial cause of the man taking his life." A romantic relationship between Martha Lane and Creed Conn cannot be proven, and she did live far away in Brownsville, Oregon. But, a close relationship of trust between the two did exist, and Conn's choice of her nephew, Frank Payne, as a clerk could have been indicative of something.

Henderson wrote that, "Every circumstance showed that Conn took his own life." *Circumstance* being the operative word. A coroner's jury typically would arrive at their verdict in a very subjective way, and speculation and conjecture about the circumstantial elements of Conn's financial life during the month before the death were considered to be "facts in the case."

The jury was well aware of Conn's financial difficulties. Creed Conn had recently borrowed money from his brother, Lafe, who testified as a witness. The undercompensated Frank Payne was a witness. George Lovegrove, secretary for the ZX Ranch, was a juror and had spent the two weeks prior to discovery of the body appraising the contents of Conn's store. Jackson himself was a witness at the inquest, and would have known about Conn's recent efforts to sell his timber claim in order to pay off some debts. The coroner himself, Farnham Harris, was the brother of Clarence Z. Harris who was a juror and a witness for the inquest, and was owed money by Conn since January for having lodged his team and teamster at Harris Station at Summer Lake.

Another juror who did double duty as a witness at the inquest was Clifford Smith, who had married the widow Lydia Partin in 1897. Lydia and her former husband, Marcus, were good friends of Andrew and Martha Lane, and the two women presumably became even closer friends when both of their husbands died premature deaths. Cliff Smith was the man who purchased the Horning ranch when he was forced to sell out to recoup his losses on the timber deal. Considering his wife's friendship with Martha Lane, Smith probably knew a lot more than most people about the large sum of cash that was missing from Conn's account, and could easily have convinced the jury that Conn was in deep financial trouble.

The author was not able to find a scrap of evidence to show that Conn ever spent Martha Lane's money, and Virgil repaid her on October 1 after he had liquidated some of Creed's assets. In fact, there is plenty of evidence that Conn did not have or use the money. He had numerous nagging debts when he died, like the one to clerk Payne whom he owed about four months of back pay. There is no evidence that Conn himself made any large purchase around the time that he disappeared, but Ray Van Buren Jackson did.

Jackson should have been more or less broke by the spring of 1904. One year before, his brother, William, had sued him to recover money and Ray was forced to sell some property that he owned in Harney County to repay the loan. He had just relinquished his timber claim at the end of 1903, probably because he could not raise the cash to pay for it, and Oregon teachers were the lowest paid teachers in the entire country at the time. On June 21, 1904 Jackson was stopped trying to enter the Cascades Forest Reserve south of Lowell by ranger Addie L. Morris, who wrote in his report:

> *Tuesday 21/*
> *I patrolled down to west side of reserve. Put up 3 fire warning on the road & wrote out application for R.B. Jackson permit to drive 250 head of cattle cross reserve. Time 9 hours, distance 24 miles.*

From the surrounding context of Morris' diary, he seems to have encountered Jackson as he was patrolling the forest boundary southeast of Cottage Grove near Crowbar Point, a rise near Oakridge that was named for the crowbars driven into the rock to prevent the road from sliding into the river. Jackson had probably come from either Cottage Grove or Disston and was planning to take the cattle up the Willamette River and over Pengra Pass to Odell, Crescent, and on to either

Lake or Harney County. Morris did not name anyone other than Jackson. That would seem to indicate that Jackson was in charge, and the cattle probably belonged to him because the permit was issued in his name. Morris was reprimanded by by Forest Supervisor Smith C. Bartrum for his irregular dealings with Jackson.

> *"I am just in receipt of your letter of recent date referring to the permit of Mr. Jackson, to drive 250 head of cattle across the reserve," wrote Bartrum. "I wrote you in regards to this matter yesterday asking to give the dates when they would want to cross the reserve, as this is very necessary, the proper thing to have done was to instruct Mr. Jackson to notify this office a few days before leaving for the reserve at which time he would then know exactly the date he would reach the reserve, and it would also give me time to issue the permit and send to him or to you at Lowell, a permit must be used within the lifetime of said permit, of course there may be times that this cannot be done exactly, and good judgment must then be exercised, but where ever it is possible to carry out the rules and regulations with exactness it must be done, or otherwise the service will become a farce."*

Bartrum ended his letter with, "The proper course to pursue is for them to make application to the Supervisor in advance for this privilege, and not wait until a forest ranger stops them." Morris' diary showed him to be a conscientious ranger who took his job very seriously and tried to do everything 'by the book.' He was no doubt influenced by Jackson to behave the way that he had. Jackson probably produced a torrent of pitiful wailing in order to get across the reserve, or may have bribed or conned the forest officer in some other way. "A sociopath who is about to be cornered by another person will turn suddenly into a piteous weeping figure whom no one, in good conscience, could continue to pressure," wrote Stout.

Another suggestion that Jackson entered into the cattle business between 1902 and 1909 came from a brief biography in his obituary, which placed the beginning of his ranching partnership with Frank Dobkins around that time.

In 1904, a fully matured beef would sell for about $28, but since Jackson was bringing a large number of animals east in the early summer, the herd was probably comprised of younger animals that he wanted to feed and fatten on the desert and then sell at a profit in the fall. A young steer, under one year of age, would have gone for about $12 to $15 in those days, depending upon the breed, quality, and size of the animal. A person could buy 250 head of young steers for $3,000 to $3,750.

The amount of money that Martha Lane lost, the amount that disappeared from Conn's bank account, was $3,270.

The murder of John Creed Conn occurred fairly early in the 'career' of Ray Van Buren Jackson, but because of the level of organization and forethought that went into the crime, and the amount of effort that he put into avoiding detection when he killed, it was likely that Conn was not his first victim. Many serial killers exhibit a pattern in their lifetime in which the first and last sets of victims are murdered near the killer's home, just as were Conn and Wallende, and later, the two Bradleys.

SOURCES:

"Reign of Terror," *Oregonian*, May 10, 1904.

"Was Not Suicide," *Oregonian*, June 9, 1904.

Probate file of John Creed Conn, Lake County Courthouse, Clerk's Basement South Storage Room:Probate [Case Files], 1875-1927, Lakeview, Oregon.

"An Illustrated History of Central Oregon," Western Historical Publishing, 1905, Spokane, WA, p 856, 921

U.S. Census Bureau, Twelfth Census of the United States, 1900, Paisley, Lake County, Oregon.

Bureau of Land Management, records of the General Land Office, land patent of Frank West, serial #ORLAA 063680. Land is in township 28 South, range 14 East, sec 22, West half of SE quarter. http://www.glorecords.blm.gov/ PatentSearch

"Death of Ethel Martin," *Lake County Examiner*, April 7, 1904.

U.S. Census Bureau, Twelfth Census of the United States, 1900, Silver Lake, Lake County, Oregon.

"Mysteriously Disappeared," *Roseburg Plaindealer,* March 17, 1904. Article was picked up from the *Central Oregonian* at Silver Lake.

Homestead patent application file of Roy B. Jackson, serial #1032174, Bureau of Land Management, records of the General Land Office, National Archives and Records Administration, Washington, D.C.

"Whereabouts of J.C. Conn Yet Unknown," *Prineville Review*, March 24, 1904.

U.S. Census Bureau, Thirteenth Census of the United States, 1910, East Cottage Grove, Lane County, Oregon.

"Creed Conn is Missing," *Lake County Examiner*, March 10, 1904.

"Has J.C. Conn Killed Himself," *Plaindealer*, March 14, 1904.

"Marriage Records, vol. 2, 1895-1909, County of Lake, Lakeview, Oregon," 1995, Oregon Youth Conservation Corps, Lakeview, Oregon, p 35

Howard family history, Boydstun-Stephenson Collection, Lake County Museum, Lakeview, Oregon, p 5-6.

"Ballistic Fingerprinting," Wikipedia article, http://en.wikipedi.org/wiki/ Ballistic_fingerprinting

"Murder or Suicide," *Oregonian*, June 12, 1904.

"Body is Found," *Lake County Examiner*, April 28, 1904.

"State Offers Big Reward," *Burns Times-Herald*, May 28, 1904.

"Rewards Offered," *Lake County Examiner*, May 26, 1904.

"Range Men Must Settle," *Oregonian*, May 13, 1904.

"Roscoe Knox, Early Pioneer," *Crook County News*, Pioneer Edition, August 4, 1939.

"A New County Judge," *Deschutes Echo*, May 2, 1903.

Harney County History Project, oral history interview #381, Shelby Petersen, August 4, 1991, p 4, 9.

Harney County History Project, oral history interview #66, Ray Shaver and Russell Emery, August 16, 1991, p 6.

Interview with R. L. "Link" Hutton, title unknown, *Lake County Examiner*, December 6, 1934.

"Colt Single Action Army," Wikipedia article: http://en.wikipedia.org/wiki/ Colt_Single_Action_Army

"Settlers in Summer Lake Valley," by Teresa Foster, 1989, Maverick, Bend, Oregon, p foreword, 98, 114-118, 148.

"Sheep Herder Shot in the Hand," *Crook County Journal*, February 2, 1905.

Bill for services rendered to the County of Lake in holding an inquest over the remains of J.C. Conn, dated at Lakeview May 2, 1904, by coroner Farnham E. Harris. Schmink Museum basement storage, Lakeview, Oregon.

In the Mater of the Estate of J.C. Conn, Deceased, Probate file of John Creed Conn, Order Appointing Appraisers, April 9, 1904. Probate Case Files, 1875-1927, Clerk's Basement South Storage Room, Lake County Courthouse, Lakeview, Oregon.

"The ZX Ranches in Oregon," by Becky Womack, Lake County, Oregon History & Genealogy, vol 3, Lake County Historical Society, Lakeview, Oregon, p 11-13.

"First in Heart," *Oregonian*, July 14, 1904.

"Robert Ressler," Wikipedia article (biography), http://en.wikipedia.org/wiki/ Robert_Ressler

"Weather Report for March," and "Weather Report for April," *Lake County Examiner*, July 21, 1904.

"Bad Men Do What Good Men Dream," by Robert I. Simon, M.D., American Psychiatric Press, Inc, Washington, D.C., p 29-31, 317.

"Profilers," by John H. Campbell and Don DeNevi, 2004, Prometheus, Amherst, New York, p 138-141, 263, 265

"Visualization of Gunshot Residue Patterns on Dark Clothing," Journal of Forensic Sciences, vol 51, Issue 5, p1091-1095, August 31, 2006. Abstract available online at: www3.interscience.wiley.com/journal/118609301/ abstract.

"Local News," *Lake County Examiner*, April 21, 1904. News item about the sale of Horning's ranch was picked up from the *Central Oregonian* at Silver Lake.

"J.C. Conn's Body Found," *Crook County Journal,* April 28, 1904.

"W.L. Jackson vs. R.V. Jackson, *Harney Valley Items,* May 2, 1903. Default and judgment and order for sale of attached property.

U.S. Census Bureau, Ninth Census of the United States, 1870, Coles Valley, Douglas County, Oregon.

Timber and Stone patent application file of John C. Conn, serial #ORLAA 058633 , Bureau of Land Management, records of the General Land Office, National Archives and Records Administration, Washington, D.C. Patented October 22, 1904.

"The School Teachers of Oregon," editorial, *Roseburg Plaindealer*, May 16, 1904.

Diary Book 4, March 1904-September 1904, Addie L. Morris, Cascade Reserve Ranger 1899-1905, p 15 June 21, 1904. Letter of S.C. Bartrum, Forest Supervisor, to Addie L. Morris, June 24, 1904.

"Lane County Historian," Lane County Historical Society, vol XIX, no. 3 & 4, Winter 1974, Eugene, OR, p 65.

"Marriage Records, vol. 1, 1875-1895, County of Lake, Lakeview, Oregon," 1995, Oregon Youth Conservation Corps, Lakeview, Oregon, p 7.

Homestead patent application file of Lydia Partin, widow of Marcus Partin, serial #ORLAA 066393, Bureau of Land Management, records of the General Land Office, National Archives and Records Administration, Washington, D.C.

"Pioneer Rancher Takes Own Life," *Harney County American*, February 4, 1938.

"Local Items," *Lake County Examiner*, April 21, 1904. News item about Horning's sale of his ranch to Cliff Smith.

"The Sociopath Next Door, the Ruthless Versus the Rest of Us" by Martha Stout, PhD, copyright 2005 by Martha Stout. Used by permission of   Broadway Books, a division of Random House, Inc., New York, p 3-7, 47, 51, 90-91, 96, 107-109, 127.

"Reign of Terror"
Dateline: Lakeview, Or, May 6 (Special)
Published: *Oregonian*, May 10, 1904

A reign of terror exists in Lake County. In the face of a daring defiance of law that approaches civil war, the peace officers are powerless. thus far about $25,000 worth of property has been sacrificed. On February 2 a band of 3000 sheep was killed. On March 4, a prominent merchant of Silver Lake, Or., J.C. Conn, died from two bullet wounds, which the verdict of the Coroner's jury held to be self-inflicted. Certain circumstances connected with his death lead to the strong suspicion that he was murdered. On April 28 another band of 2700 sheep was annihilated. The perpetrators have issued notice that they will kill anyone who offers a reward or who attempts to make an arrest. They have warned other sheep owners to move their bands from the cattle range of northern Lake County or suffer the consequences.

The circumstantial evidence leading up to the belief that the death of Creed Conn was a murder and that it was committed to conceal the identity of the outlaws is shown in the following narrative.

The particular prejudice against the first sheep killed, the McKune band, was that it came from California into Oregon pastures. It had been on the road since last October for the Winter grazing grounds of the desert. There were 9000 sheep at that time, but a bare 3000 returned to California. Upon the receipt of the news of the killing of the first band of sheep, a great wave of indignation swept over the county. The Lakeview, Paisley, and Silver Lake papers were loud in their demands that the men be found and punished. District Attorney L.F. Conn announced that he would take steps to bring the parties to justice. The belief was general that he would seek the co-operation of his brother, Creed Conn, who lived among the outlaws and knew each one of them personally. The killing took place only ten or 12 miles from his store, among the buttes of the desert, near Christmas Lake. He had sold the ammunition and the guns that killed the sheep. To the outlaws Creed Conn's attitude and subsequent movements would be a constant source of wonderment and fear.

Shortly after the killing of the sheep, Creed Conn made a trip to Lakeview, 120 miles, and was in consultation with his brother Lafe. What took place between the two brothers is not known.

But the outlaws probably argued like this: "It is unusual to make a trip to Lakeview in this Winter weather. He has gone to give us away. He simply wants to make a record for his brother as Prosecuting Attorney. What do you think of a man that would do that after he has fed off of us all these years? He should be given an object lesson."

A Warning to Creed Conn

Therefore a few nights after Creed Conn's return from seeing his brother in Lakeview, an old barn, a mile and a half from Silver Lake, with snow on the ground and everything wet, and on one about, took fire and burned up Creed Conn's freight wagons, valued at $600. There was special objection to these wagons because they were used to haul wool to market. Their burning should have been an admonition to Creed Conn not to talk. But after the fire he went right off in the storms of February and had another consultation in Lakeview with the Prosecuting Attorney. Instead of keeping him quiet, the burning of his wagons seemed to have only an inciting effect.

On his way home to Silver Lake, Creed Conn journeyed leisurely. He stayed over Sunday at Paisley, February 28. He declined to discuss either the sheep-killing or the barn-burning, and talked with no one unless he did with his brothers, Virgil and George, both merchants of Paisley. No one noticed anything unusual about him except that he was thoughtful. But Creed Conn had always been reticent about his business.

The next day after he arrived home, Tuesday, one of his fine horses took sick suddenly and died. Creed Conn had one of the best freight teams in Oregon. It was said the horse was poisoned and Conn was afraid the others might suffer the same fate. He had the horses in a pasture three miles from town and it was his practice each morning to walk out to look after them.

Friday morning, March 4, about 8 o'clock, after getting his mail and eating breakfast in company with Prof. Jackson, who noticed nothing unusual in his demeanor, he left Silver Lake to go to the horses as was his custom.

Right after him went the stage, and if Conn had taken the road where his body was found seven weeks later the driver would have observed him. another team at that same time passed over the road and the ill-fated man was not seen.

Shortly after crossing the bridge upon leaving town, a single shot was heard among the willows along the creek by two witness, Ward and Parker, from different points, but they both located the shot in the one place.

That was supposed to be the shot that killed Conn, and it was evidently fired a mile from where his body was found. If he had been killed where he lay, the shot could not have been heard. If any hunter had fired the shot he would probably have made himself known in the long search that was made for the body.

Shot Through the Heart

This shot passed through the upper part of the heart, cut the spinal cord and the bullet lodged in the backbone. If death was not instantaneous, it must have ensued within a very few minutes. There was no powder burn to show that the weapon had been held close to the body. The line of the shot shows at what angel the weapon was held. If it had been fired by a right-handed man himself, and Conn was right-handed, the course of the bullet would probably inclined the other way, and the clothing would have been powder-burned.

When the body was found there were two bullet wounds. The second had struck about three inches above the first, passed entirely through the body and buried itself six inches in the ground. The body had not moved after this shot was fired. The testimony of the physicians at the inquest was that the shot through the heart was fired first, but they said they did not know when asked what was the manner of death. The upper shot had left a powder-burn showing that it was fired at close range. The body was lying on its back the arms thrown up over the head, the legs straight and feet close together, and the clothing neatly arranged as if by some one after depositing the body.

Under the left arm with the grass growing around it was Conn's own revolver, a .38, with two chambers empty.

In one pocket was found $30 in bills, showing that no robbery was intended. A gold watch also helped to identify the obliterated features.

In the vest pocket was found a bottle of laudanum which had never been opened. The merchant carried this in stock in his store, and a physician said he had prescribed it for Mr. conn's use in the treatment of some bodily ailment.

Suicide the Verdict

The Coroner's jury that gave the verdict was made up entirely of cattlemen. After hearing the evidence a verdict of suicide was returned, which was entirely unsatisfactory to Mr. Conn's friends, who do not hesitate to assert that politics influenced the verdict. They say it is remarkable that a man should shoot himself twice. The physicians, Dr. Hall and Dr. Witham, testified that the shot through the heart was the first one fired and was probably discharged while the man was standing. Even had he fired this himself when he fell, the gun would have dropped from his nerveless grasp and he could not have picked it up again to fire the second shot. Nor would he have arranged his legs so neatly on the ground, but would have tumbled in a heap.

The last band of sheep killed, on April 28, was feeding near Benjamin Lake, 50 miles east of Silver Lake. It was what is known as a dry band and contained odd numbers from different owners. Parker, Price & Mulkey and O'Farrel are the losers.

A party of nine men on horseback rode up at 3 o'clock in the afternoon with barley sacks over their faces. The herder was a stranger. He offered to take the sheep away if they would give him two hours. They refused, tied a barley sack over the man's head, telling him not to remove it on peril of his life, and commenced to shoot the sheep. They killed 2300 outright, and scattered the other 400 to be prey for the coyotes. The herder then made his way to Silver Lake and notified the owners.

The killing of the first band was done at night by unmasked men. They used 12 heavy juniper clubs and several guns, and there may have been 15 men in the party.

Creed Conn left an estate valued at about $30,000. His heirs are nine brothers and one sister. He belonged to the Masonic order.

"Was Not Suicide"
Dateline: None
Published: *Oregonian*, June 9, 1904

New information at hand throws additional light upon the death of J.C. Conn in Lake County and leaves no doubt that a crime was committed. Mr. Conn disappeared on the morning of March 4, and his dead body was found April 21, a mile and a quarter west of Silver Lake, near the bank of a small creek and not 150 yards from the public highway. When he was missed his brothers put out searching parties that scoured all the country for miles. It was thought by some that the man had been murdered and his body buried in the sagebrush, and careful search was made for a new-made grave. Rafts were built on all the streams and the bottoms thoroughly dragged. The same thorough investigation was made in the very field where the body was found. The body lay on a small sandy knoll within a fenced field and it could have been seen from any point for some distance. The place is easily identified. Why was it that the searchers did not discover the body sooner?

Another circumstance is more convincing. all through March the weather was very severe and stormed almost every day. The precipitation was unprecedented in that part of the country for that month. It rained or snowed almost continuously until the last day of March. Persons out in a storm would become thoroughly soaked in a few hours and drenched to the skin. If the body of J.C. Conn had lain on that knoll all that time, would it not too have become rain-soaked as to the clothing? He had just paid a note for $450 in Lakeview a few days before his death, and this note was found canceled on his person. It wasn't even wet. He wore a white starched shirt and cuffs. Never a drop of moisture had touched these articles of apparel where he lay. They were as smooth as the day he put them on. Rain would have wrinkled them. Other papers in his pocket had never touched water, and all these are still in evidence. Where was the body of J.C. Conn during all those storms of March? It surely never lay in that pasture.

Body Had Been Hidden

There is another thing. The body after being exposed to the elements for seven weeks was still well preserved. The skin underneath the clothing was still clear white. Only the hands and face were blackened. It goes to show that the body had not been exposed to the elements but had been concealed in a manner to preserve it.

The morning he disappeared the ground was frozen very hard, but there was no snow. How far into frozen ground will a bullet from a .38-caliber gun penetrate after passing through a human body? The bullet underneath Conn's body was found buried six inches in the ground. It is believed that it was fired there when the ground was thawed out.

How long had the body lain where it was found? It must have been some time, for the April grass had started to grow up around where the revolver lay. the gun must have been deposited there before the grass had made much headway. But from April 1 till April 21 never a drop of rain fell in Lake County.

It is further believed that Conn did not have his revolver with him when he was killed. It was not his practice to carry a gun. He always kept a weapon in his store, but it was not his custom to lug it around with him. Why should he have taken a gun with him that particular morning? It is true that it was his own revolver that was found underneath his left arm with two empty shells in the chamber. One was underneath the hammer just as it was left after the last shot was fired.

Conn Had No Gun With Him

Conn was last seen Friday morning. Nothing was thought of his absence until the next day, and search was not instituted til Sunday. Thus two nights had intervened without any investigation. Then it was discovered that Conn's gun was missing, and it was argued that he must have taken it with him. But later this gun that was thought missing, a new Smith & Wesson, was found underneath some books where it had been all the time.

But Conn had another revolver, an antiquated .38 that had been discarded years before and was never used. It was kept in his desk at the store. This was old-fashioned and had to be cocked before it could be fired. Was a man already mortally wounded with a bullet through his heart likely to stop to cock this weapon to fire another shot? It was this revolver that was found underneath the dead man's arm. If Conn had planned to do the deed himself which gun would he have been likely to choose, the new Smith & Wesson or the antiquated six-shooter?

Conn carried with him the keys to the store. His clerk also had a set of keys. If Conn was murdered, his body examined and those keys found, could not some one that night have entered his store, taken the revolver, and nt be detected? No one slept in the store.

Laudanum Bottle Never Opened

This might also account for the presence of the bottle of laudanum in his pocket, for the bottle was the same as that carried in stock in the drug department of his store. The bottle had never been opened. It was this laudanum that influenced the jury most strongly for a verdict of suicide. But it is believed that Conn himself had taken this laudanum with him, for a physician had prescribed its use to allay hemorrhages with which he was troubled.

There seems no doubt that the body of Conn was searched after his death. A daily journal, or diary, that he always carried with him is missing. In this he made memoranda of all his daily transactions. It is believed that in this book he had made notes bearing upon the recent sheep-killing, and that it bore damaging evidence against the perpetrators. The book may have been appropriated to destroy such entries.

That persons were interested in stifling investigation in this matter is shown by the fact that one local newspaper received notice to cease agitation or swing from a limb, and a Silver Lake merchant, who had expressed himself very freely, received one morning in his mail a piece of rope and a block of matches.

From information received by the Governor, and from letters to private persons in this city, it is learned that the situation in Lake County is greatly improved. The publicity given the matter through the Oregonian, and the action of Governor Chamberlain in offering rewards has inspired the people to vindicate the law. There is no longer fear of anarchy. Indeed, it is to be believed that the fear (text omitted by compositor of the *Oregonian*) jury. That was all they were waiting for before taking further action. The verdict was made known on Monday, April 25. Almost immediately they arranged for another raid, and on Thursday killed the second band of sheep. They imagined that the Coroner's verdict settled the matter; that under the constitution they could not again be placed in jeopardy of their lives. They could easily have spirited Conn's body away and buried it in the mountains, but they wanted vindication. Those fellows firmly believed that the authorities in Lake County dared not take action. Lawabiding citizens talked about the matter only with bated breath and in fear and trembling. No one knew who was a sympathizer.

It is strange that the Governor in his proclamation overlooked the killing of the first band of sheep on February 2. It was the men who did that slaughtering that murdered Conn.

First Bullet Not Found

It is to be regretted that at the Coroner's inquest a complete autopsy was not made and the first bullet fired into Conn's body through the heart, located. If it had been found to be a 38-caliber bullet it would simply have indicated that some other 38-caliber gun was used by the assassin. If it had been found to be any other sized bullet it would have settled the matter beyond controversy, but the jury thought such and examination was not necessary. The inquest seems to have been only perfunctory. It is understood to be the intention of the relatives to take up the remains and make interment at Roseburg, when the autopsy may be completed.

This also brings out the fact that a citizen of Silver Lake was very punctilious in furnishing the Roseburg Plaindealer with all the evidence to sustain the theory of suicide. He has no doubt been surprised by the vigorous denouncement of the crime by that paper in its later issues.

It is also stated that the searching parties in the early days of March had to abandon their hunt on account of the heavy rains. The streams became so swollen they could not drag them, and it was inconvenient to look through the sagebrush. And yet through all that downpour the body of Conn lay there in the open and never a hair was wet.

The public need expect to hear of no more outrages of this character from Lake County.

"First in Heart"
Dateline: Ashland, Or., July 13 (Special)
Published: *Oregonian*, July 14, 1904

The charitable view that the public took of the Coroner's jury that rendered the verdict of suicide in the death of J.C. conn in Lake County was that the men on the jury had not fully weighed the evidence, that they were honestly deceived by the efforts to make it appear a case of self-destruction. Silence on their part was commendable, but a last one comes forward and tries to defend the action of the jury.

This juror, E.K. Henderson , in a communication to the Lakeview Herald says: "There was not a particle of evidence to show that he was murdered. On the contrary, every circumstance showed that J.C. Conn took his own life."

Is there another case on record where a man shot himself twice, first through the heart? It is true that some suicides have shot twice, but the first bullet had done but little injury.

At the Coroner's inquest these facts were brought out. The first bullet was fired through the upper part of the heart and lodged in the spinal column. Death in any event must have resulted from his wound in a very few minutes. There was no powder burn on the clothing or skin from this shot. The second shot passed through the body three inches above the first and struck no vital organ.

If but this shot alone had been fired the man could have recovered. Powder burns were left by this shot, showing that the gun must have been held close to the body when it was fired. The body never moved after this shot was fired. If it had been fired first, not being in a vital part, the body would have moved when the second shot was fired. The evidence of the two physicians at the inquest was positive on these points. In their opinion the man was standing when the first shot was fired.

Effect of Shot Through Heart

Was there ever an experience in the Army where a soldier shot through the heart did not fall? Even the savages, for whom the British invented the dumdum bullets, never failed to drop when an ordinary bullet cut the hear.

A soldier wounded through the heart falls from his horse, his gun drops from his had. He never raises the weapon to fire again. His fingers are nerveless, and he could not pull the trigger if he tried.

J.C. Conn was thus wounded and fell. He did not tumble in a heap as every soldier does who receives his death wound through the heart. But he lay down carefully, pulled his had down tight over the back of his head, arranged his clothes neatly and smoothly, placed his legs close together then found his revolver where it had fallen when he fell, picked it up, cocked it and fired a second shot through his body. He did all this practically after he was a dead man. We must believe this if we accept the verdict of suicide. He did what was impossible for a dying man to do. Yet, in the face of all this Mr. Henderson says, "Every circumstance showed that J.C. Conn took his own life."

Consistency of the Verdict

Even taking Mr. Henderson's version of the matter the case is surrounded by doubt. Let us suppose for the moment that Conn was really murdered. From the evidence developed at the inquest the jury could not point to any one man and say, "You did the deed." It was just as wrong for them to malign the dead as it would have been to arraign the living. It is admitted that there was nothing done that could have been done by some one other than Mr. Conn himself. If it was possible for Mr. Conn to have taken his own life it was also possible for some one else to have taken it. The only verdict the jury could have rendered consistently was that the deceased came to his death by unknown hands.

Mr. Henderson complains of the article in The Weekly Oregonian of May 12, and says it "reflects severely upon the citizens of Silver Lake and contains a number of false statements." One of these false statements is that the distance of the slaughtered band of sheep from Silver Lake was underestimated. Is it at all material whether the distance was ten miles or 50? Could they not have obtained the cartridges some place other than Conn's store? Is there any reflection in that statement upon the good name of the people of Silver Lake?

Personnel of the Jury

"The Coroner's jury that gave the verdict was made up entirely of cattlemen." This is the statement in the Oregonian. Mr. Henderson answers: "In fact, there were but two men on the jury who own any cattle. Does a man have to own cattle to be a cattleman? It is true that but two were cattle-owners, but the other four were all employees of cattlemen and one of them is secretary of the largest cattle company in the county. But why should this statement have aroused Mr. Henderson's ire? It is the custom in all important cases to give the occupation of the jurors, and no significance need attach to this. The Oregonian drew no inference from this fact. It is Mr. Henderson who makes "the base insinuation: that the "cattlemen would try to shield the guilty parties if possible."

Mr. Henderson says: "That politics had anything to do with the case is too absurd to refer to." Mr. Moore, the Democratic candidate for Prosecuting Attorney, who denounced the killing of the sheep, received by 24 votes in Silver Lake precinct, the lowest vote of all, and Mr. West, another Democrat, candidate for Assessor, who did not denounce the sheep-killing, and who was one of the men who rendered the verdict of suicide, received the unanimous 98 votes of his precinct.

Lafe Conn Defeated for Office

Lafe Conn, the Prosecuting Attorney who announced that he would do all in his power to bring the sheep-killers to justice, was defeated for renomination. And yet Mr. Henderson ridicules the idea that politics had anything to do with the case.

But these details are immaterial and unimportant. The point is, Who fired that first bullet through the heart of J.C. Conn? and how is Mr. Henderson warranted in his summing up of the case in saying "The evidence clearly and beyond any reasonable doubt showed suicide." The very fact of the two bullets in the body shows a reasonable doubt. The absence of all motive for suicide shows another. The fact that he left no word of his intentions nor disposition of his property is a third reason.

The fact that two men from different points heard the shot that is supposed to have killed Conn, a mile from where his body was found and has never been explained is another cause for doubt. The fact that Conn, if he had traveled the road to where his body was found, should have been seen by the stage driver and others adds further cause for doubt.

Points That Are Overlooked

Mr. Henderson takes up none of these points, but confines himself to a general denial. Does he show the spirit of the impartial investigator, the Judge who is anxious to see that justice is meted out? Is he not rather an attorney who tries to present but one side of the case? Why is Mr. Henderson taking such an interest in the matter of suppressing an investigation? The innocent demand investigation, they wand vindication. Mr. Henderson spent much effort in showing the distance to the slaughtered band of sheep was further than estimated, but every material point he calmly ignored.

Since Mr. Henderson's letter was written the further evidence has been brought to light that papers in the pockets of the deceased had never been soiled by water, although the body was supposed to have been exposed to all the soaking rains of March. A great uproar has gone forth from Mr. Henderson and his partisans because The Oregonian reported in a subsequent article that no rain fell in Lake County in April up to the time of the finding of the body. It is true that two small showers descended, but so gently that they would not wet through a man's clothing. This is evidenced by the fact that the papers in the pockets had never been wet, although it is admitted the body lay there through much of April. But again this point is immaterial to the main one of, Who fired that bullet through the heart of J.C. Conn?

No Powder Burns About Heart

Speaking of the first shot through the heart, that there were no powder burns, Mr. Henderson says: "This statement is absolutely false, as the testimony of the two examining physicians, which is a matter of record, will show." Why does not some one publish the evidence before the Coroner's jury? The Lake County papers have each published a different version of the evidence. Is the evidence being suppressed? It is not known that any private citizen has seen this public document. But it is a certain fact that the jurors, the examining physicians and the Coroner have stated in private conversation that there was no powder burn around that first shot through the heart.

The Silver Lake newspaper after a prolonged silence has started a great hubbub over the revelations in The Oregonian. It says: "That the editor of this, the only paper published in Silver Lake ever got notice to cease agitation, or swing from a limb, is a lie." The Oregonian in its article stated a local paper in the county. There are four local papers in the county. Why does the Silver Lake paper single itself out as the one? There was nothing in The Oregonian articles to indicate that it was meant.

The Silver Lake paper begins: "The persistent, indefensible and malicious attacks on the good name of the majority of our citizens and especially the jurors who rendered the verdict in the Conn case, which have appeared in The Daily Oregonian lately, are, as every one acquainted with the facts believes, gotten up for the sole purpose of hoodwinking the agents of the insurance company against which the estate of the deceased gentleman is supposed to hold a policy." The Silver Lake paper doesn't even pretend to know that such a policy is held by the estate. It says it is "supposed" to hold one. What if it turns out that the estate holds no such policy, will the Silver Lake paper say there was the motive for such an "attack on the good name of its people? As a matter of fact Conn carried no life insurance.

The attack upon the good name of the people of Silver Lake would be not so much in the crime itself as in allowing the murderers to go unpunished.

"Drive Out Sheep"
Dateline: Prineville, Or., Dec. 10 (Special correspondence.)
Published: *Oregonian*, December 12, 1904

Six thousand head of sheep slaughtered, of an approximate value of $20,000, without a single indictment from the grand jury, is the record of the past season in Central Oregon.

Criminal operations of such magnitude seem serious, and are serious, although one living among the conditions is apt to overlook this phase, for the reason that business interests of all kinds are very badly impregnated with the feeling from one or the other of the viewpoints, and during the past two years sympathy or criticism has been dealt out with caution, and in all cases the ears receiving them must be known.

The feeling becomes more acute as each ranging season opens, and as a result of the continued depredations, many of the sheepmen have found it necessary to dispose of their herds.

Examination of the Sheep

Although the first organized bands of sheepshooters were for the express purpose of protecting the range from so-called outside sheep, their efforts have never been directed at anything but the apparent extermination of home sheep, that all public range could thus be conserved for the individual use of the cattleman, to the exclusion of all other classes of stock.

At different times in the past the cattle interest have been accused of having an organization which had been responsible for these depredations, but each time the answer would come back:

"We are not guilty, and cannot possibly furnish you a clew, unless it is some irresponsible parties who have wantonly killed your stock without cause."

This answer has been a makeshift to herald to the outside world, in lieu of anything more definite, but the past season has demonstrated that such is not the case, but instead it has been proven that the counties of Crook, Lake and Grant are the homes of organized bands of sheepshooters, organized from among representative cattlemen, who co-operate with one another in their depredatory acts.

Conspiracy is Widespread

The Silver Lake shootings of last Spring furnished an example of the distances traveled by some in co-operating with others of the band, when cartridge boxes were found with a Prineville firm's cost mark on them, although the scene of the shooting was 125 miles from here. At that time two affairs followed each other in quick succession, resulting in the slaughter of over 4000 head of sheep, and were probably also responsible for the death of Creed Conn, the Silver Lake merchant, whose definite knowledge of the affair became known and feared through his criticisms.

The writer has been fortunate in getting the story of a sheep shooting affair from a participant, and the fact that it was unsolicited enables him to give it without any qualms of consoence*. His story follows:

Tale of a Sheep-Shooter

"About 3 o'clock in the afternoon the scouts that had been posted during the entire day had ascertained that he herder was alone and unarmed, and that we ran no chances in getting possession of his band. This was done by our party, numbering some dozen men, after we had indulged in a few preliminaries such as firing off our guns and giving vent to a few oaths, just to make the poor cuss stand pat, for if he had attempted to run we would have had to kill him. He was bound and gagged to prevent his getting away and giving the alarm, and was then placed by the side of a tree.

"The band of sheep, numbering about 2000, was then driven to a corral on deeded land which was done for a double purpose, as we could then shoot without their scattering, and we could also point to the carcasses and say: 'Well, they were on deeded land and whoever killed them did so merely as an act protecting their own property.' We then knelt our knees on the ground, that every shot from our 30-30's might take effect in more than one sheep, and thus save ammunition. In this manner more than 1500 shots were fired, and as a result 1200 sheep were killed.

"Those of the band that succeeded in getting away were without a herder for two days, and many succumbed to the attacks of the coyotes.

"Yes, we had our faces blackened so that we could not be recognized, and it was a veritable picnic. Had everything our own way from start to finish. You're d___d right, that sheepman will never get within miles of our range again, that's a sinch."

Not All Cattlemen Implicated

The shooting described was that in which Morrow & Keenan, of Willow Creek, representative sheepmen of this county, suffered a loss of about 1000 head of thoroughbred sheep, and illustrates the methods pursued by the sheep shooting crowd. I do not mean to say that all cattlemen are implicated in these affairs, but there are certainly few exceptions. It has been said that when a cattleman refuses to countenance their acts he incurs their enmity and is rated with a sheepman. Other cattlemen who do not care to run the chances of detection by active participation "show their colors" by contributing cartridges, and sometimes information, thus "working in with the gang."

Such acts are very naturally tending to destroy a legitimate industry of this section that has the full protection of the law the world over, save in a few isolated Western localities. The past season has witnessed over 50,000 sheep of

Crook County's total of 200,000 pass into outside hands, and if the attitude of the cattlemen does not change, in another season this number will be more than doubled. In the end, all ranges contested for will pass into the hands of the cattlemen, and, as nearly the whole of Central Oregon's ranging lands come under this head, it means the practical extermination of an industry that has brought more dollars, two to one, into this section than any other two industries. Certainly the ends do not justify the means, but unless conditions change, what can be done?   C.B.W.

* "Consoence" is not a word in the English language, so must contain typographical errors. The word "consonance," fits the context of the sentence.

Appendix B

This appendix contains other items of interest that are important sources of information for the Conn murder. All were transcribed exactly and in their entirety.

Crook County Journal
April 28, 1904

J.C. Conn's Body Found

Body of Silver Lake Merchant is Found in the Brush with Bullet Hole in the Head

The body of Creed Conn, the Silver Lake merchant who mysteriously disappeared several weeks ago and which was supposed to have been washed down Silver Creek during the high water, was found last week by Fred Autin, an employe of one of the cattle firms in that vicinity. The body was found in the sage brush about a mile and a quarter from town. A bullet hole in the right temple showed the manner of his death. The body was badly decomposed from its long exposure to the weather. Coroner Harris was summoned and an inquest held, the jury returning a verdict of self-inflicted death.

Nearly every resident in the vicinity of Silver Lake was examined at the inquest which developed the fact that Mr. Conn had shot himself twice in his successful effort to take his life. A bottle of laudanum was also found in his pocket, but its contents were intact. One bullet had passed through the body and was found imbedded two inches in the sand near where the dead man lay.

Mr. Conn disappeared on the morning of March 4, and although a systematic search was made for him no clue to his whereabouts was found until last Thursday morning. It was supposed from the first that he had committed suicide and that his body had been washed down Silver Creek. A love affair is supposed to have been a partial cause of the man taking his life.

Oregonian
June 12, 1904

Murder or Suicide

Juryman Says Verdict in J.C. Conn Case is Supported by Facts

Silver Lake, Or., June 1, 1904-- (To the Editor.)-- The Weekly Oregonian of May 12 published an article headed "Reign of Terror, Daring Defiance of Law in Lake County," etc., which reflects severely upon the citizens of Silver Lake, and contains a number of false statements. The writer states that McKune's sheep were killed only "ten or 12 miles from his (J.C. Conn's) store." The fact is the distance was at lease 50 miles. "He (Conn) had sold the ammunition and the guns that killed the sheep." that is a broad assertion, to say the least. Mr. Conn's clerk informs me that at no time within the past year has there been one-half the amount of cartridges in the store that were found where the sheep were killed.

The reference to the Coroner's jury is the part to which I particularly take exception. The correspondent says, "certain circumstances connected with his (J.C. Conn's) death lead to the strong suspicion that he was murdered."

Being one of the jury I beg leave to differ. There was not a particle of evidence to show that he was murdered. On the contrary every circumstance showed that J.C. Conn took his own life. Mr. Venator the Assistant District Attorney, made a most searching examination of all the witnesses and he was unable to find a single fact or circumstance that would point to murder. "The Coroner's jury that gave the verdict was made up entirely of cattlemen." I presume he means to insinuated that the cattlemen would try to shield the guilty parties if possible. Here, where the jurymen are well known, this base insinuation needs no refutation. In fact there were but two men on the jury who own any cattle. Clarence Harris of Summer Lake, who keeps all his cattle in a pasture and has no interest in the range, and myself, who own land in Silver Lake Valley and keep what few cattle I have in the pasture and like Mr. Harris have no interest whatever in the outside range.

The verdict "was entirely unsatisfactory to Mr. Conn's friends, who do not hesitate to assert that politics influenced the verdict." If Mr. Conn's friends are not satisfied with the verdict they have no one to blame but themselves. Lafe Conn was present at the inquest an assisted in the examination of the witnesses, as was also his brothers, Virgil and George, and if they knew of any evidence that would have caused a differing verdict they should have introduced it. The evidence clearly and beyond andy reasonable doubt showed suicide. That politics had anything to do with the case is too absurd to refer to. Politics was not mentioned. Three of the jury were Republicans and three were Democrats.

Another statement, "there was no powder burn to show that the weapon had been held close to the body." This statement is absolutely false, as the testimony of the tow examining physicians, which is a matter of record, will show. The entire jury who viewed the remains will also attest the fact that the clothing above both wounds was badly powder burned, although the body had lain in the rain and snow for over a month. One ball had gone through the body and been imbedded in the ground, where it was found. It exactly fitted the revolver which lay by his side. The revolver was identified beyond doubt to be the property of J.C. Conn.

The evidence all showed that Mr. Conn came to his death by his own hands, and there was not a single circumstance to justify the sensational story of your correspondent that he was foully murdered. Respectfully,

E.K. HENDERSON.

The following is the complete and unedited text of the coroner's bill to the county for services rendered in the inquest. Jurors and witnesses were also paid by the county:

State of Oregon,
ss.
County of Lake,

I, F.E. Harris being first duly sworn depose and say that the within named services were duly rendered by the parties named and that the several amounts claimed are justly due said parties.

(signed F.E. Harris)

Subscribed and sworn to before me this 2nd day of May, 1904.

(signed W.J. Moore)
_____Notary Public for Oregon.

Lakeview, Oregon May 2nd, 1904.
Lake County, Oregon, Dr.
To the following named parties in the several amounts set opposite the names of each for services rendered in holding an inquest over the remains of J.C. Conn, deceased:
To F.E. Harris for 5 days services in going to and returning from Silver Lake and holding inquest over the remains of J.C. Conn, deceased, $25.

To Summoning 6 Jurors at 50 cents,	3.
" Swearing 6 Jurors at 10 cents,	.60
"Subpoenaing 14 witnesses at 50 cents,	7.00
"18 miles traveled in summoning witnesses and juriors, @10¢	1.80
"200 miles actually traveled to and from Silver Lake, @ 10¢	20.00
Total---------------..----------	$58.80

Bill of F.E. Harris examined and approved in the sum of $55.00

To Frank Payne, witness fees,				$1.50
"Mrs. R.H. Mosby, "	"	and mileage,		1.70
" T.V. Hall,	"	"	"	1.50
"A.A. Witham, "	"			1.50
"George Parker, "	"			1.50
" R.B. Jackson, "	"			1.50

" R.E. Ward,	"	"	and 12 miles traveled,	2.70
" N. Bullard,	"	"		1.50
" Ferd Austin,	"	"	and 3 miles actually traveled,	1.80
" J.M. Welch,	"	"	" 3 miles " "	1.80
" C.C. Harris,	"	"		1.50
" L.F. Conn,	"	"		1.50
" J.I. May,		"	"	1.50
" Cliff Smith	"	"		1.50
To W.D. West for services as juror,				1.00
"Jas. Sullivan,	"		"	1.00
" E.K. Henderson,		"	"	1.00
" C.C. Harris,	"	"		1.00
" Cliff Smith,	"	"		1.00
" Geo. Lovegrove		"	"	$1.00

and for extending 5800 words of evidence at 25¢,
$14.50

$15.50

Acts Chapter 20, verses 16 through 38 were the basis for a sermon delivered by Reverend Jimmy Howard to the Baptist congregation of Silver Lake during the month when Creed Conn was missing. The exact date when the sermon was delivered is not known, although it was during April of 1904, and may have been heard on the night of the inquest. What follows is the King James bible version of Howard's selected verses. Creed Conn was a Baptist.

16 For Paul had decided to sail past Ephesus, so that he would not have to spend time in Asia; for he was hurrying to be at Jerusalem, if possible, on the Day of Pentecost.

The Ephesian Elders Exhorted

17 From Miletus he sent to Ephesus and called for the elders of the church.

18 And when they had come to him, he said to them: "You know, from the first day that I came to Asia, in what manner I always lived among you.

19 "serving the Lord with all humility, with many tears and trials which happened to me by the plotting of the Jews;

20 "and how I kept back nothing that was helpful, but proclaimed it to you, and taught you publicly and from house to house,

21 "testifying to Jews, and also to Greeks, repentance toward God and faith toward our Lord Jesus Christ.

22 "And see, know I go bound in the spirit to Jerusalem, not knowing the things that will happen to me there,

23 "except that the Holy Spirit testifies in every city, saying that chains and tribulations await me.

24 "But none of these things move me; nor do I count my life dear to myself, so that I may finish my race with joy, and the ministry which I received from the Lord Jesus, to testify to the gospel of the grace of God.

25 "And indeed, now I know that you all, among whom I have gone preaching the kingdom of God, will see my face no more.

26 "Therefore I testify to you this day that I *am* innocent of the blood of all *men.*

27 "For I have not shunned to declare to you the whole counsel of God.

28 "Therefore take heed to yourselves and to all the flock, among which the Holy Spirit has made you overseers, to shepherd the church of God which He purchased with His own blood.

29 "For I know this, that after my departure savage wolves will come in among you, not sparing the flock

30 "Also from among yourselves men will rise up, speaking perverse things, to draw away the disciples after themselves.

31 "Therefore watch, and remember that for three years I did not cease to warn everyone night and day with tears.

32 "And now, brethren, I commend you to God and to the word of His grace, which is able to build you up and give you an inheritance among all those who are sanctified.

33 "I have coveted no one's silver or gold or apparel.

34 "Yes, you yourselves know that these hands have provided for my necessities, and for those who were with me.

35 "I have shown you in every way, by laboring like this, that you must support the weak. And remember the words of the Lord Jesus, that He said, 'It is more blessed to give than to receive.'"

36 and when he had said these things, he knelt down and prayed with them all.

37 Then they all wept freely, and fell on Paul's neck and kissed him,

38 sorrowing most of all for the words which he spoke, that they would see his face no more. And they accompanied him to the ship.

Appendix C

The Organized Hedonistic
'Comfort' or 'Enterprise' Serial Killer

(The "comfort" killer is a subtype of the hedonistic type of serial killer.)

Serial killers are not all alike, but we can find a reference to the type that Ray Jackson was in the FBI's Crime Classification Manual:

"Material gain and a comfortable lifestyle are the primary motives of comfort killers. Usually, the victims are family members and close acquaintances. After a murder, a comfort killer will usually wait for a period of time before killing again to allow any suspicions by family or authorities to subside. Poison, most notably arsenic, is often used to kill victims."

This type of serial killer may have "previous convictions for theft, fraud, dishonesty, non-payment of debts, embezzlement, and other crimes of similar nature."

Traits Found in the Serial Killer Personality:

This list was published in the book, "The Psycho-pathology of Serial Murder,*" extracted from the revised Hare Psychopathy Checklist published in 1991. Most, if not all of the following traits are found in the serial killer personality, and the reader should be able to match most or all of these traits to the behaviors of Ray Van Buren Jackson, found within this book:

-Glibness and superficial charm
-Grandiosity
-Continuous need for stimulation
-Pathological lying (includes use of aliases)
-Conning and manipulativeness
-Lack of remorse or guilt
-Shallow affect
-Callous lack of empathy
-Parasitic lifestyle
-Poor behavioral controls
-Promiscuity

-Early behavior problems
-Lack of realistic, long-term goals
-Impulsivity
-Irresponsibility
-Failure to accept responsibility for actions
-Many short-term relationships
-Juvenile delinquency
-Revocation of conditional release
-Criminal versatility

* "The Psychopathology of Serial Murder," by Stephen J. Giannangelo, 1996, Praeger, Westport, Connecticut, p 9-10.

Selected Traits of the Organized Serial Killer
Found in the book, "Profilers" :

"Similarly, too, the organized offender brings his own weapon to the crime and takes it away once he is finished.... ballistic evidence may connect him to the murder, and so he takes it away from the scene."

Not all organized killers get rid of the bodies. The Hillside Stranglers left bodies in places where they could be found. "Their desire seems to have been an egotistical one--to flaunt the bodies in front of the police rather than to conceal them in an effort to prevent tracing the killers through identification of the victim.... An organized offender may sometimes stage a crime scene or death scene in order to confuse the authorities."

Organized offenders are reasonably attractive, outgoing, and gregarious. They often are bullies and like crowds. They pick fights in bars and are troublemakers.

They externalize hurt, anger, and fear and 'act out' in school. They commit aggressive and senseless acts.

"Organized killers feel superior to nearly everyone.... believing themselves to be the smartest, most successful people to have come down the pike."

"After the crime, they often follow the progress (or nonprogress) of the investigation in the news media."

Organized killers "have had multiple sex partners. As good con artists with excellent verbal skills, they are often able to persuade women to have sex with them.... However, they are unable to sustain normal, long-term relationships. Their lives are characterized by having many partners, none of whom stick with them for very long."

Organized killers "are angry at their girlfriends, at themselves, at their families, and at society in general. They feel that they've been mistreated during their entire lives and that everything is stacked against them.... They all believe that society has conspired to keep them down."

* "Profilers," by John H. Campbell and Don DeNevi, 2004, Prometheus, Amherst, New York, p 138, 140-144.

INDEX:

Bingham, Cyrus J., "Cy", 83, 94
Black Canyon, 84
Black, Clarence, 173
Blackburn, Elmer, 193-194
Blackburn, Henery, L., "Lester", 195
Blackburn, Marcus B., "Mark", 192-196
Blackburn, Thomas, 194
Blakely, James M., 98-99, 101-105, 156, 158, 160
Bloss, John, 179
Blue Mountains Forest Reserve, 61-62, 66, 83, 87, 142-143, 161
Board of Railroad Commissioners, 195
Boggs, James A., 35, 142, 144, 160-161, 163
Boneyard Spring, 242
Bonham, Carlos, 101
Bonham, Della Keerins, 102
Bonnieview Ranch, 107
Book Cliffs Raid, 85
Booth, Ann LaBrie, 176
Booth, Floyd, 178
Booth, James H., 176-178
Booth, John O., 176
Booth, Judge William A., 178
Booth, Rennie, 37
Booth, Robert A., 177-178
Booth, Robert A. Jr., 176
Booth, Senator Robert A., 176
Booth-Kelly Timber Company, 176-178
Boston Common, 92
Boston Tea Party, 92
Boyce, Sam, 63
Bradley family, 223, 241
Bradley Meadows, 223, 240-241
Bradley, Ada, 237-238, 240
Bradley, Grace, 228, 240
Bradley, Harold, 221-234, 237-238, 240, 242-243, 249-250, 256, 261-262, 278.
Bradley, Hosmer, 237-241
Bradley, Ira R., 222, 228, 233, 236-243, 249, 256, 261, 278
Bradley, Leah, 237
Bradley, Lean, 237
Bradley, Lora, 237
Bradley, Ruth, 237
Braly, David, 197
Brattain family, 44
Brattain, Eldon M., 35
Breese, Dick, 141
Brink, Mason E., 157, 159
Brooks, G.W., 70
Brown, Gilbert, 127-128, 198
Brown, William W., 62-63
Brown, William W., "Bill", 140, 142, 152, 223, 231, 237, 240-242
Brownsville, Oregon, 192, 275
Buck Creek, 62-63, 182, 259, 276
Buick, Charles D., 10

Department of Agriculture, 84, 91
Department of the Interior, 56-57, 59-60, 62-63, 84, 87-88, 92, 103, 146
Dillard, H.A., 104
Dillard, Oregon, 255
Disston, Oregon, 276
Division R, 60, 83, 87-89, 91, 103
Dixon, Edward, 62
Dobkins, Eliza J., "Jane", 201-203
Dobkins, Emma, 201-203, 205
Dobkins, Frank, 201, 203, 205-207, 212, 277
Dobkins, infant, 203
Dobkins, Margaret, 203
Dobkins, William, M. 201-203
Donovan family, 225
Donovan Ranch, 226
Dosch, Arno, 95
Double O Ranch, 197, 205
Dufur, W.H.H., 102
Dunbar, Secretary of State, F.I., 23
Duncan Livery, 180
Duncan, George Sr., 50-51, 173-174
Duncan, Ida, 169, 175
Duncan, Ida Vanderpool Anderson, 119
Duncan, Warren, M., 10, 119-121, 169, 175, 177-178, 181, 247
Dunham, Amos, 105
Dunham, Claude, 105
Dunlap, Sheriff Horace, 32, 144
Dunning, Al, 46, 171
Duvall, Curtis, 200
Easterly, Lenora, 254
Egli Ranch, 225, 230
Egli, Louisa, 212
Elder, Jason S., 32
Elder, Ralph, 107, 150
Elkins, Charles M, 158
Elkins, Frank, 101
Elliott, Larkin, 100, 152-153, 156-157, 163
Elliott, Mrs. Larkin, 101
Elliott, William F., 152
Ellis, H.C., 207
Embody, Charles W., 129
Embody, John, 179
Emery, Everett, "Slivers", 199
Emery, George, 180
Emery, Russell, 171, 199, 205
Emmitt, Senator Ralph, 46, 50
Escallier, Alex, 109
Escallier, Julius, 34, 109
Farrell, Thomas, 118
Fife, Oregon, 62
Five Mile Creek, 86
Forbes, Bertha, 207
Forbes, P.L., 207

Ford, John, 38
Forest Service, 91-92
Foster, Frank, 213
Foster, Guy, 199
Foster, Isaac, 197
Foster, Teressa, 120, 199
Fox Valley, 55
Franklin, Benjamin, 92
Frazier, Sheriff C.W., 213-214
Fremont National Forest, 127
French Settlement, 45
French, Peter, "Pete", 197
Fulton, Charles W., 102
Gale, Oregon, 116, 119
Gesner, Dr. Van, 135-136, 139-140, 142-154, 156-157, 159-163, 172, 269
Geyer, Al, 179-180, 182
Gibson, Dirk C., 260, 273
Gibson, H.S., 194
Gibson, Jess, 197, 206, 230, 241, 274
Gibson, William S., 241
Gilfry, George, 171-172
Gilfry, Louisa A., 171-172
Gladstone Depot, 193
Gladstone Park, 193
Glaze, Til, 104-105
Glazier, Eugene, 209
Glazier, Rosetta "Etta" Cane, 209
Goddard, Calvin, 261
Godon, Louise, 33
Goose Lake Forest Reserve, 90
Gordon, Mrs. Lenor I., 196
Gould, Deputy Sheriff, 238
Gowdy, Grace Bradley, 223
Gowdy, James H., "Bert", 127, 129
Graham, Richard, 104
Grand Mesa, 85
Gray Creek, 107
Gray Prairie, 71, 145, 150
Gray, Bruce, 37, 73, 107
Gray, Claud, 213
Gray, Edward, 197, 201-202, 230-231, 235, 237, 241
Gray, John H., "Henry", 60, 99, 107, 109, 141-142, 148-152
Gray, Otto, 37, 73, 107, 145
Gray, Rebecca, 145
Gray, Roy, 145
Greene, A.R., 63
Grimes, Holt, 213
Grindstone Creek, 74
Hach, Henry H., 126
Hall, Dr. Thomas V., 10, 138, 250, 265-267, 272
Hall, John H., 146
Hamilton, Ole, 125, 130-131
Hamilton, Thomas C. "Cull", 10, 19

Titles by Melany Tupper:

Trip, Nomadic in America 2001

High Desert Roses,
Significant Stories from Central Oregon
volume one 2003

The Sandy Knoll Murder,
Legacy of the Sheepshooters 2010

Forthcoming Books by Melany Tupper:

High Desert Roses,
volume two

The sequel to The Sandy Knoll Murder
(title to be announced)